Teaching Decoding in Holistic Classrooms

J. LLOYD ELDREDGE

Brigham Young University

MERRILL
An imprint of Prentice Hall
Upper Saddle River, New Jersey / Columbus, Ohio

Library of Congress Cataloging-in-Publication Data

Eldredge, J. Lloyd (Joseph Lloyd).
   Teaching decoding in holistic classrooms / J. Lloyd Eldredge.
      p.   cm.
   Includes bibliographical references and index.
   ISBN 0-02-332230-6
   1. Reading (Elementary)—Phonetic method. 2. Language experience
approach in education. I. Title.
LB1573.3.E43 1995
372.4'145—dc20   94-32491
                                                              CIP

Editor: Linda James Scharp
Production Editor: Sheryl Glicker Langner
Text Designer: Angela Foote
Cover Design: Proof Positive/Farrowlyne Assoc., Inc.
Production Buyer: Pamela D. Bennett

This book was set in New Baskerville by Carlisle Communications, Ltd. and was printed and bound by
R. R. Donnelley & Sons Company. The cover was printed by Phoenix Color Corp.

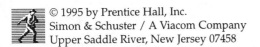

© 1995 by Prentice Hall, Inc.
Simon & Schuster / A Viacom Company
Upper Saddle River, New Jersey 07458

Printed in the United States of America

10 9 8 7 6 5 4 3 2

ISBN: 0-02-332230-6

Prentice-Hall International (UK) Limited, *London*
Prentice-Hall of Australia Pty. Limited, *Sydney*
Prentice-Hall of Canada, Inc., *Toronto*
Prentice-Hall Hispanoamericana, S. A., *Mexico*
Prentice-Hall of India Private Limited, *New Delhi*
Prentice-Hall of Japan, Inc., *Tokyo*
Simon & Schuster Asia Pte. Ltd., *Singapore*
Editora Prentice-Hall do Brasil, Ltda., *Rio de Janeiro*

For my wife (Cherie), my seven
children (Lloyd, Steve, Gaylene,
Kristin, Brad, Michelle, Nicole), my
mother, and my fourteen grand-
children who make my life worthwhile.

About the Author

J. Lloyd Eldredge is a professor in the College of Education at Brigham Young University. He is currently serving as the Graduate Coordinator of the Elementary Education Graduate Program at BYU, and teaches both graduate and undergraduate literacy courses. Dr. Eldredge is a former elementary school teacher, school principal, and school superintendent. He has also served as the Utah Director of Chapter I, the Utah Director of Early Childhood Education, and the Utah Director of Elementary Education.

His interests are in whole language and emergent literacy. He was one of the first educators to implement and research "whole language" practices in the public schools. The editors of *The Reading Teacher* acknowledge his article on "alternatives to traditional reading instruction" as the first "whole language" article published in that journal. During the past twelve years he has focused his research on phonemic awareness, a reconceptualization of decoding instruction in the early years of schooling, whole language, oral reading, and the effects of various forms of "assisted reading" strategies (dyad reading, group assisted reading, and taped assisted reading) on young and "at-risk" readers. His work has been published in many journals, including *Journal of Educational Research, Reading Research and Instruction, Journal of Reading, The Reading Teacher,* and *Reading Research Quarterly.*

Preface

Teaching Decoding in Holistic Classrooms was written to help preservice and practicing teachers teach decoding in the classroom. It has been designed to support holistic teaching practices.

This book describes decoding strategies that will help children develop decoding knowledge while engaged in writing and reading activities that are relevant to them. In addition to commonly known holistic strategies, such as the shared book experience, writing using invented spelling, and the Language Experience Approach, we present other, less well-known, strategies, including dyad reading and group assisted reading. These strategies are unique because they allow students to read interesting but "frustrational level" text and at the same time improve their decoding and comprehension abilities.

The first four chapters present research evidence to support the positions taken on whole language, decoding, phonemic awareness, phonics, and word recognition. These chapters support the teaching practices and strategies described in the book. The strategies introduced in the last seven chapters have been tried and tested in experimental classrooms. Studies have shown these strategies to have a positive effect on children's attitudes, and on their reading and writing achievement.

The whole language philosophy has had a worldwide impact on schools' literacy programs, perhaps greater than that made by any other educational trend. However, many teachers are confused regarding the role of decoding in holistic classrooms, particularly the role of phonics instruction. Some whole language enthusiasts state that phonics and whole language are incompatible and cannot coexist, while others claim that holistic approaches without some phonics support will not help students achieve literacy. Since whole language is not a prescribed method or program, educators have implemented it differently from school to school, and its implementation is expected to evolve and change as we learn more about how young children become literate.

Part of the confusion regarding the role of decoding in holistic, meaning-based approaches is that either there are many whole language philosophies in existence, or *the* whole language philosophy is still emerging. This conclusion is supported by the various, sometimes contradictory, definitions of whole language found in the educational literature. There is currently no clearly defined description of whole language that would be acceptable to all who claim to be involved in the movement. For example, Ken and Yetta Goodman's well-known whole language model and the "child-centered" programs found in New Zealand and Australia are not the same, even though many educators in the United States often assume otherwise. The New Zealand and Australian models seek to achieve an instructional balance between skills and meaning, while whole language "purists" advise against teaching skills, particularly in isolation.

The evolution of whole language in the United States was, in large measure, a reaction against the "skill and drill" reading programs introduced in the early part of the twentieth century. These programs continued until they gained almost "sacred cow" status in the latter part of the century. This book does not support these approaches. However, it doesn't support the position of whole language "purists," either. Many of these "purists" tell teachers that children will learn all they need to know about the alphabetic principle when they are engaged in meaningful writing and reading activities. Some theorists tell teachers to ignore phonics, or advise them to teach phonics only when children demonstrate a need for it. These practices are neither consistent with, nor supported by existing research.

The different perceptions of what constitutes holistic practices are centered for the most part around the teaching of skills, particularly phonics. While these differences are bothersome to many whole language enthusiasts, and in some cases spawn futile, divisive debate, there are some commonly held beliefs about whole language that keep the basic philosophy alive. It is this core of beliefs that this book seeks to support.

Holistic teachers believe that children learn *about* reading and writing by attempting to read and write. Therefore, they involve children in meaningful reading and writing experiences *before* children develop the skills needed to be independent readers and writers. They also believe that when children experience meaningful language activities, they not only learn from the experiences, but also learn to enjoy reading and writing as well. So, holistic teachers use shared book experiences, taped assisted reading, and other "connected-text" reading and writing strategies to help children achieve independence. If they are unable to spell words correctly as they write, teachers either transcribe their work or encourage them to "spell" words by sounds.

Traditional decoding approaches emphasize the *teaching* of skills over the *application* of skills. They can also take so much classroom time (remember phonics workbook pages?) that little time is left for children to read and write. *Teaching Decoding in Holistic Classrooms* describes how to teach decoding through direct instruction in as few as 10 minutes a day. Because so little time is required for these brief, total-class lessons, teachers are able to allocate more classroom time for children to *use* language, thus achieving a better "balance" for children and teachers alike.

Acknowledgments

My interests in literacy development heightened while I was serving as a young elementary school principal in the Granite School District, a suburban district near Salt Lake City, Utah. It was at that time that I became emotionally involved with certain children who were to soon move on to the junior high school, but were unprepared for the experience. These children had struggled in school for years because they had been incapable of dealing with the normal reading and writing tasks required of them. I can still remember the conferences I had with the parents of the children. A common thread ran through all of the stories they told. Their child's reading difficulties had surfaced early—by first grade. Efforts to correct the problem by the child's teacher, the child, and the parents were unsuccessful. The problem continued to worsen over the years. Year after year the child and his or her parents sought remedies for the problem. Year after year their attempts were unsuccessful. When the time arrived for the child to move on to the junior high school, the parents panicked and redoubled their efforts to help. They requested help from me that I could not deliver. I promised myself at that time that I would study the issues related to literacy development until I could respond appropriately to such pleas for help. I owe much to the children and parents at the Hillsdale Elementary School who helped me focus on this important problem. I thank and acknowledge parents, children, and colleagues at the West Kearns, Taylorsville, and Robert Frost Elementary Schools for their contributions to this book as well.

I owe a debt of gratitude to my students and colleagues at the Brigham Young University, and the teachers and administrators in Utah, who have helped me in my research efforts, and who have challenged many of the conclusions I have drawn from my studies. I am especially indebted to Robin Steed at BYU for her pioneering work in the area of phonemic awareness, and for her willingness to share her knowledge with me. Her input and reactions to the book have been invaluable.

I am grateful to the following reviewers whose input and valuable suggestions contributed greatly to this text: Dorothy A. Wedge, Fairmont State College; Leo Schell, Kansas State University; William S. O'Bruba, Bloomsburg University;

Timothy R. Blair, University of Central Florida; Edward W. Holmes, Towson State University; Melissa J. Rickey, Eastern Montana College; Timothy Rasinski, Kent State University; and Patricia P. Kelly, Virginia Tech. Thank you for your time and efforts.

To Linda Scharp, I express appreciation for her willingness to support a project of this kind, and for her counsel and advice regarding the book. I thank Sheryl Langner and her associates for their meticulous attention to detail in the preparation and production of the manuscript.

It is my hope that all who read the book will find the information interesting, useful, and challenging. Furthermore, I hope that readers can visualize the practical applications of the information presented herein. Most importantly, it is my hope that the book might contribute in some small way to the solution of literacy problems facing us all.

Contents

5

Developing Phonemic Awareness through Stories, Games, and Songs 50

6

A Formal Phonemic Awareness Training Program 71

9

Teaching Decoding Informally through Reading and Writing Activities 122

10

Teaching Phonics in Ten Minutes a Day 146

11

Assessing Decoding and Reading Comprehension   167

Chapter 1

Whole Language

What Is Whole Language?

Whole language is not an educational program, but a philosophy about learning, language development, and children that drives such programs. Definitions of whole language are often vague and elusive. For example, according to Goodman (1986), "a whole language program is an educational program conducted by whole language teachers" (p. 5). Rich (1985) described whole language as "an attitude of mind which provides a shape for the classroom" (p. 719). Newman (1985) said that whole language was so complex and comprehensive that it defied definition. Farris and Kaczmarski (1988), while attempting to describe what teachers do in whole language classrooms, suggested that the whole language framework tends to be abstract because it deals primarily with attitudes and beliefs.

Whole language is based on the premise that language acquisition (both oral and written) is natural, not in the sense of being innate or inevitably unfolding, but in the sense that when individuals unfamiliar with a language are placed in an environment where that language is an integral component, they will learn language with little or no direct instruction, (Altwerger, Edelsky, & Flores, 1987, p. 145). Whole language proponents believe that reading and writing abilities develop when there is a reason for them to develop. Individuals constantly exposed to written language, in authentic situations, react to those experiences naturally, and learn more about the language in the process.

Whole language is also based on other beliefs, such as that reading, writing, speaking, and listening are reciprocal processes that should not be separated for purposes of instruction; that children should have opportunities to read "authentic" or "natural" text rather than text material that is "watered down" through the use of readability formulas; that literacy experiences for children should be meaningful; and that children should be given opportunities to learn to read and write as they learn about the world in which they live—that is, the content children study should be relevant to them, and literacy development will occur as children read and write about that content.

The Evolution of Whole Language

Psycholinguist Kenneth Goodman is often given the credit for pioneering the whole language movement in the United States (Goodman, 1992a; Fountas & Hannigan, 1989). In fact, credit should go to many people within and outside of the United States—among them Don Holdaway, Marie Clay, Jerome Harste, Frank Smith, Dolores Durkin, Lucy Calkins, Carol Chomsky, Donald Graves, Jane Hansen, and Donald Murray.

Goodman's work was influenced by language theorists and educators in New Zealand, Australia, Great Britain, and Canada. The literacy programs developed by these individuals involved children in early informal reading and writing activities focused around their natural interests. Goodman claimed that these programs were influenced by principles of progressive education advocated by John Dewey with which he fully agreed: "I believe in a view of education that starts with a learner's strength and builds outward from it. I share Dewey's view that the classroom is not preparation for life; it is life itself. I believe learning is both personal and social and that optimum learning occurs when learners are engaged in functional, relevant, and meaningful experiences" (Goodman, 1992a, p. 192).

Goodman based his whole language model on miscue research that he began in the early 1960s. He rejected the notion that reading was a hierarchical set of skills, dealing with reading as a holistic process. In 1976 he used the term *psycholinguistic guessing game* to describe the tentative information processing strategies he believed readers used as they read (Goodman, 1992a). He claimed that readers looked for various clues in a sentence as they tried to construct meaning from print. The meanings of words (semantic clues), a word's function (syntax clue), and the beginning letter of a word (phonics clue) enabled readers to "guess" a word they didn't recognize. Goodman's major concern was reading for meaning; he considered decoding errors insignificant as long as those errors were syntactically and semantically appropriate to the text message.

Goodman emphasized the need for teachers to use more oral language activities and read-alouds to help students use semantics, syntax, and phonics cueing systems to make sensible predictions from text. Goodman believed that children would learn to read and write in the same natural way that they learned to speak in the home. He encouraged teachers to make language learning in the schools as easy and natural as it seemed to be in the home. He believed that children should be immersed in a language-rich environment and provided with many authentic reasons to use reading and writing. He was violently opposed to teaching reading skills, stating that "all programs for teaching reading, writing, spelling, or any other important ability that reduce it to a simple skill sequence and isolate what is learned from functional use violate the most basic premises of whole language" (Goodman, 1992a, p. 197).

Goodman was against direct instruction. He believed that teachers used direct instruction without considering how it affected or was affected by everything else. He wrote, "[W]hat DI advocates usually mean is direct focus on 'skills' which can be easily and immediately tested with an 'objective test' for 'mastery.' Whole language is concerned with the kind of learning that is much more complete and important than what can be tested in the DI manner" (1992a, p. 197). Goodman's strong position against skills and phonics was largely responsible for separating educators in the United States into camps for and against whole language.

Goodman wasn't the only one in the United States inspired by successful literacy programs in other English-speaking countries, and he was not the only one with an impact on the whole language movement here. During the late 1970s, many educators in the United States began to respond to the ideas espoused by Marie Clay and Don Holdaway in New Zealand, and by various educators in Australia, Canada, and Great Britain. These educators began to stress the importance of integrating the teaching of reading and writing; of providing young children with meaningful reasons to use the written language; and of immersing them in a language-rich environment. More and more teachers began using children's literature books in the classroom instead of basal readers. Whole language, as it was called, began to evolve in the United States.

According to Goodman (1992a, p. 195), the term *whole language* was popularized in Canada. Educators there wanted a label to differentiate their developing educational philosophy from the popular skills models. Thompson (1992, p. 135) stated that the term was used by Jerome Harste and Carolyn Burke, Dorothy Watson, Ken and Yetta Goodman, Orin Cochran, and Ethel Buchanan in the late 1970s. However, the term was never universally adopted by supporters of this emerging "child-centered" literacy movement. Even some of the educators from whom Goodman received much of his inspiration avoided attaching the label to their literacy philosophies and/or programs. Nevertheless, the term "whole language" caught on with many educators in the United States and language immersion programs in other countries were soon referred to by this label. Thus, whole language definition problems in the United States emerged; confusion regarding the role of skills followed; and futile, divisive debates "for" and "against" whole language flourished.

Whole language evolved relatively quickly in the United States, equaled in popularity by only a few previous educational trends. Furthermore, it has had a positive impact on both teachers and students. The evolution was, in large measure, a reaction against "skill and drill" teaching approaches introduced in the early part of the twentieth century in the form of basal reading programs. These programs were based on principles of learning advocated by behavioristic psychologists. The basic basal approach was simple: identify all of the decoding, vocabulary, and comprehension skills necessary to be a good reader and then teach them to children. Program designers provided teachers with lists of skills to be taught, and tests to assess whether children possessed the skills. The designers instructed teachers in how to teach children the skills, and also how to manage the assessment data obtained from the diagnostic tests so they could group children with common skill needs together for instruction.

In skill and drill programs, so much classroom time was taken giving tests, recording test results, and teaching skills that children had little time left to read. Children didn't like reading, and teachers didn't enjoy teaching it. By the mid

1980s many teachers were ready for alternative teaching perspectives, and the ideas associated with whole language found a receptive audience. The impact of whole language was unbelievable. In Goodman's own words, "What has been an evolution elsewhere has been seen as a revolution here" (1992a, p. 195).

We must note here, however, that Goodman's whole language model and the "child-centered" programs found in other English-speaking countries are often different. Generally speaking, the models of literacy development implemented in these countries, particularly in New Zealand and Australia, seek to achieve a balance between skills and meaning (for example, see Goldenberg, 1991). For this reason, the New Zealand and Australia literacy models are now becoming more popular with teachers in the United States than is Goodman's whole language model. In addition, Goodman's model and the "grassroots" whole language programs that have evolved in the United States are not always identical. Whole language is not a prescribed method or program; educators have implemented it differently from school to school, and its implementation is expected to evolve and change as researchers learn more about how children become literate (Gunning, 1992, p. 387).

Multiple Whole Language Philosophies

Recently an associate of mine, speaking of whole language, said, "Getting whole language enthusiasts to define whole language is like trying to nail jello to a tree." His comment reflected his frustration with the various, sometimes contradictory, definitions of whole language found in the educational literature. For example, some whole language advocates state that direct instruction and whole language are compatible (Spiegel, 1992; Newman & Church, 1990; Fountas & Hannigan, 1989; Slaughter, 1988) while others are either violently opposed to direct instruction, or implicitly communicate that it is undesirable (Goodman, 1986, 1989; Doake, 1987; Altwerger et al., 1987).

Bergeron (1990, p. 312) analyzed 64 articles dealing with whole language and found that whole language was defined differently in each article. It appears that the philosophy is still emerging, and there isn't a clearly defined description of whole language in existence today that would be acceptable to all who claim to be involved in the movement. The different perceptions of whole language, for the most part, are centered around the teaching of skills, particularly phonics. While these differences are bothersome to many whole language enthusiasts, and often spawn debate, there seem to be some commonly held beliefs about whole language that keep the basic philosophy alive.

Classroom Practices Associated with Holistic Literacy Education

Certain classroom practices are associated with holistic educational philosophies. A description of these practices helps us form an image of this approach to literacy education. The term *holistic* is used here rather than "whole language" for two reasons: First, "holistic" represents the position taken by many teachers involved in the child-centered, activity-centered literacy movement that is rapidly growing in the United States. Second, the term does not elicit negative reactions from educators who have rejected the "purist" view of "whole language." Therefore, *whole language* will be used hereafter to describe the position taken by whole language purists, and *holistic* will be used to describe the position advocated in this book.

Two words of caution are appropriate here. First, because whole language "is a philosophy rather than a method, no two teachers do the same things, unless they deliberatively plan together" (Thompson, 1992, p. 140). Second, item nine following is not consistent with the whole language philosophy as espoused by Ken Goodman. This practice *is* consistent with a holistic approach to literacy development, but to purists, "whole language is an all or nothing proposition" (Moorman, Blanton, & McLaughlin, 1992, p. 7) and the practice would be unacceptable to them (Goodman, 1992b).

1. Rather than teach reading, writing, spelling, and handwriting as separate subjects, holistic language teachers integrate the teaching of the language arts into a single period. They recognize the interrelatedness of reading, writing, speaking, and listening. They recognize that all of these language processes are used as individuals attempt to communicate with each other, and growth in one area facilitates growth in the others. Holistic teachers therefore provide children with opportunities to talk, write, listen, and speak to each other, and to the teacher, while learning about themselves, others, and the world in which they live.

2. Teachers use children's oral language as the vehicle for helping them make the transition to the written language. Children are given opportunities to write messages, letters, and stories, using their own words and sentence patterns, even before they can accurately read, write, or spell.

3. Teachers encourage students to write as soon as they enter school. Children may dictate experiences or stories for others to write, as is done in the Language Experience Approach to reading instruction; however, holistic teachers emphasize children's doing their own writing, following their belief that children's writing skills develop from scribbling to invented spellings to eventual mature writing.

4. In addition to using children's written documents as reading material, holistic teachers frequently use literature books, rejecting vocabulary-controlled, sentence-controlled stories in favor of those containing predictable language patterns. They choose the best children's literature available to read to and with children. Classrooms are stocked with interesting information books and storybooks, and teachers encourage children to choose from those books the ones they desire to read.

5. Holistic teachers organize literacy instruction around themes or units of study relevant to students. Children use all of the language arts (listening, speaking, reading, and writing) as they study a particular theme. Many teachers also integrate the teaching of music, art, social studies, and other subjects into these units of study.

6. Language learning and its use is largely based on personal relevance. Holistic teachers believe in intrinsic motivation, and when children enjoy good literature, create stories, write letters, keep personal journals, and share their written documents with others, language learning becomes intrinsically rewarding.

7. Social interaction in whole language classrooms is essential and visible. Holistic teachers believe that literacy development depends on having opportunities to communicate. Since communication is not possible without social interaction, these teachers give children opportunities to read other children's compositions, and to write, listen, and speak to each other.

8. Holistic teachers give children opportunities to both teach and learn from each other. They often work collaboratively on a common interest or goal. They react to each other's written products, and they share favorite books with each other.

9. Holistic teachers control literacy instruction. It may be student centered, but it is also teacher guided. While whole language purists reject direct instruction (Newman, 1985) and phonics (Watson, 1989), holistic teachers recognize that some direct instruction, including instruction in phonics, is not incompatible with student empowerment, nor with any of the other whole language practices described in this chapter. The assumption of primacy of either "skills over meaning" or "meaning over skills" simply does not make sense (Goldenberg, 1991; Eldredge & Butterfield, 1986; Eldredge, 1991).

10. Teachers emphasize holistic reading and writing experiences—children spend most of the classroom time available on meaningful reading and writing experiences rather than on skills instruction preparing them to read and write. Writing instruction is primarily focused on holistic writing, with a secondary emphasis on spelling, handwriting, grammar, and other related skills. Reading instruction is focused on holistic, connected, reading experiences. Immature readers of any age are involved in holistic reading strategies such as "taped assisted reading," "echo reading," and "Language Experience Approach" (LEA), and Don Holdaway's "shared book experience" (see Chapter 9). These experiences help children read materials they are unable to read by themselves. In addition, whole language teachers provide opportunities for readers at all developmental levels to have holistic reading experiences in books and other materials they can read independently.

Advantages of a Holistic Approach

Holistic teaching is an educational trend that affects everyone involved with schools and concerned about literacy. It is a movement that offers great hope to teachers, children, and parents. The following holistic teaching practices are supported by research and are associated with effective literacy programs:

Basic Instructional Practices.

1. Literature books replace basal readers as the major medium of instruction. Children enjoy reading literature books more than basal readers, and their

achievement is better (Cohen, 1968; Cullinan, Jaggar, & Strickland, 1974; Eldredge & Butterfield, 1986; Eldredge, 1991). Teachers select books for children that accommodate a wide range of student interests, and students are allowed to select books they want to read.

2. Teachers encourage students to read extensively. Involving children in actual reading may well be the major component that affects growth in reading achievement (Reitsma, 1988; Allington, 1977, 1980, 1984; Fielding, Wilson, & Anderson, 1986). Not only do students who read extensively become better readers through the "practice," but increased reading improves writing abilities, as well (Devries, 1970; Mills, 1974).

3. Students read favorite books over and over again. Teachers encourage children to practice their oral reading skills so they can read favorite books to younger children, peers, and parents. Repeated readings of moderately difficult text tend to produce student growth in word recognition, reading fluency, and reading comprehension (Herman, 1985; Samuels, 1979; Taylor, Wade, & Yekovich, 1985).

4. Teachers involve immature readers of all ages in holistic reading practices such as taped assisted reading, "shared book experience," "dyad reading," and "group assisted reading." Children learn to read by reading, and a teacher's prime concern must be to do as much reading as is necessary with children until they can make progress on their own (Smith, 1976, p. 297).

Holistic reading strategies help students read interesting, relevant material, too difficult for them to read independently. In addition, consistent use of these connected-text reading experiences enables students to repeatedly see written words as they are read for them, which eventually has a positive impact on their sight vocabulary skills (Bridge & Burton, 1982; Bridge, Winograd, & Haley, 1983; Eldredge & Quinn, 1988; Eldredge, 1990a), reading fluency (O'Shea, Sindelar, & O'Shea, 1985), and reading comprehension (Eldredge & Butterfield, 1986; Eldredge, 1988–1989; Eldredge & Quinn, 1988; Eldredge, 1990a; Eldredge, 1991).

Grouping Practices. Student dyads, total class activities, and small heterogeneous groups replace traditional reading groups. Not only do children enjoy their experiences in these grouping patterns, but they feel better about themselves and learn more than when placed in traditional basal reading groups (Eldredge & Butterfield, 1986).

Some teachers use an individualized approach, where children select the books they want to read, either individually or with another student, and read at their own pace (Eldredge & Butterfield, 1986). Others use a literature units approach, where teachers purchase multiple copies of specific literature books they believe students might want to read; in this situation students choose books from a limited number of options. Still others use a core literature approach, where students read books teachers believe all students should read. These literature books are chosen because teachers believe that they teach important concepts about "the human condition." Many teachers use a combination of all of these approaches.

Each orientation to literature-based reading instruction seems to work best with a particular grouping scheme. When using the individualized reading approach, student conferences and ad hoc groups are popular. (An *ad hoc* group is a temporary group formed for a specific purpose, such as to discuss a concept or book, or to learn about a specific aspect of the language. The group disbands after achieving its purpose.)

When using a literature units approach, teachers prepare "book talks" for specific books to help students choose what they want to read from those available, telling students enough about the book to help them know whether they want to read it. After the teacher has presented talks for five or six books, each student chooses one book to read. "Reading response" groups are formed consisting of all the students who chose a particular book. These groups involve students in both pre- and postreading activities designed for that book.

With a core literature approach, either the entire class reads a book at one time, or small groups read it at different times during the school year. Total class instruction is used in the former situation, while smaller heterogeneous groups are used in the latter.

Encouraging Writing. Holistic teachers encourage children to write daily for "intrinsic" purposes, on topics relevant to them. Not only do children learn to write well when given meaningful opportunities to write, but their reading abilities are also enhanced when writing is a part of a literature-rich environment (Calkins, 1982; Graves, 1983).

Holistic teachers also stress writing content over form during drafting and revising. Teachers encourage children to write down anything they can say, even when they do not know how to spell the words they want to use. Children write better when they are free to focus on what they want to say (Clarke, 1988).

In addition, children are encouraged to spell words by sounds (invented spelling) when they want to use words they cannot spell. Clarke (1988) found that first-grade students not only wrote better when they had the freedom to spell without emphasis on standard forms, but their word recognition abilities and reading achievement improved significantly as well. Spelling words according to their sounds focuses children's attention on the individual phonemes in words and requires them to apply their knowledge of letter–sound relationships. Both phonemic awareness and phonics knowledge are related to word recognition abilities. Therefore, it is not surprising that researchers find that writing has a positive impact on the word recognition abilities of young children when they are encouraged to use invented spelling as they write (Tierney & Shanahan, 1991).

Integrating Reading and Writing Instruction. Studies indicate that reading and writing are interrelated processes (Doctorow, Wittrock, & Marks, 1978; Taylor & Berkowitz, 1980), and growth in one process tends to facilitate growth in the other. Success in writing can be predicted by reading scores (Evanechko, Ollila, & Armstrong, 1974), and increased reading results in improved writing (Stotsky, 1983). It has also been demonstrated that writing activities in a literature-rich environment (Graves, 1983), writing activities using invented spelling (Clarke, 1988), and writing activities designed to improve reading comprehension (Stotsky, 1983; Holbrook, 1987) enhance reading abilities. Many language arts researchers have concluded from their research that writing and reading should be taught together (Graves, 1983; Shanahan, 1988).

Reading and writing are interrelated in a complex relationship. Sometimes we observe good readers who are poor writers, and good writers who are poor readers. Further studies are needed to understand the exact nature of the reading–writing connection (see Tierney & Shanahan, 1991). However, reading and writing, when used together, involve students in a greater variety of reasoning operations than when either is used alone (Tierney & Shanahan, 1991, p. 272), enhancing literacy development in the process. In addition, teaching writing and reading together has been shown to motivate poor readers who have been "turned off to reading" (Dionisio, 1983).

Holistic teachers use themes of interest to students as a springboard for both reading and writing activities. Many holistic researchers and practitioners have found that thematic units offer a splendid opportunity to integrate both reading and writing (Reutzel & Cooter, 1992).

Teachers also frequently use students' oral language productions, during the first year of schooling, to help children discover relationships between the oral and written forms of the language. Students' own vocabulary and sentence patterns are easier for them to write and read than adult vocabulary and syntax patterns. Therefore, the transition from oral to written language is relatively easy for young children when they participate in the Language Experience Approach (LEA) to reading, or when they engage in the writing process. In language experience activities children see their speech written down by teachers or other literate individuals before they attempt to read it, and when young children write they encode their own speech for themselves and others to read.

Most of the research on language experience approaches suggests that they not only have special advantages for beginning readers, but they are as effective as basal programs in teaching young children how to read (Hall, 1981). Writing activities where children are encouraged to use invented spelling are known to have a positive impact on reading development (Clarke, 1988; Tierney & Shanahan, 1991; Robinson, 1991).

Understanding Text Structure and Meaning.

Learning Elements of Story Grammar. Teachers focus children's attention on the basic elements of story grammar when stories are read to or with them. Children are asked to make predictions about setting, characters, and storyline from book titles, book covers, and story previews before reading a story, and/or to identify basic story grammar elements after reading. Story schema seems to influence both what individuals recall from a story, and what they anticipate while reading a story (Mandler & Johnson, 1977; Fitzgerald, 1984). When needed, teachers provide less proficient students with instruction on story grammar. Fitzgerald and her colleagues found that instruction on story structure positively influenced poorer students' reading and writing of narrative text (Fitzgerald & Spiegel, 1983; Fitzgerald & Teasley, 1986).

Prior to reading stories to or with young children, teachers also spend time on appropriate vocabulary/schemata issues that may affect the comprehension of the story (see Tierney & Cunningham, 1984).

Inferring Intended Meaning. Teachers prepare students to use their own prior experiences and the writer's cues to infer the intended meaning of specific text material. While children derive benefits from reading books they choose to read even when teachers do not intervene in any way, many holistic teachers consciously involve students in pre- and postreading activities designed to enhance their reading comprehension of specific material (for an extensive review of the reading comprehension research on this issue see Tierney & Cunningham, 1984).

Judith Irwin (1991) has written a scholarly, definitive book on how to teach reading comprehension processes. Her definition of reading comprehension reveals the complex nature of the process and identifies those elements of the process subject to teacher intervention:

> Comprehension can be seen as the process of using one's own prior experiences and the writer's cues to construct a set of meanings that are useful to the individual reader reading in a specific context. This process can involve understanding and selectively recalling ideas in individual sentences (microprocesses), inferring relationships between clauses and sentences (integrative processes), organizing ideas around summarizing ideas (macroprocesses), and making inferences not necessarily intended by the author (elaborative processes). These processes work together (interactive hypothesis) and can be controlled and adjusted by the reader as required by the reader's goals (metacognitive processes) and the total situation in which comprehension is occurring (situational context). (p. 9)

For students to engage in the thinking processes involved in comprehending text they must be able to integrate their knowledge of various aspects of written language. Students' ability to think and create meaning while reading is either facilitated or hindered by decoding, syntax, semantic, and discourse (text structure) knowledge they must use while reading. If knowledge is weak in any of these areas, comprehension suffers. On the other hand, if knowledge is strong in all of these areas, student thinking improves. Effective teachers consistently seek to enlarge these basic knowledge sources through meaningful literary experiences. Therefore, teachers who are knowledgeable about the impact of decoding, syntax, semantic, and discourse knowledge on reading comprehension selectively choose appropriate prereading and/or postreading activities to enhance student comprehension. For example, teachers and students commonly engage in prereading activities designed to build specific schemata/vocabulary knowledge prior to reading text material requiring the use of that knowledge.

Teachers have various opportunities to enhance students' comprehension of specific text material throughout the day. For example, whenever students read content-area books (science, social studies, health, etc.), successful teachers make those reading experiences more meaningful for them through well-chosen prereading and/or postreading activities. In addition, teachers occasionally provide similar experiences for students when several of them are reading the same children's literature book (Giddings, 1992). However, such activities never treat children's literature as basal text, nor do they take much classroom time.

In summary, effective holistic teachers provide students with the knowledge needed to engage in specific thinking processes while reading, and teach them how to employ those processes, when necessary, to improve their comprehension of both narrative and expository text.

Learning to Think. Holistic teachers help students to develop their own comprehension processing strategies through meaningful experiences with expository text such as social studies, health, science, or other content-oriented material. Teachers use scaffolding processes such as "think-alouds," "modeling," and "reciprocal teaching" (see Chapter 7) to help children develop their individual thinking strategies (for example, see the model proposed by Gordon, 1985). It is one thing to prepare students to read and understand a specific book, and another to help them develop their own thinking strategies that they can employ when reading any book (see Tierney & Cunningham, 1984, pp. 629–634).

Learning to Decode. Teachers provide primary-grade students daily with brief, total-class systematic decoding instruction. Holistic teaching strategies seem to have a more powerful effect on students' reading development, and their attitudes towards reading, when those strategies are supplemented with brief, but appropriate instruction on decoding (Eldredge & Butterfield, 1986; Eldredge, Quinn, & Butterfield, 1990; Eldredge, 1991).

Results of Research on Whole Language

Because whole language has been defined as a set of beliefs (Farris & Kaczmarski, 1988), rather than a set of specific teacher practices, some educators and researchers find it difficult to define, implement in a classroom, and evaluate. Because little evidence exists that all whole language educators are following the same set of beliefs (Bergeron, 1990), and whole language advocates do not seem to agree on the practices that are, and are not, consistent with the philosophy (Thompson, 1992), research findings on the effectiveness of whole language are understandably inconsistent. However, if one wants to talk about the effectiveness of *specific practices* generally associated with whole language, as in the preceding discussion, research findings are less equivocal.

Several educators have criticized the quality of whole language research. Thompson (1992), speaking of whole language research, made the following statement:

Teachers should be made aware that the evidence upon which WL [whole language] assumptions are founded is not experimental research. When WL advocates pronounce the existence of "plenty of research," they imply experimental comparisons of treatments favoring WL. Beware! It is descriptive research which WL advocates are referencing. Descriptive research, some of which is "kid watching" as Yetta Goodman refers to it, is used to describe rather than to compare. If teachers accept WL philosophical assumptions for operating their reading and writing activity programs, they should be apprised that they are operating on a set of beliefs that are based on intuitions rather than hard experimental evidence. . . . [T]here is a paucity of experimental research. (pp. 144–145)

McKenna, Robinson, and Miller (1992), and Almasi, Palmer, Gambrell, and Pressley (1991) have concluded that the "whole language" construct still remains untested because most whole language investigations completed so far have not met the standards accepted for either quantitative or qualitative research.

Because of these ambiguities, educators are still divided regarding both the merits of whole language programs and the conclusions drawn from whole language research (Stahl & Miller, 1989; McKenna, Robinson, & Miller, 1990; Edelsky, 1990; Schickendanz, 1990; Stahl, 1990; McGee & Lomax, 1990). Some educators plead for additional research to help alleviate the impasse (McKenna et al., 1990), while others are concerned with the type of research that may be used to resolve the issue, feeling that quantitative research may not be the appropriate tool to use to evaluate the effects of "a philosophy" (Edelsky, 1990).

Assumptions of the Whole Language Philosophy

The whole language philosophy is based on two assumptions: 1) reading is a "psycholinguistic guessing game," and 2) oral and written language are equivalent language forms. We may challenge each of these assumptions on the basis of current research.

Reading Is a Psycholinguistic Guessing Game. Goodman (1967) developed his "psycholinguistic guessing game" concept by watching children read. From his observations he concluded that children selectively used three cueing systems—graphophonic, syntactic, and semantic—as they sought meaning from written text. He embraced a theory of reading that placed more importance on readers' use of prediction, print sampling, and context than upon word recognition abilities. He reasoned that meaning-oriented readers do not need to process every letter of every word or even to recognize all words in a text to get meaning from print. Readers who seek meaning as they read will focus on the syntax and semantic cues more than on the graphophonic cues.

Goodman therefore based his model on the premise that readers predict words by means of cues provided by context and then confirm or refute their predictions by the print samples that follow. His message to teachers is simple: Teachers should help students develop and use prediction skills, deriving the meanings of words from context cues and confirming or refuting their predictions with further reading. Because meaning is the major reading focus, teachers should not be too concerned about decoding errors as long as those errors are syntactically and semantically appropriate to the text being read.

Refutation: Readers Rely on Graphic Cues. Research indicates that the alphabetic principle is more important in the reading process than the "psycholinguistic guessing game." Goodman argues that poor and beginning readers rely on phonics to identify unfamiliar words, while good readers rely less on graphic cues and more on contextual information. However, research conducted over the past fifteen or more years does not support his claim.

First, the use of context to recognize words is not a variable that separates good readers from poor readers, nor is it a cause of reading failure (Stanovich, 1992). Even less skilled readers make substantial use of contextual information to help them identify written words (West & Stanovich, 1978; Stanovich, West, & Freeman, 1981; Simpson & Foster, 1986; Nicholson, Lillas, & Rzoska, 1988).

Second, studies have shown that the effect of context on word recognition speed decreases with age, grade level, word recognition ability, and stimulus quality (see Stanovich, 1984, 1986 for reviews).

Third, *poor* readers tend not to fully analyze the interior components of words; i.e., they seem to lack concern for word details beyond the beginning of the word (Venezky, 1976).

Fourth, eye movement studies have revealed that the time required for *fluent* readers to recognize words in and out of context is nearly the same, and that word length and word familiarity, not context, account for much of the variation of eye fixations (see Just & Carpenter, 1987; Rayner & Pollatsek, 1989; Adams, 1990; Stanovich, 1991).

Fifth, research indicates that *fluent* readers sample the letter sequences in words rather completely, even when reading fairly predictable words (Just & Carpenter, 1980, 1987; Rayner & Pollatsek, 1989). Good readers do not reduce their sampling of letter sequences in words when context is present, nor are they in the habit of skipping difficult words (Stanovich, 1992).

Sixth, even though fluent readers are better than poor readers in language prediction abilities, they rely less on context to identify words as they read (Perfetti, Goldman, & Hogaboam, 1979).

Seventh, research suggests that while good readers use both graphic and contextual cues when reading, words' *spelling patterns* are most important to fluent reading (Tulving & Gold, 1963). Better readers are so fast and accurate at word recognition that they do not need to rely on contextual information. It is only when graphophonic knowledge breaks down that good readers resort to contextual information for word identification (Stanovich, 1980; Tulving & Gold, 1963).

Research also helps us understand why Goodman observed young children using all three cueing systems (graphophonic, syntax, and semantic) to identify unfamiliar words. Readers with undeveloped word recognition skills would need to compensate for that deficit by using contextual information. As readers' word recognition skills improve, context would have less effect on recognition speed as context would only be referred to when word recognition fails. Biemiller (1970) supports this reasoning, finding in a longitudinal study of first graders' oral reading errors that progress in reading was determined in part by how early children began to shift their attention to the letters within words. In addition, Perfetti's (1985, 1986) verbal efficiency theory maintains that children will have difficulty reading if they cannot recognize individual words quickly and accurately. Research supports his position (see Adams, 1990; Gough, Ehri, & Treiman, 1992).

New theories of reading suggest that word recognition is much more important than Goodman's "psycholinguistic guessing game" theory acknowledges. Researchers now generally believe that (a) written words are identified by their spellings (orthography); (b) meanings of words (semantics) are associated with their pronunciations (phonology); and (c) meaning ambiguities (problems distinguishing meanings of multiple-meaning words) are resolved by the context in which the words occur. The brain processes all of these sources of information in parallel, or simultaneously, but it is the "orthographic processor," using Adams's (1990) words, "that kicks the system in." This parallel distributed processing that good readers employ while reading occurs very quickly. The brain is capable of recognizing written words and associating meaning with them in a fraction of a second.

Oral and Written Language Are Equivalent. Whole language purists in the United States and Canada believe that oral and written language are equivalent language forms, and that children can learn to read and write as naturally as they learn to understand and speak oral language. They do not view written language as being secondary to oral language (Edelsky, 1990), and assume that students can learn to read and write by being immersed in meaningful reading and writing situations, just as they learned to listen and speak by being immersed in meaningful oral language experiences. To support this assumption, they cite various studies to show that young children can learn both oral and written language *naturally* as toddlers (Baghban, 1984; Harste, Woodward, & Burke, 1984; McGee, Lomax, & Head, 1988).

Whole language purists further assume that the rules governing the structure of language, including the alphabetic principle (phonemic awareness and phonics knowledge), are discovered by children as they are meaningfully involved in activities requiring them to use oral and written language (Ferreiro & Teberosky, 1982; Lindfors, 1987); that is, the phonemic awareness and phonics knowledge needed by literate people is "caught" implicitly while using the language, and does not need to be explicitly "taught." These purists recognize the need for children to develop and refine a knowledge of the alphabetic principle, the principle that reveals how speech is coded into written language, but are violently opposed to the direct teaching of the principle (Watson, 1989; Altwerger et al., 1987; Goodman & Goodman, 1979; Goodman, 1989).

Refutation: Oral and Written Language Are Not Equivalent. Knowledge of the alphabetic principle is not generally acquired "naturally." Research supports the view that children develop some literacy abilities by being immersed in holistic reading and writing activities. However, certain aspects of the written language are not easy for children to learn naturally, and existing research suggests that these aspects (phonemic awareness and phonics knowledge, for example) often need to be made explicit to children if they are to become effective writers and readers (Adams, 1990; Bradley & Bryant, 1983; Lundberg, Frost, & Peterson, 1988).

Phonemic awareness is the conscious ability to segment spoken words into their constituent phonemes. Writing with invented spellings requires phonemic awareness because students must be able to hear the individual sounds in words before they can try to match those sounds with letters. The ability to segment individual phonemes in words correlates highly with reading achievement, and training programs that foster this ability appear to speed up overall reading development (Evans & Carr, 1985). *Phonics knowledge* is knowledge about the relationships that exist between speech sounds and printed letters. Byrne and Fielding-Barnsley (1989) found that both phonemic awareness and phonics knowledge were needed for a reader to learn the alphabetic principle, which must be acquired for successful reading. They wrote that "it appears from our research that the major hurdle for young learners in understanding the basic principle of alphabetic writing is the realization that the speech stream is composed of a small stock of interchangeable units, the phonemes. . . . [E]xplicit instruction in letter–phoneme relations, added to phonemic awareness, makes it likely that the child can compute the representational function of those letters" (p. 320). We will discuss phonemic awareness and phonics issues more extensively in Chapter 2.

The position taken in this book is that written and oral language are not equivalent language forms (see Liberman & Liberman, 1990), and that while many children manifest emerging literate behaviors while engaged in relevant reading and writing experiences, they do not learn to read and write in the same *natural,* subconscious way as they learn to speak and listen. Written language involves a *code* (the alphabet), which makes it significantly different from oral language. This code *represents* the oral language. Therefore, oral language is primary, and written language is secondary. Which language form do we learn first? Which language form is absolutely necessary in order for people to live together in groups? Remember, no societies exist on the earth today without an oral language, but many still do not have a written language. Since a written language uses an alphabet to represent sounds from oral language, logic would suggest that children need to understand *explicitly* how the sounds in spoken words relate to the print in written words. Making these aspects of language explicit to children need not consume much classroom time, and need not be boring and meaningless to them.

Many educators are now questioning the incidental teaching of phonemic awareness and phonics, a popular approach in some whole language classrooms. Schickedanz (1990), for example, wrote, "Whole language approaches seem to provide precious little help in making graphic-phonemic information explicit to children. . . . My work with 3-, 4-, and 5-year-old children leads me to believe that literacy development is facilitated when adults make phonemic segmentation explicit" (p. 129). Stahl (1990) amplifies this point:

Many of the theoretical underpinnings of whole language . . . are based on research done with the acquisition of oral language. Only if you believe that written language is a parallel language system, developing in a manner similar to that of oral language, can you use that theory and research base to discuss the acquisition of reading. It is this belief that supports whole language. This belief seems to be based as much on faith as on research. The evidence that children grow in their use of written language from exposure to a supportive environment is based largely on case studies. Although such studies can provide useful insights, there is other research evidence that many children do not learn to read "naturally." (pp. 148–149)

Thompson (1992, p. 139) emphasized, "While no doubt some students can learn from immersion, most students profit best from direct instruction, and some cannot learn without it."

In a recent clarification of her view on emergent literacy, Adams (1991) used strong words about the concept of immersion as proposed by whole language purists:

For some people, the term *emergent literacy* alludes to the notion that literacy development is an enormously complex process—that only as its many components mature and merge together can literacy in any real sense "emerge." . . . But then there are the other interpretations of the term. Don Holdaway defines it as a stage that occurs when the child has begun to recognize letters but still can't sound out words. That's very different. And in a third usage, which is one that I cannot endorse, emergent literacy is linked to the idea that literacy will naturally blossom forth if only the child is surrounded by a rich and joyful world of print. (p. 210)

Experimental studies suggest phonemic awareness is best acquired through early, explicit training (Bradley & Bryant, 1983; Lundberg et al., 1988), and Teale (1991, p. 186) says that children will "be in big trouble" if decoding is taught only incidentally. Phonemic awareness and phonics knowledge are prerequisites to conventional literacy, and the ability to deal with the codes of alphabetic languages does not simply and automatically emerge (Sulzby & Teale, 1991).

Whole Language Application Activities

1. Summarize, in writing, the classroom practices generally associated with whole language.
2. Describe your personal position regarding whole language. Is it consistent with existing research?
3. Summarize, in writing, holistic teaching practices supported by research.
4. Interview several "whole language" teachers. Ask them to define whole language. Record and compare their responses. How similar are their definitions?
5. Visit one or two "whole language" classrooms. Observe children and teachers in action. How are reading, writing, spelling, grammar, handwriting, and listening taught in these classrooms?

Chapter 2

Decoding

The Coding System in Written English

A twenty-six letter alphabet code is used in English to represent the oral language in written form. Each spoken word in the language is comprised of individual sounds called *phonemes,* and the twenty-six letters (called *graphemes*) in the written code are used in a variety of ways to represent those phonemes. For example, the word *tack* is comprised of three separate phonemes /t/ /a/ /k/. The letter *t* represents the phoneme /t/, the letter *a* represents the phoneme /a/, and the letters *ck* represent the phoneme /k/. However imperfect the system may appear, a word's letter sequences in the English language represent its phoneme sequences.

When individuals use the written language to communicate, they *encode* the words in their sentences, paragraphs, and larger units of discourse, representing the sounds of each word by written symbols. When individuals read, they *decode* words one after another by different means, using their language knowledge, schemata, and thinking abilities to construct meaning from the message; that is, readers translate written code into words, making it possible for them to use other abilities and knowledge to apprehend the oral language equivalent of the written message.

Defining Decoding

Decoding is a term that means different things to different people. Some definitions are extremely narrow, while others are quite broad. For example, some individuals use the term *word recognition* to describe the process students use when they recognize words instantaneously, and *decoding* to describe the process they use when they "sound out" words, thus excluding word recognition from their definition. Others use *decoding* to refer to word recognition, and the term *recoding* to refer to the process used to sound out words. Still others use the term to refer to both word recognition and sounding out words.

Decoding is defined fairly broadly in this book, as the process readers use to translate written language into either verbal speech or inner speech, regardless of the strategy used for the translation. We use this definition because the reading theory embraced here is based on the premise that readers generally translate written words into internal speech as they read (Cunningham & Cunningham, 1978; Tannenhaus, Flanigan, & Seidenberg, 1980; Taylor & Taylor, 1983; McCutcheon, Bell, France, & Perfetti, 1991). This premise is derived from research on the effects of speech upon the development of word meanings (see Taylor & Taylor, 1983). Young children initially attach meanings to words from speech (i.e., each word's unique sounds). Readers translate written words into inner speech because inner speech calls to mind the attached meanings and aids comprehension while reading.

Let us recapitulate the language development process children go through, and the effects of the auditory channel on the development of word meanings. Children first learn to understand speech, and then they learn to speak. After speech is reasonably well developed, children learn to read. Reading initially is taught orally to children. It is only after children learn to read orally that they are able to engage in silent reading. Even after children learn to read silently, they spend most of their time using oral language. Therefore, listening and speaking are practiced much more than reading and writing. People are more accustomed to, and have more practice with, the auditory channel for communication, and it is through the auditory channel that people (apart from those with hearing impairments and the deaf) learn to attach meanings to most words.

Children attach meanings to spoken words early in life through trial and error. As they listen to their parents and others trying to communicate with them, they perceive sounds, or sometimes think they do, and attach meanings to them based upon how the adults in their environment use them. Children attempt to replicate the sounds of words so they can communicate with others through speech, sometimes making mistakes that adults find amusing; but through trial and error, children learn to listen and speak. Through early, meaningful, receptive and expressive language experiences children begin to refine their listening and speaking abilities, and can eventually use the spoken language effectively to communicate with others.

Children learn to differentiate words from one another by their unique sound sequences (phonemes). It is the individual phonemes in a word, occurring in a specific sequence, that set it apart from all other words (homophones excepted). Therefore, children learn to identify individual words by processing specific sound sequences through the auditory channel. Children attach meanings to the words, based upon their sounds, and both the sounds and the meanings attached to them are stored in *lexical memory*. Huey (1908), speaking of inner speech, said, "Although it is a foreshortened and incomplete speech in most of us, yet it is perfectly certain that the inner hearing or pronouncing, or both, of what is read, is a constituent part of the reading of by far the most people" (p. 117).

When children begin to read they must use all of their language abilities and knowledge to make sense of the messages contained in written text. However, before they can employ this knowledge, they must be able to decode, or translate the text's written symbols into words. It is the words in the spoken language to which children have attached meanings, and it is the words in written text that bring those meanings to mind when reading. Therefore, when individuals read they do *not* go directly from the print to meaning, as some believe. They go from the graphic representation of the word to the word itself to the meanings attached to the word. For good readers, these connections occur nearly simultaneously.

Many studies demonstrate clearly that readers, when reading silently, are sensitive to the auditory components of words (see Taylor & Taylor, 1983). Readers take more time to read words containing many syllables than words of equal graphemic length containing fewer syllables. Readers also detect more misspellings in words when the spellings are not phonetically compatible with the spoken word, and they detect fewer misspellings when the misspellings are phonetically compatible with the spoken word.

Readers store inner speech in short term memory until they can integrate it and comprehend it as a clause or sentence. Poor readers cannot use inner speech or auditory images to hold linguistic material in short term memory as well as good readers do because of inadequate decoding (translating) abilities. Apparently, this ability to hold inner speech in short term memory does not develop quickly (see Taylor & Taylor, 1983).

The theory of reading embraced in this book suggests that proficient readers simultaneously process orthographic (spelling), phonological (speech), and meaning (syntax and semantic) information while they read, making predictions about immediate and subsequent text, and checking those predictions against the actual text. Because readers encounter written words first, it is their orthographic and phonological processors (see Adams, 1990) that initiate this parallel distributed processing, which in turn leads to reading comprehension. Decoding therefore plays an important role in reading (see Chapter 1).

The Relationship of Decoding to Reading

Decoding is not equivalent to reading, since readers sometimes can decode words without understanding them. At other times readers can decode, but may not be able to organize meaningfully the ideas presented among or between sentences. At still other times readers can decode, but cannot create mental pictures from the message, make inferences from text clues, or critically evaluate the message. Decoding is clearly not reading, but it is necessary for reading (Adams, 1990), for if print cannot be translated into language, then it cannot be understood (Gough & Tunmer, 1986, p. 7).

Reading fluency is directly related to reading comprehension (Nathan & Stanovich, 1991; Eldredge et al., 1990). *Reading fluency* has been defined by cognitive psychologists as the ability to recognize words accurately, rapidly, and automatically (see Perfetti, 1985; LaBerge & Samuels, 1974; Stanovich, 1980, 1986). Individuals who are fluent decoders (who recognize words automatically without giving conscious attention to them), generally comprehend written text better than those who are poor at decoding. In fact, inadequate decoding seems to be a hallmark of poor readers (Carnine, Carnine, & Gertsen, 1984; Lesgold & Curtis, 1981; Jorm & Share, 1983). Good decoders find it easier to comprehend written text than poor decoders simply because they have less difficulty in translating print into language.

Cognitive psychologists reason that people have finite cognitive capacity to devote to any given task (Kahneman, 1973), and that since comprehension processing utilizes so much of this capacity (Freedman & Calfee, 1984), ways must be found to decrease the capacity needed for decoding and increase that available for comprehension. Readers who are poor decoders, will use too much of the cognitive capacity needed for reading in attempts to translate the written symbols into words. Fluent readers will use less of their cognitive capacity for decoding, leaving more for comprehension.

Different Decoding Levels

Decoding, as used in this book, includes both a fast translation process called *word recognition,* and slower processes called *word identification.* Word recognition is the primary decoding process used by proficient readers, and implies an accurate, rapid, and automatic recognition of written words. The utilization of various word identification strategies, along with some word recognition, is associated with less proficient readers. Once readers have developed reading fluency their decoding efforts do not interfere with comprehension processing as some researchers suggest (Johnson & Baumann, 1984; Barr, 1972; Cohen, 1974–1975), but rather enhance it. Less fluent readers find comprehension difficult, then, not because of an overreliance on decoding, as whole language purists suggest, but because of insufficiently developed decoding skills.

Teachers can enhance children's word recognition development by (a) providing them with meaningful experiences with written language that (b) focus their attention on the letter sequences of specific words. When children perceive the relationships existing between the sounds of spoken words and the letters in written words, word recognition occurs more rapidly than when they do not perceive such relationships.

Quantitative and Qualitative Dimensions. Children develop word recognition skills only through practice, and the more meaningful the practice is to children, the more likely they will continue to practice. Word recognition practice has both a quantitative and a qualitative dimension. The quantitative dimension is based on the belief that the more experiences children have associating spoken words with the letter sequences representing them, the greater their word recognition development will be. The qualitative dimension is based on the belief that when teachers provide children with experiences that focus their attention on words' letter–sound relationships, the greater their word recognition development will be.

Students can develop word recognition through the use of such informal decoding strategies employed by holistic teachers as shared book reading, dyad reading, group assisted reading, tape assisted reading, repeated reading, writing with invented spellings, and the Language Experience Approach to reading. These strategies are effective if students pay attention to the words' letter sequences as they read or are read to, and, in the case of writing, if they try to recall the letter sequences of words as they write them. Informal decoding strategies such as these (with the exception of writing) provide children with *quantitative* word recognition practice. Writing with invented spellings is probably more qualitative than quantitative.

Children may also develop their word recognition abilities through meaningful phonics instruction. Such instruction can enhance phonemic awareness and can help children learn how the sounds in spoken words are related to the letters in written words. In fact, carefully organized phonics instruction focuses children's attention on words' letter sequences more than any other type of activity (Adams, 1990). Planned phonics activities, therefore, provide *qualitative* word recognition practice.

There are advantages to using Goodman's "psycholinguistic guessing game" with young children. However, these advantages are related to other areas of the reading process rather than to the recognition of unknown words. Goodman's model does not require young children to look closely enough at the letters of unknown words to enable them to associate their unique letter sequences with the words. Hence, encounters with unknown words, when using this strategy, do not provide children with either quantitative or qualitative word recognition practice. For example, when teachers ask children to "guess" an unknown word based on syntax, semantic, and graphophonic contextual information, they generally need to look only at its initial letter to make an intelligent guess, providing that they are able to recognize the other words in the sentence and can use their knowledge of syntax and semantics. Try using the guessing game yourself. Read the following sentence: "The beautiful black cat p_ _ _ _ _ gently as her master petted her." Ask yourself, "What action word (syntax focus) beginning with the letter *p* (graphophonic focus) would make sense (semantic focus) in this sentence?" Did you respond with "purred"?

Readers may identify words that they do not immediately recognize by using a variety of word identification strategies, some of which they develop themselves, and others that teachers teach them to employ. Among those strategies are (a) identifying words by analogy (b) identifying words through contextual information (c) identifying words by "sounding them out" (phonics), (d) identifying words through recognition of morphemic units (roots, prefixes, suffixes, or inflectional endings), and (e) identifying words by locating syllable boundaries and sounding out the syllables (syllabic analysis and phonics). Readers are decoding when they use any of these word identification processes, even though these are considered to be interim strategies, employed only because word recognition abilities have not developed sufficiently for accurate, automatic, rapid decoding.

In summary then, decoding involves either word recognition; identifying words by analogy; identifying words through the use of contextual clues; sounding out words using phonics; identifying words through the recognition of familiar root words, prefixes, suffixes, or inflectional endings; or identifying syllabic boundaries within multisyllabic words and sounding out the separate syllables. The goal of all decoding instruction should be to help readers develop word recognition abilities because accurate, rapid, automatic recognition of printed words is directly related to reading comprehension, and is a hallmark of all good readers. Word identification strategies are a means to the end, not ends themselves.

Decoding Application Activities

1. Describe, in writing, the role of "inner speech" in the reading process.
2. Summarize, in writing, the relationship of decoding to reading.
3. Summarize, in writing, the quantitative and qualitative dimensions of word recognition practice. Describe how teachers can provide both types of practice for students.
4. Interview two or three teachers. Ask them to define *decoding*. Compare their responses. How do they compare with each other? How do they compare with the definition of decoding in this text? How do they teach decoding in their classrooms?
5. Visit a second- or third-grade classroom. Ask the teacher to identify the two best and the two poorest readers in the classroom. Listen to these students read. Observe the decoding strategies they use. Ask them some questions about what they have read. How do their decoding abilities relate to their reading comprehension?

Chapter 3

Phonemic Awareness and the Alphabetic Principle

The English language uses an alphabetic writing system whose underlying assumption is that each *phoneme,* or speech sound of oral language, has its own distinctive graphic representation. There is not a one-to-one relationship between the 42 or so speech sounds that comprise spoken English and the 26 letters of its alphabet; some letters must be used in combination with others to represent fully these basic sounds. This connection or relationship between letters and sounds is known as the *alphabetic principle.* The principle reveals how the sounds in spoken words (the smallest elements of phonology) are represented by the letters in written words (the symbols of the alphabet). The alphabetic principle provides students with the key to understanding how the oral and written forms of the language relate to each other.

Students need two sources of knowledge for them to understand the alphabetic principle. First, they need to be aware that spoken words are comprised of phonemes (the smallest units of sound within words), and second, they need to understand the relationship existing between these units of sound and the alphabetic letters (*graphemes*) representing them. When individuals become aware that spoken words are comprised of phonemes we say that they have *phonemic awareness.* When individuals are able to associate letters with these phonemes we say that they have letter–sound knowledge or *phonics knowledge.* Individuals who understand the alphabetic principle must have developed some level of phonemic awareness and phonics knowledge. Educators and researchers are currently debating the exact nature of this knowledge and how much is needed to be a successful reader. However, there should be no debate about the importance of both phonemic awareness and phonics knowledge in writing and reading. Reading acquisition research suggests that knowledge in both areas is causally related to literacy development.

Phonemic Awareness

What Are Phonemes?

A *phoneme* is the smallest unit of sound in a word. The word *man* has three phonemes: /m/ /a/ /n/. The word *sleep* has four: /s/ /l/ /e/ /p/, even though there are five letters in the word. A single phoneme change in a word results in a meaning difference because word meanings are determined by the phonemes. For example, consider how the phoneme differences in the following word pairs affect word meanings: p**e**n, p**i**n; so**d**, so**b**; **b**at, **f**at; and **c**attle, **r**attle. When individuals hear these words they automatically attach different meanings to them, even though they may not realize that a subtle difference of just one phoneme sets each of them apart from all other words. As stated earlier, except in the case of homophones, the unique sequence of phonemes in a word distinguishes it from all other words used in the spoken language.

Words are not our only means of communication. Meanings are also conveyed to us through the use of signals or signs, such as pictures, symbols ($), door bells, or dog barks. In general, however, nonlinguistic systems are not as efficient as language. Because the signals used in nonlinguistic systems differ holistically from one another, recipients must perceive each signal or sign individually. In addition, the number of possible different signals in a nonlinguistic system is limited, which places limits on what that system can communicate. Words, however, are created by phoneme sequences, and individuals can produce an extremely large number of words by creating new sequences. The English language contains hundreds of thousands of words; almost all of them are perceived by their unique sequence of phonemes, but each is not holistically different from other words. Liberman, Shankweiler, and Liberman (1989) described this phenomenon in the following words:

> Language is different in a most important way. Meanings are not conveyed directly by signals that differ holistically, but rather by words that are distinct from each other in their internal structure. This structure is formed of a small number of meaningless phonological segments we know as consonants and vowels, and governed according to a highly systematic combinatorial scheme called phonology. The consequence is that words can (and do) number in the tens of thousands. Moreover, there is a perfectly natural basis for accommodating new words, since the phonological system, which all speakers of the language have in common, automatically recognizes a new, but legal, structure as a word that stands to have meaning attached to it. (pp. 7–8)

Liberman et al. (1989) claimed that words, whether spoken or printed, are always phonological structures. They stated that listeners or readers "may very well be unsure of [a word's] meaning—indeed, may even have got the meaning wrong—but if they have the phonological structure, they have [an] adequate basis for ultimately getting its meaning properly sorted out. As for going directly to meaning . . . independently of phonology—surely that is done when a person sees a picture, for example, or hears the roar of a lion, but not when one perceives a word as it is spoken or read" (p. 8).

Phonemes, therefore, are the smallest units of sound in a word that determine the meaning we attach to it. As children learn to speak a language, they are not consciously aware of its phonological structure because the biological specialization for speech manages the production and perception of phonemic structures below the level of consciousness; awareness of phonemes in words is not an automatic consequence of speaking a language. It is only when children attempt to make the transition from oral to written language that a conscious awareness of phonemes becomes necessary—children cannot understand the alphabetic transcription used in the written language if they are unaware of the phonological structure that transcription represents.

What Is Phonemic Awareness?

Phonemic awareness, sometimes referred to incorrectly as phonological awareness, has been defined in a variety of ways. Cunningham, for example, defined phonemic awareness as the ability to examine language independently of meaning, and to manipulate its component sounds (Griffith & Olsen, 1992). Isabelle Liberman defined it as the ability to analyze the internal structure of the word into its phonemic constituents (Shankweiler, 1991). Blachman (1991) defined it as an awareness of and the ability to manipulate the phonological segments in words. Yopp (1992) defined phonemic awareness as having control over the smallest units in speech, the phonemes. Griffith and Olsen (1992), said that phonemic awareness is the realization of sound segments in words; a realization that speech can be segmented into phonemes. They said, "It is an understanding of the structure of spoken language" (p. 518).

All definitions of phonemic awareness focus on children's understanding of the nature of spoken words. Do children understand that words can be broken into smaller-than-syllable sound sequences we call phonemes? If they do, then they are becoming phonemically aware. Can they count the phonemes in spoken words? If they can, they possess a higher level of phonemic awareness. Can they segment or isolate the separate phonemes in words? If so, then they are phonemically aware at a still higher level of understanding. In fact, it is the isolation level of phonemic awareness (being able to vocalize the separate phonemes in single syllable words) that we generally associate with successful reading and writing. Researchers disagree regarding the difficulty children have in completing various phonemic awareness tasks. However, most would agree with the following statement:

> The phonemic awareness tasks easiest for children are those requiring them to rhyme words or to recognize rhymes. Blending phonemes and syllable splitting (e.g., segmenting the beginning sound of back /b/ from the remainder -ack) are intermediate-level tasks. The most difficult phonemic awareness tasks are those that involve completely segmenting the phonemes in spoken words and manipulating phonemes to form different words. (Griffith & Olson, 1992, p. 517)

Technically, individuals could be phonemically aware and not even know the letters of the alphabet, because phonemic awareness involves speech sounds, not the letters representing them. In fact, the earliest phonemic awareness training programs we know of focused on phonemes without reference to letters (Zhurova, 1963; Elkonin, 1963, 1973). These early experiments established a strong connection between children's levels of phonemic awareness after training and later successful reading. Subsequent studies, patterned after these earlier ones (Olofsson & Lundberg, 1985; Torneus, 1984), not only found a strong connection between children's levels of phonemic awareness and later reading achievement, but also a strong connection to spelling. However, as successful as these experiments were, subsequent studies have revealed that children best develop phonemic awareness when they are taught to associate the letters in written words with the phonemes they represent (Hohn & Ehri, 1983; Bradley & Bryant, 1985; Ball & Blachman, 1991).

The Difference between Phonemic and Phonological Awareness

Phonemic awareness and phonological awareness refer to different concepts. Speaking of this issue, Morais (1991) said: "The study of the relations between acquisition of literacy in an alphabetic writing system and phonemic awareness has been hampered to some extent by ambiguity [in defining terms]. Phonological awareness subsumes at least the following: awareness of phonological strings (a global, nonanalytical level of awareness); awareness of syllables; awareness of phonemes (also called segmental awareness); and awareness of phonetic features" (p. 6).

Phonological awareness, then, is a general term that refers to an awareness of the following aspects of language:

- words within sentences
- rhyming units within words
- beginning and ending sounds within words
- syllables within words
- phonemes within words (phonemic awareness)
- features of individual phonemes (how the mouth, tongue, vocal cords, and teeth are used to produce each phoneme)

Some forms of phonological awareness seem to be acquired with ease at an early age, while other forms do not seem to emerge unless circumstances require them (Peterson & Haines, 1992). Bradley and Bryant (1985) claim that awareness of rhyme seems to occur almost spontaneously in even very young children, whereas awareness of phonemes is very difficult for them to acquire. Most researchers believe that children's awareness of the phonological structure of speech is developmental in nature. Children first become aware of words, then syllables, and finally phonemes (Liberman, Shankweiler, Fischer, & Carter, 1974; Rozin & Gleitman, 1977; Leong & Haines, 1978).

It has been found that literacy instruction is not necessary for the development of all forms of phonological awareness. Studies convincingly demonstrate that awareness of syllables and awareness of phonological strings can be developed in many children before instruction (Liberman et al., 1974; Bradley & Bryant, 1983; Maclean, Bryant, & Bradley, 1987). However, Morais (1991) claims that phonemic awareness does not generally develop in the absence of explicit instruction on a graphic code that represents the phonemic information. His claim is supported by other researchers (Morais, Cary, Alegria, & Bertelson, 1979; Read, Zhang, Nie, & Ding, 1986).

How to Know if a Child Is Phonemically Aware

The following examples indicate various levels of phonemic awareness:

When presented with the spoken phonemes /m/ /a/ /n/, the child is able to identify the word *man*.

When presented with the spoken word *back,* the child is able to tell you that there are three sounds in the word.

When presented with the spoken word *box,* the child is able to tell you that /b/ is the beginning sound of the word.

When presented with the spoken word *toss,* the child is able to tell you that /s/ is the ending sound of the word.

When presented with the spoken word *cat,* the child is able to say the three phonemes in the word, /k/ /a/ /t/.

Individuals who can perform such tasks demonstrate that they are able to (a) focus on words independently of their meanings, and (b) have control over the smallest units of their speech. Such individuals are considered phonemically aware.

Why Phonemic Awareness Is Important

Phonemic awareness, understanding the internal structure of spoken language, would be irrelevant were it not for the fact that phonemes are the units encoded by the letters of the alphabetic languages used throughout the modern world. For children to learn to write and read they must learn how spoken language maps onto written language, and phonemic awareness helps them grasp this understanding (Ball & Blachman, 1991). Phonemic awareness is a prerequisite for phonics knowledge, spelling development, and word recognition, and is a predictor of later reading and spelling achievement.

Prerequisite for Phonics Knowledge, Spelling Development and Word Recognition. Phonemic awareness is not a synonym for phonics, but without it there would be no phonics knowledge, and phonics instruction would not make much sense. Children cannot connect letters to sounds if they cannot hear the phonemes in speech.

Studies of invented spellers suggest that an understanding of the alphabetic principle is necessary for spelling development since children must assign letters to represent sounds in the words they spell (Beers & Henderson, 1977; Read, 1971; Morris, 1983). The link between phonemic awareness and spelling development is supported by, among others, Juel, Griffith, and Gough (1986) and Lundberg et al., (1988), who found a causal relationship between phonemic awareness and growth in spelling ability of first- and second-grade children.

Preschool, kindergarten, and first-grade children with the poorest phonemic segmentation skills are likely to be the poorest readers and spellers (Ball & Blachman, 1991; Tangel & Blachman, 1992). Juel (1988) found that phonemically unaware poor readers entering first grade remained poor readers at the end of fourth grade. She concluded that their lack of phonemic awareness contributed to their slow development of word recognition (Juel, 1988). Researchers generally agree that early problems in phonemic awareness reflect children's inability to break the alphabet code, resulting in poor word recognition and spelling strategies (Blachman, 1991). Children must be phonemically aware when trying to learn those essential literacy skills requiring them to manipulate phonemes—specifically phonics, spelling, and word recognition skills.

Predictor of Later Reading and Spelling Achievement. Zhurova (1963) and Elkonin (1963, 1973) provided the first published evidence regarding the relationship between phonemic awareness and reading. Since that time, studies conducted in both the United States and abroad have shown that children's phonemic awareness abilities are significantly related to their success in reading and spelling.

Phonemic awareness and phonics knowledge provide a foundation for reading and writing. Reading and writing obviously involve more than constructing and recognizing written words; however, individuals could not read or write at all without being able to encode (represent phonemes by letters) and decode (translate letters into spoken words). These abilities require phonemic awareness and phonics knowledge; phonemic awareness and phonics knowledge are thus the raw materials of both reading and writing.

Many educators believe that young children should overlearn lower-order processes involving the manipulation of phonemes (the sound–spelling skills involved in writing, and the spelling–sound skills involved in reading) (LaBerge & Samuels, 1974; Scardamalia, 1981). These educators claim that it is only when these lower-order processes become automatic that children's conscious attention can be concentrated on the higher-order processes of comprehension when reading and composing when writing.

In summary, two decades of research suggest that some skill in phonemic analysis is (a) directly related to the issue of understanding the pronunciation clues of written language; (b) necessary for phonics knowledge; (c) necessary for spelling development; (d) related to efficient reading; and (e) a key feature of becoming conventionally literate (Sulzby & Teale, 1991, p. 746). Researchers also have linked indirectly phonemic awareness to reading comprehension, finding a causal link between phonics knowledge and reading comprehension (Tunmer & Nesdale, 1985; Eldredge et al., 1990).

Phonemic awareness is one of the hallmarks of a good reader. Good readers outperform poor readers in a variety of tasks measuring phonemic awareness, even when differences in intelligence and socioeconomic background are controlled (Rosner & Simon, 1971; Torneus, 1984; Zifcak, 1981). The ability to segment individual phonemes in words correlates highly with reading achievement, and training programs that foster this ability appear to speed up overall reading development (Evans & Carr, 1985).

How Children Develop Phonemic Awareness

Phonological Awareness Can Develop Naturally in a Print-rich Environment. The written language, predominant in the environment (signs, labels on food, letters, notes, books, magazines, and even print on TV), influences young children's language development, including their phonological awareness. As they interact with this written language, they discover important concepts about it that contribute to their emerging literacy. The development of the following concepts indicates that children are becoming literate:

1. words are represented by print
2. written word boundaries are established by spaces
3. print goes from left to right
4. there are legitimate reasons why we read and write
5. we create written words by using letters of the alphabet

When parents read nursery rhymes and books emphasizing alliteration to their children, they develop an awareness that words are made up of sound elements (Griffith, 1991). In fact, the ability to recite nursery rhymes is strongly related to beginning levels of phonological awareness in 3- and 4-year-old children (Maclean et al., 1987). Children do not develop an awareness of phonemes in rhymes or syllables, however, until they have a genuine need to use them.

Phonemic Awareness Is Enhanced through Writing. Writing creates a natural need for phonemic awareness, although this need does not surface in young children's initial writing efforts. Children don't use phonemes or letters in their beginning writing; they use scribbles and pictures to represent speech instead. When they do learn that alphabet letters are used in writing, they begin to use them, although without initially understanding that letters and sounds are related to each other. It is only after considerable time that young children's writing reveals understanding of the alphabetic principle. We are not exactly sure how this occurs, but we know that children's involvement with books and their attempts to write influence this development.

Studies of invented spellers (Read, 1971, 1986; Beers & Henderson, 1977; Morris, 1983) indicate that children go through predictable stages in their writing development. When they begin to write words according to their sounds (invented spellings), children must segment words into phonemes and assign letters to represent them. Therefore, the creation of invented spellings by young children indicates that they have started to become aware of the internal structure of both spoken and written words (Tangel & Blachman, 1992). As children's phonemic awareness and phonics knowledge increase, their invented spellings become more sophisticated.

Some educators have suggested that phonemic awareness and phonics knowledge emerge when children attempt to write with invented spellings. However, a more likely scenario is that, as children write with invented spellings, their skills in phonemic awareness, phonics knowledge, and word recognition increase through the experience. This assumption is supported indirectly by various studies. Ehri and Wilce (1987) revealed that teaching children to generate phonetic spellings of words resulted in improved phonemic segmentation skills. Clarke (1988) found that first-grade students encouraged to use their invented spelling skills not only wrote better, but their word recognition ability and reading achievement improved significantly as well. Tierney and Shanahan (1991) found a positive influence on the word recognition ability of young children encouraged to use their phonemic awareness and phonics knowledge to spell words by their sounds.

Research suggests that precocious children can spontaneously invent spellings without any formal instruction (Bissex, 1980; Burns & Richgels, 1989; Read, 1971, 1986). These children seem to deduce the alphabetic principle on their own, and as a result, generally become successful readers (Ferroli & Shanahan, 1987; Mann, Tobin, & Wilson, 1987). Several studies have also shown that some normally achieving students have created invented spellings without formal instruction in the written language (Bissex, 1980; Paul, 1976). We do not know all of the circumstances surrounding these accomplishments. However, we do know that children do not generally develop the phonemic awareness and phonics knowledge necessary for invented spelling without some interaction with print and some parent or teacher feedback or intervention. There is no reason to suppose that children who have created invented spellings without formal instruction accomplished this feat without exposure to print and adult input.

Children Do Not Develop Phonemic Awareness through Speech. Phonemic awareness does not normally develop in an environment where only the oral language is used. If we could explicitly hear phonemes when we speak or listen to others, we might develop phonemic awareness naturally as we use our language. However, we neither represent nor perceive spoken words as a sequence of independent phonemes, but store and retrieve them as a holistic pattern of interacting phonemic elements described as gestures, features, or articulatory routines (Ferguson, 1986; Jusczyk, 1986; Menyuk & Menn, 1979; Studdert-Kennedy, 1986, 1987). This is reflected in the fact that individuals learning a new language frequently have difficulty isolating individual words when listening to native speakers. More will be said about gestures and articulatory routines later in this chapter. In short, we do not isolate phonemes in the words we speak. We do not say, "/k/ /a/ /t/" and "/d/ /o/ /g/." We say, "cat" and "dog." Because phonemes are not isolated in spoken words they are not easy to detect, and we do not naturally become phonemically aware by just speaking and listening. In fact, if we didn't need to read and write there would probably be no need to ever become consciously aware of the individual phonemes in words.

Formal Instruction Develops Phonemic Awareness. Individuals do not become aware of phonemes either by speaking or by listening to others speak. Young children lack a conscious awareness of phonemes—preschoolers, for example, cannot tell you that the word *milk* has four separate sounds (Liberman et al., 1974).

The realization that speech can be segmented into phonemes and that these units can be represented in print is believed to be a fundamental task facing the beginning writer (Read, 1986) and reader (Liberman, 1971, 1983). However, children do not ordinarily develop phonemic awareness without specific instruction, and even then rarely before age 5 or 6 (Liberman, 1989). Explicit awareness of phonemes requires children to focus their attention on the formal attributes of words rather than on their meanings, which is a metalinguistic task difficult for young children. Jean Piaget has labeled this ability to shift attention from one aspect of a stimulus to another aspect as *decentering* and considered it to be a hallmark of the concrete operations stage of cognitive development that begins between the ages of 5 and 7. While intensive training efforts prior to age 5 have successfully taught children to segment or categorize on the basis of words or syllables (Content, Kolinsky, Morais, & Bertelson, 1986; Fox & Routh, 1976; Treiman & Breaux, 1982), these efforts have not produced awareness at the phoneme level (Fowler, 1991).

Many children need formal phonemic awareness training to make the transition from oral to written language. Liberman and Liberman (1992) wrote of phonemic awareness and phonics knowledge, "It is now quite firmly established that neither experience with speech nor cognitive maturation is sufficient to acquaint a person with the principle that underlies all alphabets" (p. 354). Clay, discussing invented spelling, said, "Undoubtedly children can invent for themselves something like written English, but not all children will invent it" (1983, p. 122). Chomsky (1971), speaking of invented spelling over twenty years ago, said, "For those children whose phonetic awareness doesn't yet permit this kind of composition, the thing to do is to work on developing the awareness" (p. 299). Fortunately, more and more educators are realizing that many children need training in phonemic awareness for them to be successful writers and readers. It is only when children receive specific training, or become involved with the written language in a way that requires the use of phonemes, that phonemic awareness begins to develop.

Understanding Coarticulation and Learning to Isolate Phonemes. Developing phonemic awareness is not an easy task because phonemes are not discrete language units children can easily hear. Phonemes are *coarticulated* (overlapped or merged) with other phonemes as we speak, so even a spectrographic analysis of human speech cannot detect them (Liberman, Cooper, Shankweiler, & Studdert-Kennedy, 1967). Consider, for example, the three phonemes in the word *man*. They are so thoroughly coarticulated that they produce a single unified segment of sound, rather than the three separate sounds /m/, /a/, and /n/. Spectrographs can pick up syllables and phones, but cannot pick up the coarticulated phonemes within these language units.

Once children become aware of phonemes and are able to count them, their challenges are still not over. They must be able to isolate them in order to spell, and recognize the letters representing them in order to read. However, once writers and readers understand how phonemes are mapped onto letters, they quickly master the mechanics of writing and reading; children then are able to focus their attention on constructing meaning through writing, and reconstructing meaning through reading.

Some teachers help students understand the alphabetic principle by teaching them to "sound out" words. To sound out a word, children first must isolate all of the word's phonemes, and then quickly blend them together. However, neither children nor adults can isolate coarticulated phonemes without some articulatory distortion. This distortion occurs largely because many consonant sounds cannot be isolated without an accompanying schwa sound. (The schwa sound is the /u/ sound you hear at the beginning of the word *up.*) For example, in the word *box,* you get /bu/ when you try to isolate the sound of *b,* even though the letter doesn't represent that sound. So when you try to isolate all of the phonemes in the word *box* you get the sounds /bu/ /o/ /ks/, and if you blend the isolated sounds back together you get a distorted version of the word /bu/ /oks/ rather than /boks/. (Actually, the phoneme represented by the letter *b* is coarticulated with the phoneme represented by the letter *o,* so the sound we really hear at the beginning of the word is /bo/ rather than /bu/ /o/.

The word distortion that occurs when isolating phonemes implies that our alphabetic representation of spoken words does *not* specify, on a segment by segment basis, how the speech organs are to be articulated and coarticulated so as to produce the sounds of speech—even though some individuals assume otherwise. The letters in written words are, in fact, an abstraction from speech, and do represent phonemes, but because of coarticulation this representation is hard for children to apprehend. Therefore, the difficult task facing emerging readers is to match the alphabetic transcription to the *abstract* phonological structure of the word it represents.

Dealing with an abstract phonological structure is difficult for beginning writers and readers. However, there is a logical reason why phonemes are articulated and coarticulated with other phonemes to form spoken words. Perhaps the best explanation comes from the work of Isabelle Liberman (1983). For nearly twenty years she and her colleagues studied the problems beginning readers encounter in learning to read. They concluded that in order for children to be successful readers, they must first become aware of the internal phonological structure of words (i.e., become phonemically aware); and second, they must see how these phonemes map onto print (Liberman et al., 1989). Liberman and Liberman (1992) stated, "We take it as given . . . that in teaching children to read and write, our aim must be to transfer the wonders of phonology from speech to script. In our view, this can be done only if the child comes to understand the alphabetic principle. . . . [To teach this principle successfully,] we must first . . . understand how the phonemes are produced and perceived in speech, for only then can we see precisely how far these processes must be different in writing and reading" (p. 349).

Liberman and Liberman (1992) concluded that in all languages, utterances are formed by stringing together two or three dozen consonants and vowels in various ways. These strings inevitably run to considerable lengths, so, as a practical matter, there had to be a way of producing them at some reasonable rate. For example, speech would be impossibly tedious if, instead of saying *strict,* we could only say /s/ /t/ /ru/ /i/ /k/ /t/. Not only would communication be slow, but our sentence comprehension would be extremely difficult, if not impossible, due to the strain on our working memory limits. The Libermans concluded that speech and language became possible only because coarticulation of phonemes evolved—specialization for the rapid and effortless production and perception of phonological structures.

> We and some of our colleagues believe that the strategy underlying this specialization was to define the phonemes not as sounds but as motor control structures we choose to call gestures. Thus, the phoneme we write as *b* is a closing and opening at the lips; the phoneme we write as *m* is that same closing and opening at the lips, combined with an opening of the velum, and so forth. In fact, the gestures are far more complex and abstract than this . . . . but for our purposes the important consideration is only that the gestural strategy permits coarticulation. That is, it permits the speaker to overlap gestures that are realized by different organs of articulation (as in the case of lips and tongue in /ba/) and to merge gestures that are produced by different parts of the same organ (as in the case of the tip and blade of the tongue in /da/). The consequence is that people can and do regularly speak at rates of 10 to 20 phonemes per second. (Liberman & Liberman, 1992, p. 350)

The Libermans explained that language would pay a terrible price if it were not based upon phoneme articulation and coarticulation. If each phonological segment were distinctive then communicating phonological structures at rates of 20 phonemes per second would merge the sounds of language together into an unanalyzable buzz. Therefore, coarticulating several segments of the phonology into one segment of sound is extremely efficient for speech, even though beginning writers and readers may have difficulty apprehending such segments. Understanding this specialization helps us understand why many children do not develop phonemic awareness without some adult intervention.

Phonemic Awareness Application Activities

1. Summarize, in writing, the alphabetic principle.
2. Describe how phonemes affect word meanings.
3. Describe phonemic awareness and summarize its importance in reading and writing.
4. Visit a first-grade classroom. Obtain permission to assess three or four children's phoneme counting ability. Assess each student individually, using the following steps:
   (a) Tell each student that there are two sounds in the word *on.*

(b) Say each phoneme in the word *on*, slowly. As you say /o/ hold up one finger, and as you say /n/ hold up a second finger.

(c) Ask the student to tell you how many sounds are in the following words (don't isolate the phonemes for the student): *at* (2), *man* (3), *last* (4), and *shop* (3).

(d) Record your results. Ask the teacher to rank the children you tested according to their reading ability. Compare your phoneme counting results with her rankings.

5. Obtain a stopwatch. Time yourself as you read the following sentence: "I think it is difficult to isolate sounds in words." Ask another person to listen to you and time yourself again as you read the sentence by phonemes: "I th-i-nk i-t i-s d-i-f-f-i-c-u-l-t t-o i-s-o-l-a-t-e s-ou-n-d-s i-n w-or-d-s." Ask the person listening if they understood what you said. Compare the time required to read the sentence by words and by phonemes. What does this experience tell you about the importance of phoneme coarticulation?

6. The evidence supporting the relationship of phonemic awareness to reading and spelling is overwhelming. If you desire to review some of this evidence read the following documents: Blachman, 1983, 1984, 1989; Blachman & James, 1985; Bradley & Bryant, 1983, 1985; Calfee, Lindamood & Lindamood, 1973; Fox & Routh, 1975, 1980; Helfgott, 1976; Juel, 1988; Juel, Griffith, & Gough, 1986; Liberman, 1973; Liberman, Shankweiler, Fischer, & Carter, 1974; Lomax & McGee, 1987; Lundberg, Olofsson, & Wall, 1980; Mann & Liberman, 1984; Rohl & Tunmer, 1988; Share, Jorm, Maclean, & Mathews, 1984; Stanovich, Cunningham, & Cramer, 1984; Tunmer & Nesdale, 1985; Wagner, 1986; Wagner & Torgesen, 1987; Williams, 1986.

You may also want to review the following documents indicating that phonemic awareness is considered to be the best predictor of reading achievement presently existing: Adams, 1990; Blachman, 1989; Fox & Routh, 1984; Golinkoff, 1978; Lundberg, Olofsson & Wall, 1980; Mann, 1984; Stanovich, 1985; Vellutino & Scanlon, 1987.

Chapter 4

Phonics and the Alphabetic Principle

Defining Phonics

Word meanings are not found in words, but in the people who attach meanings to them. It has been said that words do not "mean," only people "mean." Instead of saying, "Words do not mean the same thing to all people," it is more correct to say, "People do not mean the same by all words." We discussed various meanings of the word *decoding* in Chapter 2, and defined decoding for this book as the process readers use to translate the written language into oral or inner speech. Phonics is one of the tools used in this translation process. It is not the goal of decoding, it is a tool to help learners achieve the goal: word recognition.

Phonics means different things to different people. Over the years various educators have coined such terms as "intensive phonics," "phony phonics," "analytic phonics," "synthetic phonics," "implicit phonics," and "explicit phonics" to communicate their specific notions about phonics, and to express their preferences regarding how it should be taught.

We use the term *phonics* in two different ways in this book: (a) to refer to a knowledge individuals acquire about the language, and (b) to describe approaches utilized to help students acquire that knowledge. The two usages are different, and if individuals do not differentiate between them, confusion results. For example, when discussing the impact of students' phonics knowledge on word recognition, some individuals might confuse students' phonics knowledge with specific approaches used to teach the knowledge. So instead of associating the effects of the knowledge with the outcomes observed, they associate the effects of a teaching approach with the outcomes. Researchers and educators who want to study the influences of each on reading must differentiate between phonics knowledge and the various strategies employed to acquire that knowledge.

Phonics as we use it here refers to both a knowledge, and an instructional approach. *Phonics knowledge* refers to an individual's knowledge of letter–sound relationships as they are influenced by syllable patterns. This knowledge helps students see how the spoken and the written forms of the language relate to each other, and the acquisition of this knowledge is dependent upon phonemic awareness. Phonics knowledge is directly related to the acquisition of word recognition, which is directly related to reading comprehension. Phonics knowledge can be assessed by asking students to read different pseudowords containing all of the phonics elements, organized in patterns identical to those used in real words.

Phonics instruction, as described in this book, involves the teaching of letter–sound relationships, segmentation of letter sounds, and blending of letter sounds. It more nearly represents explicit than implicit phonics programs, but differs from explicit programs in the following ways.

1. The instruction is process or strategy oriented rather than skills oriented.
2. Instruction takes little classroom time, about ten minutes per day.
3. Instruction does not involve the use of workbooks or ditto masters.
4. It is inexpensive.
5. It teaches children how to determine vowel sounds in words based upon each word's written syllable pattern.
6. It avoids distortion of phonemes.
7. Instructional methods are designed to support holistic approaches to literacy development.

Differentiating between Implicit and Explicit Phonics Approaches

Studies and debates about how phonics should be taught, or if it should be taught, occupy considerable space in the literature. One position is based on the premise that children need to be explicitly taught how sounds in speech are represented by letters in written language, while the other position is based on the belief that explicit phonics instruction is probably not necessary. At one time the debate centered on the question, "Should early instruction in reading be based upon a 'look and say' approach or should it be based upon phonics?" Later on the question was, "Should we use analytic phonics programs or synthetic programs to teach young children how to read?" Chall's (1967) "great debate" was, "Should we teach 'code emphasis programs' or 'meaning emphasis programs' in the early years of schooling?" And again, in *Becoming a Nation of Readers* (Anderson, Hieber, Scott, & Wilkinson, 1985), a major issue was, "Are implicit phonics programs better, no different, or less effective than explicit phonics programs in the primary grades?"

The labels "implicit phonics," "analytic phonics," and "meaning emphasis programs" reflect essentially one position regarding phonics instruction, while "explicit phonics," "synthetic phonics," and "code emphasis programs" reflect an alternative position. The names have changed over the years, but the basic issues have not.

Implicit Approaches

Advocates of implicit phonics approaches believe that meaning is deemphasized when children are taught to focus their attention on the written coding system. While these programs do not ignore decoding instruction, their major focus is on "meaning." Implicit phonics approaches stress the acquisition of a sight vocabulary and the use of context clues, teaching only enough phonics information to enable children to identify unfamiliar words through contextual analysis.

In early versions of implicit phonics programs, children were taught to read stories where the vocabulary was carefully selected and controlled. The stories were not very interesting because the words children needed to learn intentionally occurred over and over again in the story to facilitate word recognition. Newer versions of implicit phonics programs are characterized by less vocabulary control. Usually students are involved in "shared reading experiences" where teachers read stories to them from "big books," tracing the lines, and touching words while reading the books. After children have learned to recognize a number of commonly used words, those words are "analyzed" and the sounds common to them are identified along with the letters that represent them. Phonics is taught by "analysis" (analyzing known words to learn about their parts). In short, words are taught first, and then certain phonics elements are taught within those words.

Implicit phonics approaches emphasize letter–sound relationships, but purposely avoid isolating or blending sounds represented by letters. Children using these programs are never asked to sound out unfamiliar words. Instead, they are asked to "guess" unknown words using contextual information. Because the major decoding strategy employed in these approaches is contextual analysis, consonant letters are considered more important than vowels, and are therefore taught first. Since most of the words in the language begin with consonants, and since the sound associated with the initial letter is the most important word sound to know when using context clues for word identification, this practice is consistent with the desired outcome.

Explicit Approaches

Many explicit phonics programs emphasize meaning, and some of them have a strong children's literature component so these are not the factors differentiating implicit programs from explicit ones. Explicit phonics programs are based on the premise that children must master the code early. Because first-grade children have already learned to use the oral language fairly well, educators believe that most of them possess sufficient background, vocabulary, and syntax knowledge needed for early reading experiences. However, they possess little decoding knowledge, so their early reading experiences should help them learn to decode. Hence phonics becomes important.

In explicit programs children are taught the sounds represented by letters, but they are also taught how to isolate those sounds, and how to blend them for word identification. Phonics is taught through a "synthesizing" process (parts to whole) rather than by analysis. That is, letter–sound relationships are taught first, and then letter sounds are combined in various ways to form words.

The Instructional Approach of This Book

Advocates of both implicit and explicit approaches encourage teachers to follow the instructions outlined in the manuals so children will receive the full benefits of their programs. However, if teachers follow the manuals, which encourage them to utilize workbooks, flash cards, diagnostic tests, photocopy pages, manipulatives, and so on, children have little time left to engage in other language activities. A frequently heard complaint about basal text programs is that they require so much classroom time that there is little left for children to read and write.

The formal phonics instruction presented in this book is, in a sense, unique. It is not an approach taught in either implicit or explicit phonics basals. It is designed to be used by holistic teachers who desire to spend most of the available classroom time on holistic reading and writing activities. This approach takes only ten minutes of classroom time per day. It is designed to help students associate "appropriate" sounds with letters according to syllable or word pattern. It is also designed to help them segment (isolate) sounds, and blend them as well. The approach is based upon overwhelming evidence that children must master segmentation and blending before they can transfer the results of phonics instruction to the reading of unfamiliar words (Jeffrey & Samuels, 1967; Jenkins, Bausell, & Jenkins, 1972; Muller, 1973; Fox & Routh, 1976). It is also based on research, discussed in previous chapters, indicating that phonics knowledge is directly related to the acquisition of word recognition, which in turn is related to reading comprehension.

How to Know if a Student Has Phonics Knowledge

Teachers may use three types of assessment to determine a student's phonics knowledge. The following examples indicate various levels of knowledge.

Assessment Type 1. You may present the tasks in this assessment in two ways. Approach one: *Tell the student the word.* Ask the student to say the word in two parts. Point to the vowel letter in the word. Ask the student to say the part of the word that ends with the vowel sound, and then say the part of the word that comes after the vowel. Approach two: *Do not tell the student the word.* Tell the student to say the word in two parts. Point to the vowel letter in the word. Ask the student to say the part of the word that ends with the vowel sound, and then say the part of the word that comes after the vowel.

When presented with the written word *up,* the student is able to isolate the sounds /u/ /p/, while touching the appropriate letters representing each sound.

When presented with the written word *map,* the student is able to isolate the sounds /ma/ /p/, while touching the appropriate letter(s) representing each sound.

When presented with the written word *box,* the student is able to isolate the sounds /bo/ /ks/, while touching the appropriate letters representing each sound.

When presented with the written word *last,* the student is able to isolate the sounds /la/ /s/ /t/, while touching the appropriate letter(s) representing each sound.

When presented with the written word *stop,* the student is able to isolate the sounds /sto/ /p/, while touching the appropriate letter(s) representing each sound.

When presented with the written word *witch,* the student is able to isolate the sounds /wi/ /ch/, while touching the appropriate letters representing each sound.

When presented with the written word *shop,* the student is able to isolate the sounds /sho/ /p/, while touching the appropriate letter(s) representing each sound.

When presented with the written word *lunch,* the student is able to isolate the sounds /lu/ /n/ /ch/, while touching the appropriate letter(s) representing each sound.

When presented with the written word *shrub,* the student is able to isolate the sounds /shru/ /b/, while touching the appropriate letter(s) representing each sound.

When presented with the written pseudoword *wo,* the student will say /wō/.

When presented with the written word *cake,* the student is able to isolate the sounds /kā/ /k/, while touching the appropriate letter(s) representing each sound.

When presented with the written word *soap,* the student is able to isolate the sounds /sō/ /p/, while touching the appropriate letter(s) representing each sound.

When presented with the written word *bird,* the student is able to isolate the sounds /bir/ /d/, while touching the appropriate letter(s) representing each sound.

Assessment Type 2. When presented with the written letters *ai,* the student is able to say / ā /. When the letter *r* is written in front of the letters *ai,* the student is able to say /rā/. When the letter *n* is written at the end of the letters *rai,* the student is able to say /rān/. (Note: This assessment format would be continued using all of the phonics parts and patterns discussed in Chapter 8.)

Assessment Type 3.

When presented with the written pseudoword *ef,* the student is able to say /ef/.

When presented with the written pseudoword *bazz,* the student is able to say /baz/.

When presented with the written pseudoword *cen,* the student is able to say /sen/.

When presented with the written pseudoword *milt,* the student is able to say /milt/.

When presented with the written pseudoword *scradge,* the student is able to say /skraj/.

When presented with the written pseudoword *sheb,* the student is able to say /sheb/.

When presented with the written pseudoword *swush,* the student is able to say /swush/.

When presented with the written pseudoword *plench,* the student is able to say /plench/.

When presented with the written pseudoword *naid,* the student is able to say /nād/.

When presented with the written pseudoword *girt,* the student is able to say /girt/.

Individuals who can perform the three previous assessment tasks demonstrate their phonics knowledge by (a) associating appropriate sounds with letters, (b) isolating letter sounds within words, and (c) blending letter sounds within words. Not all phonics parts were represented in the assessment tasks; however, representation of those parts was implied, and a thorough assessment would necessitate their inclusion. All four basic syllable patterns were included in assessment types one and three, and implied in assessment type two. Utilizing these patterns in both assessment and teaching is critical since the written syllable pattern suggests which vowel sound is being represented in the written word (we discuss syllable patterns more fully in Chapter 8). Students in the first assessment were asked to isolate sounds in words without distorting phonemes. Phoneme articulation and coarticulation is also a critical element in phonics assessment and teaching since sound distortions sometimes interfere with word identification, and a "grunting and groaning" approach to phonics is often negatively associated with traditional explicit phonics approaches (see the discussion in Chapter 8).

Why Phonics Knowledge Is Important

A review of decoding research provides convincing evidence that phonics knowledge is related to the acquisition of basic reading skills.

Phonics knowledge positively affects decoding abilities (Stanovich & West, 1989), and inadequate decoding is a hallmark of a poor reader (Carnine et al., 1984). Poor readers (a) read slowly (Calfee & Drum, 1986); (b) cannot decode pseudowords created according to the graphic structure of real words (Doehring, Trites, Patel, & Fiedorowicz, 1981); and (c) do not use spelling–sound patterns when attempting to identify unfamiliar real words (Biemiller, 1970). All of these indicators are directly linked to poor or inadequate phonics knowledge.

The use of contextual information while reading does not differentiate good readers from poor ones since research indicates considerable use of context by all early readers. In fact, between 70 and 95 percent of the oral reading errors of first graders are contextually appropriate (Biemiller, 1970, 1979; Weber, 1970). Two tasks that clearly differentiate good from poor comprehenders, however, are accuracy (see Tunmer & Nesdale, 1985) and speed (see Perfetti & Hogaboam, 1975) of naming pseudowords, such as *naid* and *hoach*. These differences are observed even when younger fluent readers are matched with older, poor readers (Manis & Morrison, 1985; Snowling, 1985). Pseudoword reading reflects readers' phonics knowledge (since they could not have been seen before and could not have been learned by sight), knowledge that clearly differentiates readers with good comprehension abilities from those with poor abilities.

In Chapter 2 we stated that good readers store written representations of various words in lexical memory. They have attached meaning(s) to each word, and recognize each word by a specific letter sequence. When good readers see a particular letter sequence, the word associated with that letter sequence is immediately called to mind as inner speech, along with the meaning(s) attached to it. Good readers translate written words into audio images very rapidly, and hold this inner speech in short term memory until after they apprehend complete sentences. Letter–sound relationships then, are a critical component in this process; specific letter sequences represent specific audio images. Therefore, readers who have difficulty with letter–sound relationships (phonics knowledge) will also have difficulty with word recognition.

Visual–Phonological Connections

Ehri (1992) developed a theory of sight word reading that explains how phonics knowledge affects word recognition. Her theory proposed that readers do not use a "visual route" to go from print to meaning when recognizing words by sight, but instead, they use a "visual–phonological route," going from print to pronunciation to meaning.

> The critical connections that enable readers to find specific words in lexical memory by means of this visual–phonological route are connections linking spellings to pronunciations rather than to meanings. However, connections between spellings and meanings are easily formed in the process of establishing visual–phonological routes. . . . The visual–phonological connections that readers have formed for a word make that spelling a visual symbol for its pronunciation. This means in effect that readers "see" the pronunciation when they look at the spelling, and this event creates direct links between the spelling and its meaning. Thus, readers access not only pronunciations but also meanings directly when they learn to read words by means of a visual–phonological route. (pp. 115–116)

Ehri concludes, "my view of sight word reading makes letter–sound knowledge a necessity. This knowledge is needed to form a complete network of visual–phonological connections in lexical memory" (p. 138).

Stages of Reading Acquisition

Frith's (1980, 1985) theory of reading by full or partial letter cues supports the beliefs about reading advocated in this book, supports Ehri's sight word reading theory, and explains why some children rely on contextual information for word identification.

According to Frith, there are three stages of reading acquisition: logographic, alphabetic, and orthographic. At the beginning, or *logographic*, stage readers look at words like they look at pictures, selectively focusing on some feature or aspect of a printed word to help them remember what it looks like. Lacking a knowledge of letter–sound relationships, the associations they make with the written word are largely visual. Remembering words this way is extremely difficult, and word recognition is slow and ineffective.

Children at the *alphabetic* stage have begun to perceive letter–sound relationships, but tend to focus on only a few letters in a word for purposes of identification. While children may learn many words in this manner, the method has at least two serious problems: (a) readers will eventually confuse words with common letters, and (b) readers will not develop the knowledge needed to identify novel words.

When children reach the *orthographic* stage, they realize that, because a word's full spelling is the only thing distinguishing it from all other words, they must use all of its letters for word identification. At this stage children begin to focus on the complete letter sequences in words as they read. According to Frith, children who read by partial letter cues will not be able to adequately discriminate words that contain similar letters, such as *horse–house, pin–pen,* and *peach–poach.* Therefore, since they will not be able to adequately recognize words by their unique letter sequences they must rely on contextual information in the sentence to help them read.

Other investigators subscribe to the view that children can, and do, learn to read a certain number of words well by partial letter cues, before developing phonics knowledge (Gough & Hillinger, 1980; Gough & Walsh, 1991; Gough, Juel, & Griffith, 1992). However, they claim children's progress will be hindered if they continue to learn words using partial cues, without developing phonics knowledge:

> Children could continue to learn in this way, but they face two serious problems. Although it is easy to find partial cues that distinguish a handful of words, this task becomes increasingly difficult as additional words must be added. In the end, many words can be identified on the basis of no partial cue, for every one of their proper subsets of ordered letters is shared with some other word; the only thing that distinguishes such a word is its full spelling. The result then is that learning by selective association begins easily but gets progressively harder.
>
> The second problem is that selective association provides no way of recognizing a novel word. . . . To read ordinary text, children must be able to identify unfamiliar words. (Gough, Juel, & Griffith, 1992, pp. 37–38)

The Whole Word Hypothesis

It is no secret that beginning readers read in a different manner than skilled readers. Explanations of the nature of these differences vary among educators. Some subscribe to the theory that both skilled and unskilled readers perceive words as "wholes," and that the only difference between them is the speed and ease of word perception. Skilled readers perceive words faster than unskilled readers because of their background knowledge, their attempts to make reading meaningful, and the quantity and quality of their previous experiences with written text. Other educators reject the whole word theory. These individuals believe that skilled readers recognize words by the letters that distinguish them while unskilled readers do not. They believe that unskilled readers select some cue, attribute, or feature of a word to distinguish it from other words simply because they have not learned how to associate the phonemes in spoken words with letters in written words.

The holistic word perception theory (whole word hypothesis) goes back to Cattell's (1886) studies of word perception. According to the hypothesis, words are perceived by their shapes and word length, along with some letter cues. The whole word hypothesis is very popular with whole language purists and meaning–emphasis advocates, but is not founded on solid research. Perfetti (1992) wrote, "It is now fairly clear that, whatever the appeal of the whole word hypothesis at the phenomenal level, word identification is mediated by letter perception. The individual constituent letters of the word are the units of its identification. Cues of word shape and word length appear to be of some significance, but they carry a very small share of the identification burden compared with letters" (pp. 146–147).

Advocates of the whole word hypothesis believe that beginning readers view words globally, registering each word as a gestalt. They agree that readers must know the alphabetic principle, but believe they do not need to look at all of the letters in words to recognize them. Opponents suggest that early readers perceive words by partial letter cues, not by wholes, using a process of "selective association" (Gough, Juel, & Griffith, 1992) to help them remember written words. This view is consistent with Frith's theory of reading with full and partial letter cues, and with the research suggesting that skilled readers do not view words globally, but by letters. When skilled readers read, they quickly survey each word's component letters to ensure accurate recognition (Balota, Pollatsek, & Rayner, 1985; Rayner & Bertera, 1979; Pollatsek, Rayner, & Balota, 1986). This process occurs so rapidly that some mistakenly conclude that the words must have been perceived "globally."

Several researchers (Adams, 1990; Barron, 1981, 1986) claim that phonics instruction facilitates the development of accurate orthographic representations of words simply because it forces children's attention to words' interior details. Studies show that poor readers do not fully analyze the interior components of words (Stanovich, 1992; Vellutino & Scanlon, 1984); therefore, instruction focusing children's attention on a word's letters, and the sounds representing them should help them read by full cues, achieving Frith's orthographic reading stage. Frith also claims that students using full cues to read also become better spellers because they have stored more complete orthographic representations for words in lexical memory.

Beginning readers must eventually learn that there is systematic correspondence between elements of spoken and written language to advance beyond the stage of reading where words are recognized by selective association. Children who continue to read words as though they were pictures will be limited to reading the specific words they have learned as arbitrary patterns.

Developing Word Recognition

The evidence is strong that phonics knowledge provides the foundation for the development of word recognition abilities (see also Chapter 3). Ehri and Wilce (1985) compared kindergartners' ability to learn to read nonsense words with both systematic (*msk* for *mask*) and arbitrary (*uhe* for *mask*) spellings. They found that nonreaders learned to read arbitrary spellings more readily than systematic phonetic spellings. However, beginning readers learned systematic spellings more readily than arbitrary spellings. They hypothesized that nonreaders lacked letter–sound knowledge needed to form visual–phonological connections in memory, which was verified on tests showing that the nonreaders knew only a few letter–sound relations. Ehri and Wilce speculated that beginning readers learned systematic spellings better than arbitrary spellings because they used letter–sound knowledge to form systematic connections in memory. Beginning readers' phonics knowledge was verified by tests revealing that these students knew all of the letter names and most letter sounds.

Ehri and Wilce (1983) also compared the speed with which skilled and unskilled readers in the first, second, and fourth grades read familiar real words (*cat, red*) and pseudowords (*mig, fup*), and named single digits. All subjects read real words and pseudowords over several practice trials. This practice enabled the skilled readers to read the pseudowords as fast as the real words and digits. However, even 18 practice trials did not allow poor readers to read pseudowords as fast as real words and real words as fast as digits. They hypothesized that only the skilled readers possessed adequate phonics knowledge to form complete connections between spellings and pronunciations in memory.

Reading Irregular Words. Phonics knowledge also helps children learn to read irregular words. For years educators believed (and some still do) that children learned to read irregular, or exceptional, words differently than they learned to read graphophonically regular words. However, there is now strong evidence that children learn how to read both regular and irregular words similarly, and that phonics knowledge is needed for learning both.

Orthographic irregular words contain letters that are pronounced differently than expected (e.g., come, any, Wednesday). In a sense, however, all English words are regular, and all nonwords are irregular, since the written form of the English language is based upon an alphabetic system, and alphabetic systems use letters to represent word sounds. The fact is that most English words are spelled in predictable ways; those that are spelled unpredictably are often referred to as *irregular* or *exceptional.*

One frequently heard criticism of phonics is that English is not a phonetic language. This is simply not true; phonetic languages are languages based on unique sounds, and English certainly meets this criterion. What these critics are trying to communicate is that the words in English are not always spelled in consistent ways, which is true. However, this criticism is often made by those who possess a weak understanding of English graphophonics. English spellings are much more consistent than inconsistent. Many "inconsistently" spelled words are actually borrowings from other languages that have not been conformed to English orthography. Ehri (1992) wrote of English word spellings:

> . . . few English word spellings are totally arbitrary in the sense that they contain no letters that conform to English letter–sound spelling conventions. Most spellings that are considered irregular are only partially so. For example, *island* and *sword* each contain only one irregular letter. All the other letters correspond to sounds in the words' pronunciations. In using memory processes to read these words, readers are more apt to take advantage of any available systematic relations than to ignore them and rote memorize the entire form. (pp. 111–112)

All English words are comprised of specific letter sequences that represent specific phoneme sequences whether or not the spellings are consistent. Therefore, it would seem reasonable to assume that readers store exceptional words in lexical memory in the same fashion as they store regular words. This assumption is supported by Ehri (1992) who claims that learning to recognize regular and exceptional words by sight is not a rote memory process, but a process involving the establishment of systematic connections between spellings and pronunciations of words in lexical memory (p. 137). The assumption is also supported by research indicating that children process regularly spelled words, irregularly spelled words, and pseudowords similarly (Gough & Walsh, 1991; Treiman & Baron, 1983; Lovett, 1987).

In certain situations, children with large sight vocabularies will identify unfamiliar words by analogy, searching through their store of words in memory to find a word containing a pattern similar to the unfamiliar one and using the analog, identifying, for example, the unfamiliar word *pound* by associating it with the word *found* already existing in memory. Ehri and Robbins (1992) found that children could not identify words by analogy until they possessed sufficient phonics knowledge. Educators might argue on how beginning readers may best acquire phonics knowledge, but there should be little argument about its importance in word recognition and identification. Children *must* acquire phonics knowledge if they are to progress successfully in reading.

Effective phonics instruction affects word recognition in two separate, but related, ways. (Note that we are now talking about phonics as a *method* rather than phonics as *knowledge*.) First, children who are taught how to segment and blend word sounds learn how to sound out unfamiliar written words. Words accessed in this manner are remembered better than when using contextual analysis since students pay attention to all of the letters in a word rather than just the beginning letter (Adams, 1990). Second, phonics instruction helps students learn the regular graphophonic patterns found in the written language, facilitating the recognition of other words not yet encountered in print; students who are taught to focus on all of the letter sequences within words become consciously aware of basic letter and sound patterns needed to identify words by analogy. Dank (1976) found that students learned graphophonic patterns quickly in the early grades when they were taught how to segment and blend sound in words, and Fox and Routh (1984) found that the learning of such strategies strongly affected students' later ability to acquire new words. As young children become acquainted with the principles involved in stringing letters together to form words they use this knowledge both to learn new words and to rapidly access familiar words.

Phonics Knowledge Affects Reading Comprehension

We have shown in this chapter that phonics knowledge aids development of word recognition. Word recognition, in turn, increases reading fluency; when written words are firmly rooted in lexical memory, fluency and automaticity in word recognition follow. Reading fluency, then, should facilitate reading comprehension since students who are not struggling with decoding should be able to give their full attention to the written message. These conclusions are supported by the National Commission on Reading.

In 1985, the commission stated that phonics knowledge contributed to the development of word recognition abilities, and that rapid, accurate, automatic word recognition, in turn, was needed for effective reading comprehension (Anderson et al., 1985). The commission acknowledged that decoding was not a "sufficient condition" for reading comprehension, but insisted that it was a "necessary" one. That is, while decoding is only one of the many factors influencing an individual's reading comprehension, without it there *is* no reading comprehension. Adams (1990), who also extensively studied decoding research, came to the same conclusion. She compared decoding and reading with gasoline and a car: Without gas the car does not run; without decoding there is no reading. Studies supporting this claim report strong correlations between speed and accuracy of context-free word recognition and reading comprehension, especially among children in the lower grades (see Perfetti, 1985; Lesgold, Resnick, & Hammond, 1985).

In conclusion then, we may state that phonics knowledge has a positive effect on word recognition abilities, and that this in turn leads to growth in reading comprehension (Eldredge et al., 1990; see also Anderson et al., 1985).

Explicit Phonics Instruction Is Beneficial

It has long been known that children who were taught to read with explicit phonics programs that emphasized segmentation and blending, had an advantage over children taught to read with implicit programs that ignored both (Anderson et al., 1985; Bond & Dykstra, 1967; Pflaum, Wahlberg, Karegianes, & Rasher, 1980). The causal impact of phonics knowledge on reading comprehension implied in the Eldredge et al. (1990) study is consistent with these studies since students' knowledge of the graphophonic patterns in the written language is an outcome associated with explicit phonics instruction (Dank, 1976; Norton & Hubert, 1977).

Some educators are concerned that explicit phonics instruction may have negative effects on young children's reading comprehension. As Johnson and Baumann

(1984) caution, "it may be that the excessive reliance upon code–emphasis instruction obscures the more important goal of obtaining meaning from print" (p. 595). Their concerns are supported by studies revealing that first-grade children taught by explicit phonics programs made more nonsense errors while reading than children taught by implicit programs (Barr, 1972; Cohen, 1974–1975; DeLawter, 1975; Norton, 1976). For example, when children taught by explicit phonics programs encountered an unknown word such as *horse* some read it *house* because *horse* and *house* are graphophonically similar, even though *house* simply didn't make sense in the sentence they were reading. When children taught by implicit phonics programs encountered an unknown word such as *horse* some read it *pony*. Even though *horse* and *pony* were not graphophonically similar, the word *pony* made sense in the sentence being read. From these studies researchers concluded (a) that young children taught by programs emphasizing print–sound relationships focus more on graphophonic clues when encountering unknown words than on the semantic clues; and (b) that children taught by implicit phonics programs focus more on meaning than on print clues. These researchers therefore judged that explicit phonics programs may have negative effects on reading comprehension.

This line of reasoning contains several fallacies. First, the bulk of the research evidence regarding explicit versus implicit phonics programs indicates that children get a better start in reading when taught with explicit phonics than when taught with implicit phonics (Anderson et al., 1985).

Second, researchers have discovered that children taught by explicit programs pass the stage of making nonsense errors after developing reading fluency (Biemiller, 1970), usually around the second or third grade (Carnine et al., 1984). At this point they surpass their peers taught by implicit approaches. This is consistent with the theory of automaticity proposed by LaBerge and Samuels (1974), who believe reading comprehension depends on decoding accuracy and fluency. They propose that since the human mind cannot focus on two things "equally" at the same time, children are not able to fluently grasp a text's meaning as long as they are struggling with decoding. When decoding becomes automatic, children have more attention to give to the meaning of the message.

Third, although the errors made by first-grade children using implicit programs were semantically correct, they *were* errors. Those errors demonstrated obvious defects in decoding, and poor understanding of the alphabetic principle.

Fourth, as discussed in Chapter 2, research findings indicate that good readers use both graphophonic and contextual cues when reading, and that graphophonics knowledge is more important to fluent reading than contextual cues (Stanovich, 1980; Tulving & Gold, 1963). It is only when graphophonic knowledge breaks down that good readers resort to contextual cues for word identification.

Fifth, the problem of children's ignoring semantics cues in their initial reading experiences can be resolved by teachers spending more time on holistic literacy activities in the classroom and less time on decoding. Many explicit phonics programs in past years have been excessively code oriented, and effective phonics instruction does not need to occupy much classroom time (Eldredge & Butterfield, 1986).

Types of Phonics Instruction to Provide for Children

Effective phonics instruction will have the following characteristics:

1. It will not absorb much classroom time.
2. It will not communicate to children that phonics is reading.
3. Instruction will teach children how to determine vowel sounds in words according to syllable patterns.
4. Instruction will avoid the distortion of phonemes.
5. It will teach phonics as a decoding strategy to be used rather than a set of skills to be learned.
6. Teaching will not involve the use of workbooks or photocopied masters.
7. Strategies will be based upon sound linguistic principles.
8. Instruction will support holistic literacy experiences in the classroom.
9. It will help students identify written words by sounds.

Identifying words by sounds helps children develop letter–sound knowledge, and involves them in sound segmentation and sound blending. Segmentation involves the isolation of sounds, such as isolating the /a/ and the /m/ sounds in the word *am*. Blending refers to combining sounds, such as putting the /a/ and /m/ sound together to get /am/. Knowledge of letter–sound relationships coupled with segmentation and blending abilities provide beginning readers with the foundational tools needed for accurate, rapid, automatic word recognition.

Phonics instruction should be provided in a predominantly holistically oriented learning environment. Students should spend most of their time in meaningful reading and writing experiences. Teachers should read to them; students should read stories with teachers; students should read by themselves and in small groups; and should be involved in meaningful writing experiences. The focus of holistic reading and writing should be on meaning and relevance, while the focus of explicit phonics instruction should be on the spelling–sound patterns existing in the written language. Both types of activities are important to beginning readers. Decoding at the "sounding out" level, while reading, substantially interrupts the comprehension process. It is best to provide some phonics instruction apart from students' meaningful reading experiences.

Phonics Application Activities

1. Obtain a copy of any basal first-grade teacher's manual. Browse through the manual. Determine whether it is an implicit or explicit phonics basal. Justify your determination.
2. Listen to two or three first graders read. Identify whether each child is at the logographic stage, alphabetic stage, or orthographic stage of reading. Justify your conclusions.

3. Describe to another person how you believe phonics knowledge affects reading ability.
4. Describe and justify the type of phonics instruction you believe teachers should provide for children.
5. The evidence supporting the relationship of phonics knowledge to the acquisition of basic reading skills is overwhelming. If you desire to review some of this evidence read the following documents: Hoover & Gough, 1990; Tunmer, Herriman, & Nesdale, 1988; Juel, 1988; Juel, Griffith, & Gough, 1986; Backman, Bruck, Herbert, & Seidenberg, 1984; Jorm, Share, Maclean, & Matthews, 1984; Manis & Morrison, 1985; Perfetti & Hogaboam, 1975; Snowling, 1980, 1981; Stanovich, Cunningham, & Freeman, 1984; Thompson, 1986; Tunmer, 1989; Tunmer & Nesdale, 1985.

Chapter 5

Developing Phonemic Awareness Through Stories, Games, and Songs

Phonology is the study of language sounds. *Phonological awareness* is a general term used to indicate that children are aware of the basic units of sound in the language: words, syllables, and phonemes. *Phonemic awareness* is a specialized term used to indicate that children are aware of the smallest units of sound in the language: phonemes.

Most linguists believe that children's awareness of phonology develops in a natural sequence from words to syllables to phonemes. Phonemes are the last sound units children learn to perceive, and the most difficult. Phonemic awareness does not develop as naturally as other forms of phonological awareness, but teachers can provide experiences for children that will help them become phonemically aware. The research reviewed in the previous chapters indicates that children will not become successful readers and writers without this knowledge. Phonics instruction is meaningless without phonemic awareness since children must understand what letters and spellings are supposed to represent. Phonemic awareness training must precede or accompany phonics instruction. Children must be aware of the units of sound within words (phonemes) and the letters that represent them (phonics) so they can spell (write the letters that stand for word sounds) and read (retrieve words from memory by their spellings). In this chapter we discuss different levels of phonological and phonemic awareness, and explore a few of the many different ways children's phonemic awareness can be enhanced through songs, games, and stories.

Phonological Awareness Stages

Phonological awareness develops in stages. Children first become aware of the larger units of sound, the words. Next, children become aware of syllables within words, and last of all, phonemes.

Some teachers are unaware that young children must develop word awareness. "After all, my students understand me when I speak to them. They must be aware of words," these teachers say. Yet many young children write without leaving spaces between words, reflecting the difficulty they are having with word awareness.

The difficulty young children have with word awareness might be better understood after you do a little experiment: Say the word *excitement*. Then say the sentence, "You can't come." Say the word *disenchantment.* Then say the sentence, "Don't bother me." *Excitement* is a three-syllable word. The sentence, "You can't come" is also three syllables long. *Disenchantment* and "Don't bother me" are both four sylla-bles long. To a non-English–speaking person, words and sentences with the same number of syllables are nearly indistinguishable.

People attach meanings to speech sounds. Sometimes these speech sounds rep-resent one word and other times they represent more than one word. When we speak, we speak in a fairly steady flow, pausing only to cluster words into phrases. The spaces we place between written words are not to separate each word's sounds, as some might believe; they are artificial breaks, used only to separate words, and came into common use in alphabetic written languages less than two thousand years ago (relatively recently, historically speaking). Young children frequently confuse words, syllables, and phrases in adult speech. Even when young children speak they are not always aware of word breaks. Children's word awareness problems are often difficult for teachers to understand; adults have learned to "hear" word breaks simply because they already know the words. If you have ever listened to someone speak a language that you don't understand you might have experienced the word aware-ness problem that many young children experience when they hear adults speak.

As a teacher, you can help young children develop word awareness, informally, during normal discussion periods throughout the school day. For example, you might occasionally ask, "How many words did you hear in my last sentence?" Children's responses to the question may vary because of their individual word awareness development. However, if you repeat the sentence, and ask the students to say it in unison, many of them will be able to count the words. If children have difficulty with word awareness, you may repeat the sentence and make a mark on the chalkboard after each word is said. Writing words underneath those marks will also help children visualize the connections between the spoken and written lan-guage. You also can help them discover relationships between the length of written and spoken words with such questions as, "Which words are short words?" and "Which word is the longest?"

The first level of phonological awareness, then, is word awareness. Children must come to understand what a word is. They must be able to differentiate words from syl-lables, and eventually they must be able to hear phonemes in both words and syllables.

Syllabic awareness is the second level of phonological awareness. A *syllable* is a part of a word containing one vowel sound. When we speak multisyllabic words we *say* the individual syllables because of the natural speech breaks separating them. Syllables can be isolated without distorting speech, while phonemes cannot. For this reason, syllabic awareness is easier for children to develop than phonemic awareness. How many syllables (vowel sounds) do you hear in the following words: *apple, engage, disagree, justification*?

You may use an *auditory blending* game called the "secret code" game to help chil-dren develop syllabic awareness. Begin the game by saying, "I am going to say some words in a secret code. Tell me the word, if you can discover how to break my code. The word is /pen/ /sul/." (Wait for a response.) As children become more acquainted with written words, you might write the word *pencil* on the chalkboard and underline its syllables, as the word is repeated, so students can make the connection between the spoken and written forms of the word. In the meantime, you will probably want to divide the class into two groups and have one half of the class compete with the other half to add some motivation to the secret code game.

The following words, familiar to young children, are appropriate for use in the secret code game: *bun-ny, can-dy, car-pet, fun-ny, emp-ty, but-ter, bas-ket, foun-tain, chil-dren, dol-lar.* You will easily think of other words to use with your students.

If children have difficulty hearing syllables in these words, you may want to begin the secret code game with compound words such as the following: *bed-room, air-plane, cook-book, birth-day, gold-fish, flash-light, grand-ma, play-house, snow-ball, rail-road.*

When children are able to manipulate sounds in words, we have evidence that they are more phonologically aware than when they demonstrate the ability to complete auditory blending tasks. For example, if children can respond to such directions as, "Say *cupcake* without *cake*," "Say *football* without *foot*," "Say *carpet* without *car*," or "Say *candy* without *can*," they are more phonologically advanced than children who cannot respond to those directions. You may want to play classroom games with children using these manipulation tasks.

Phonemic Awareness Levels

Demonstrating phonemic awareness involves performing the following tasks:

1. hearing and counting phonemes
2. matching phonemes to phonemes
3. isolating phonemes (segmentation)
4. blending phonemes
5. matching phonemes to letters (technically a phonics task, it has been found to enhance both phonemic awareness and phonics knowledge
6. manipulating phonemes

Some researchers claim that these tasks, in the order presented, represent phonemic awareness levels. However, there is some disagreement regarding levels of phonemic awareness. Some claim that children are able to blend phonemes more easily than isolate them if teachers segment the phonemes for them. Furthermore, children respond differently to various phonemic awareness tasks; some are able to do tasks that others cannot, but are unable to do other tasks these same children can perform.

Phonemic Awareness Tasks

Current research suggests that most children seem to hear rhyming words, and words that begin alike, before they develop the ability to hear, isolate, and blend individual phonemes in words. After developing the ability to hear rhymes and beginning sounds, most children seem to be able to perform the phonemic awareness tasks, roughly speaking, in the same order as previously listed, except that blending phonemes precedes isolating them. The following examples specify the tasks involved.

Hearing and Counting.

The teacher says, "Listen to the sounds in the word *so.* /s/ /ō/. Count the sounds in the word. /s/ /ō/."

Sound Matching.

1. The teacher places three pictures in front of the child and says, "Point to the picture that begins with /f/."
2. The teacher says, "Tell me a word that begins with /s/."
3. The teacher places three pictures in front of the child and says, "Point to the picture that ends with /p/."
4. The teacher says, "Tell me a word that ends with /t/."
5. The teacher places three pictures in front of the child and says, "Point to the picture that has a /u/ sound in the middle of the word."
6. The teacher says, "Tell me a word that has an /i/ sound in the middle."

   Note: Sound matching tasks 5 and 6 are generally more difficult for children than are tasks 1 and 2. Some children may also find matching tasks 3 and 4 more difficult than the first blending task.

Blending.

1. The teacher says, "I will say the word in a secret code. If you can break my code, tell me the word. The word is /ba/ /k/. What is the word?"
2. The teacher says, "I will say the word in a secret code. If you can break my code, tell me the word. The word is /b/ /ak/. What is the word?"
3. The teacher says, "I will say the word in a secret code. If you can break my code, tell me the word. The word is /b/ /a/ /k/. What is the word?"

Segmentation.

1. The teacher says, "I can 'machine gun' the first sound of *top.* T-t-t-top. Can you 'machine gun' the first sound of *cat?*"
2. The teacher says, "The beginning sound of *man* is /ma/. Tell me the beginning sound of *lock.*"
3. The teacher says, "The beginning sound of *man* is /m/. Tell me the beginning sound of *no.*"
4. The teacher says, "The ending sound of *lip* is /p/. Tell me the ending sound of *kiss.*"
5. The teacher says, "The word *catch* can be said in two parts: /ka/ /ch/. Say the word *pan* in two parts."
6. The teacher says, "The middle sound in the word *top* is /o/. Say the middle sound in the word *man.*"
7. The teacher says, "The sounds in the word *can* are /k/ /a/ /n/. Tell me the sounds in the word *nap.*"

Sound to Symbol.

1. The teacher places lettered squares in front of the child. One square has the letter *i* on it, and the other one has the letter *t*. The teacher puts them in front of the child and, while pointing to the appropriate letters, says, "This letter says /i/ and this letter says /t/." The teacher points to the letter /i/ and says, "Tell me the sound of this letter." While pointing to the letter *t*, the teacher says, "Tell me the sound of this letter."

2. The teacher places various lettered squares in front of the child and, while moving the appropriate squares to make words, says, "I am going to make the word *up*. This letter says /u/ and this letter says /p/. When /u/ and /p/ are put together they make the word *up*. Make the word *an*. Move and sound each letter as you make the word."

3. The teacher says, "Write the sound of /i/." After the student responds, the teacher says, "Write the sound of /t/." After the student responds, the teacher says, "Touch and sound each letter you have written and tell me the word."

Sound Manipulation.

1. The teacher places various lettered squares in front of the child and, while moving the appropriate squares to make words, says, "This word says *man*. Make it say *pan*." After waiting for the child to move the appropriate lettered squares, the teacher says, "Make *pan* say *pat*." After the appropriate student response, the teacher says, "Make *pat* say *pit*."

2. The teacher says, "Say *tan* without /t/."

3. The teacher says, "Say *tan* without /n/."

4. The teacher says, "Say *tan* with /m/ at the beginning instead of /t/."

Activities to Enhance Rhyme and Alliteration

Holistic teachers are concerned about whether learning experiences are relevant to children. They know that lessons requiring children to use language, involving activities children can relate to, enhance children's language development. When children discover that reading is enjoyable, they will try to read and learn from the attempt. When they have someone to write to, they will try to write and they will learn from the experience. When teachers and children are discussing an interesting subject, children will try to read books about it and write about it. Relevance, therefore, is one of the hallmarks of a holistic classroom, and phonemic awareness activities can and should be relevant to children.

Listening to teachers read nursery rhymes and books that play with the language is a natural way for children to learn that words are made up of sound elements. Any activity that helps children become aware of rhyming words or words that sound alike at the beginning, focuses their attention on those phonological aspects of words and enhances their phonological awareness.

Children enjoy reading books that emphasize rhyme and alliteration. Some favorites follow:

Bears on the Stairs: A Beginner's Book of Rhymes, by Muriel and Lionel Kalish, Scholastic, 1993

Each Peach Pear Plum, by Janet and Allan Ahlberg, Puffin, 1978

Peek-A-Boo! by Janet and Allan Ahlberg, Puffin, 1981

Goodnight Moon, by Margaret Wise Brown (pictures by Clement Hurd), Harper & Row, 1975

I Met a Man, by John Ciardi (illustrated by Robert Osborn), Houghton Mifflin, 1961

It Does Not Say Meow and Other Animal Riddle Rhymes, by Beatrice Shenk De Regniers (pictures by Paul Galdone), Houghton Mifflin, 1972

Jesse Bear, What Will You Wear? by Nancy White Carlstrom (illustrations by Bruce Degen), Scholastic, 1986

Fire! Fire! Said Mrs. McGuire, an old jingle adapted by Bill Martin, Jr., (pictures by Ted Schroeder), Holt, Rinehart and Winston, 1970

Across the Stream, by Mirra Ginsburg (pictures by Nancy Tafuri), Puffin, 1985

Don't Forget the Bacon, by Pat Hutchins, Puffin, 1976

Chicken Soup with Rice, by Maurice Sendak, Scholastic, 1962

Over in the Meadow, illustrated by Ezra Jack Keats, Scholastic, 1971

Busy Buzzing Bumblebees and Other Tongue Twisters, by Alvin Schwartz (illustrated by Kathie Abrams), Harper & Row, 1982

Roar and More, by Karla Kuskin, Harper & Row, 1956

Little Chicks' Mothers and All the Others, by Mildred Luton (pictures by Mary Maki Rae), Puffin, 1983

Alphabears: An ABC Book, by Kathleen Hague (illustrated by Michael Hague), Scholastic, 1984

Aster Aardvark's Alphabet Adventures, by Steven Kellogg, William Morrow: Mulberry, 1987

It's Raining Said John Twaining, translated and illustrated by N. M. Bodecker, Atheneum, 1973

After reading a book emphasizing alliteration or rhyming to children, call the children's attention to that characteristic of the book that makes it so much fun to read (rhyme or alliteration). During subsequent readings of the book, you might ask the children to clap their hands when they hear rhymes or words beginning with certain sounds. You may also want to ask the children if they can think of other words that rhyme with those used in the story. For example, in the book *Goodnight Moon,* a little rabbit is saying goodnight to everything around him. He says, "Goodnight bears, Goodnight chairs." Ask the children if they can think of other words that rhyme with *bears* or *chairs.* The children might come up with, "Goodnight stairs, Goodnight pears."

Children also enjoy rhyming games. For example, you could develop rhyming questions for them where the last word in the question either rhymes or doesn't rhyme with other words in the sentence. If the last word in the question rhymes with other words, the children would respond with a "yes" to the question. (You: "Will a bear share a pear?" Children: "Yes.") If the last word in the question does not rhyme with other words in the sentence, the response would be "no." (You: "Will a bear share a peach?" Children: "No.")

Sample questions:

Will a dog chase a frog?   Will a pig wear a big hat?
Will a clown frown?   Will Kate clean her plate?
Will Jake bake a cake?   Will Alice find the treasure?
Is the queen fifteen?   Will Dot pet the cat?
Will a bee land in a bush?   Will Sam feed the hamster?

Another rhyming game children enjoy playing requires them to supply the rhyming word:

A little white mouse
Was playing in the _____ (house).

A large black cat
Chased a fat brown _____ (rat).

Eventually, you will want children to see the text of the books, poems, and songs they read and sing (we discuss shared book, music, and rhythm experiences in Chapter 9). When doing this, emphasize the written representations of rhyme and alliteration to help them perceive sound–letter relationships.

Children enjoy participating in joint writing activities with teachers. In these activities, both together develop the ideas for the written product, but the teacher does the actual writing. Teacher and children read the finished piece aloud together. The teacher might also make copies for the children to read to their parents. Your first joint writing activity might be *couplets,* two successive lines of poetry that rhyme. Each line is approximately equal in length. For example:

In my favorite dream
I eat chocolate ice cream.

The first step in creating a couplet is to identify a topic, for example, *food.* The second is to make a list of all of the words related to the topic: *ice cream, pizza, hamburger, corn, peas, carrots, peaches, apples,* and so on. In step three, identify rhyming words for the words related to the topic, such as *peach—reach, teach, beach, preach, bleach.* Finally, use one of the rhyming sets to create a couplet:

On the beaches,
I eat peaches.

More mature children will enjoy creating limericks with the teacher. A *limerick* has five anapestic lines, of eight, eight, five, five, and eight syllables, respectively. Lines one, two, and five each contain three stresses; lines three and four each contain two. The lines rhyme aabba. For example:

I know an old fellow named Ray,
Who goes to the beach every day.
"I swim in the sea—
Because it is free.
The surfers stay out of my way."

Children also enjoy creating tongue twisters. Tongue twisters use alliteration and help children become consciously aware of common phonological elements. After children create tongue twisters they enjoy seeing how fast they can say or read them without stumbling. For example:

Robert's **r**abbit **r**an a **r**ace with a **r**accoon.

Hank **h**eld a **h**ealthy **h**amster in **h**is **h**and.

Big **b**ad **b**ashful **B**en **b**uilt a **b**anjo from a **b**undle of **b**ranches **B**en's **b**rother **b**rought **b**ack from **b**eautiful **B**ritain.

Seven **s**ad **s**elfish **s**isters **s**uddenly **s**tarted **s**inging the **s**ame **s**imple **s**ong they **s**ang to **s**ix **s**ea **s**erpents **s**o **s**lowly **s**everal **s**easons ago.

One-two-three-four poetry also uses alliteration. This type of poetry is relatively easy for a teacher and students to create. For example, after a field trip to the zoo, ask your students to list all of the animals they saw: horses, monkeys, elephants, lions, snakes. Then ask the students to think of something each animal does that begins with the same sound heard at the beginning of the animal's name: horses heave; monkeys munch; elephants eat; lions lick; snakes sit. Ask students to think of a word to describe each animal that begins with the same sound as the animal's name: healthy horses; moody monkeys; elegant elephants; large lions; slithery snakes. Finally, ask the students to think of words with the same beginning sound that describe how the animals do what they do: heave heavily; munch merrily; eat endlessly; lick lazily; sit slyly. Students put these elements together and have a one-two-three-four poem:

Healthy **h**orses **h**eave **h**eavily.
Moody **m**onkeys **m**unch **m**errily.
Elegant **e**lephants **e**at **e**ndlessly.
Large **l**ions **l**ick **l**azily.
Slithery **s**nakes **s**it **s**lyly.
We saw interesting animals at the zoo.

Using Songs to Enhance Phonemic Awareness

Young children enjoy singing. By creating new words for old familiar songs, children's phonemic awareness can be enhanced through music:

Sound Matching

Beginning Sounds—Level 1 [Song: Skip to My Lou (Modified)]

Who has a word that starts with /fi/?
Starts, starts, starts with /fi/?
Who has a word that starts with /fi/?
Skip to my Lou, my darling!

(Call on a student who knows a word that starts with /fi/. The word is repeated, and used in the song.)

Fish is a word that starts with /fi/.
Starts, starts, starts with /fi/.
Fish is a word that starts with /fi/.
Skip to my Lou, my darling!

Sample words for other beginning consonant sounds: *witch, badge, sack, fox, desk, map, jam, rat, hand, nut, lock, kick, ten, pan, cup, coat, paint, teeth, goat, kite, yard, lake, nose, home, rope, road, jail, moon, dime, face, soap.*

Beginning Sounds—Level 2

Who has a word that starts with a /k/?
Starts, starts, starts with a /k/?
Who has a word that starts with a /k/?
Skip to my Lou, my darling!

(Call on a student who knows a word that starts with /k/. The word is repeated, and used in the song.)

Cat is a word that starts with a /k/.
Starts, starts, starts with a /k/.
Cat is a word that starts with a /k/.
Skip to my Lou, my darling!

Sample words for other beginning consonant sounds: *box, sack, wig, dog, man, jet, rock, hen, nest, log, yes, kiss (cap), gum, tub, pig, zoo.*

Ending Sounds

Who has a word that ends with a /t/?
Ends, ends, ends with a /t/?
Who has a word that ends with a /t/?
Skip to my Lou, my darling!

Cat is a word that ends with a /t/.
Ends, ends, ends with a /t/.
Cat is a word that ends with a /t/.
Skip to my Lou, my darling!

Sample words for other ending consonant sounds: *cup (rope), fox, bib (robe), knife, sun (bone), duck (cake), gum (dime), bell (smile), bed (food), bug, page, horse (ice), five, nose.*

Vowel Sounds

Who has a word that has an /a/?
Has, has, has an /a/?
Who has a word that has an /a/?
Skip to my Lou, my darling!

Apple is a word that has an /a/.
Has, has, has an /a/.
Apple is a word that has an /a/.
Skip to my Lou, my darling!

Sample words for other vowel sounds: *itch, ox, up, edge—ice, ate, open, use, eat—hat, bed, big, dog, bus—face, bone, music, bike, seed.*

Sound Blending [Song: The Mulberry Bush]

Now we will say the word out loud,
The word out loud,
The word out loud,
Now we will say the word out loud,
So put the sounds to-geth-er.

(Say, "/ka/   /t/"—simple level. Children respond, **"cat."** Say, "/k/   /a/   /t/"— advanced level. Children respond, **"cat."**)
Sample words for sound blending activities: *wax, bed, sun, fog, dig, men, jam, red, hug, nap, van, lid, yes, kiss, gas, ten, pot, cut, zip, quick, gym, queen, zoom, coat, page, teeth, kite, yard, lawn, nose, horse, rope, jail, mice, dime, food, soap, beach, week.*

Sound Isolating (Simple)

Beginning Sounds [Song: The Farmer in the Dell (Modified)]

What sound starts the words?
What sound starts the words?
Hi-ho, the der-ri-o,
What sound starts the words?

(Say, **"man, moon, mouse."** Everyone repeats, **"man, moon, mouse."**)

/m/ starts the words.
/m/ starts the words.
Hi-ho, the der-ri-o,
/m/ starts the words.

(Everyone repeats, "*man, moon, mouse.*")

Sample words for isolating beginning consonant sounds: *coat, cook, cap; pain, point, pup; toy, test, tape; goat, good, gum; kiss, king, keep; yes, yell, yard; log, leg, lake; vest, van, voice; nail, nice, noise, hill, home, hat, rope, room, rain, jump, job, junk, day, dance, dish, food, foot, fish, soap, sun, sand; box, bus, badge; wet, wood, wig; cheese, chain, church; shop, shed, shirt; thin, thick, thorn; that, them, this; whip, wheat, wheel.*

Ending Sounds

What sound ends the words?
What sound ends the words?
Hi-ho, the der-ri-o,
What sound ends the words?

(Say, "*fish, wash, wish.*" Everyone repeats, "*fish, wash, wish.*")

/sh/ ends the words.
/sh/ ends the words.
Hi-ho, the der-ri-o,
/sh/ ends the words . . . *fish, wash, wish.*

Sample words for isolating ending consonant sounds: *top, cup, ape; web, job, robe; six, mix, ox; knife, off, safe; rain, bone, ten; snake, duck, book; kite, boat, rat; gum, name, home; doll, nail, smile; toad, food, mud; wig, leg, bag; cage, age, page; house, mouse, boss; rose, nose, noise; five, stove, cave; teach, couch, ditch; moth, tooth, mouth; sing, long, ring.*

Vowel Sounds

What sound is in the mid-dle?
What sound is in the mid-dle?
Hi-ho, the der-ri-o,
What sound is in the mid-dle?

(Say, "*man, cap, jam.*" Everyone repeats, "*man, cap, jam.*")

/a/ is in the mid-dle.
/a/ is in the mid-dle.
Hi-ho, the der-ri-o,
/a/ is in the mid-dle . . . *man, cap, jam.*

Sample words for isolating vowel sounds: *mail, rain, name; heat, teeth, geese; five, dime, ride; bone, road, home; cute, fuse, mule; bed, men, red; fish, dish, lid; bus, pup, nut; box, rock, top.*

Sound Isolating (Difficult) [Song: London Bridge]

> Lis-ten to the words I say,
> words I say,
> words I say,
> Tell me all the sounds you hear,
> Lis-ten to this word.

(Say, **"Cat."** Children respond, "/ka/   /t/"—simple level. Children respond, "/k/ /a/   /t/"—advanced level.)

Sample words for sound isolating activities: *witch, badge, sand, farm, dance, moon, joke, reach, house, nurse, voice, lawn, yes, kiss, gum, tooth, paint, count, quake, geese, chop, shake, peach, wish, whale, bang, thick, bath.*

Sound Substituting [Song: Little White Duck]

> There's a lit-tle white duck
> sit-ting in the wa-ter,
> A lit-tle white duck
> do-ing what he ough-ter.
> He took a bite of a lil-y pad,
> Flapped his wings and he said, I'm glad,
> I'm a lit-tle white duck
> sit-ting in the wa-ter.
> Quack! Quack! Quack!

(Say, "Sing the song again and say *quack* without /kw/"—simple level. Say, "Sing the song again and put the /z/ sound in place of the beginning sound of *quack*"—more difficult level. Say, "Sing the song again and put the /k/ sound in place of the ending sound of *quack*"—more advanced level. Say, "Sing the song again and put the /i/ sound in place of the /a/ sound in *quack*"—most advanced level.)

Using Games to Develop Phonemic Awareness

Word Awareness Games

Many times during the school day teachers and children discuss the experiences they share. These experiences are varied and might include stories read, art projects completed, songs sung, filmstrips viewed, or field trips taken. During these discussions, teachers often ask students to talk about their experiences while they write what the children say on the chalkboard. Students then usually read these sentences with assistance from the teacher. It is on occasions such as these that the first word awareness game is appropriate. The steps to the game follow:

1. Write each word of a dictated sentence on a separate word card.
2. Select a child to stand in front of the classroom and give her the first word in the sentence to hold. Select another child to stand next to the first child and hold

the second word. Repeat this process until you have the words in the sentence held by students in the correct order. For example:

| We | had | fun | baking | bread | today. |

3. Reread the sentence and touch the head of each child holding the appropriate word as it is read.
4. Tell the students that you will read the sentence again, but this time the child holding the appropriate word should raise it above her head as it is read.
5. Ask the children at their seats to close their eyes. Have one student in the sentence line turn her card over so a blank space appears.

| We | had | fun | | bread | today. |

6. Ask the children to open their eyes and guess which word is missing.
7. Repeat this process with other words in the sentence.

A second word awareness game is as follows:

1. Divide the class into two groups. Give each group the assignment to sort the words used in the sentence according to their length, shortest to longest. Give the students time to consult with each other in their groups.
2. Ask group one to send one of their members to the sentence line to take the shortest word from the student holding it. If the student selects the correct word, group one gets a point and the word is taped to the chalkboard. If he selects the wrong word, no points are given and the word is returned to the student holding it.
3. Ask group two to send one of their members to the sentence line to take the shortest word remaining. If the student selects the correct word, group two gets a point and the word is taped beneath the first word on the chalkboard. If he selects the wrong word, no points are given and the word is returned to the student holding it.
4. The game continues until all of the words in the sentence line have been taped to the chalkboard according to length. When the game is over, students, with your assistance, read the words taped on the chalkboard. You then help students perceive length relationships between spoken and written words.

Phoneme Counting Game

The phoneme counting game is designed to help children become aware of phonemes by listening to words spoken by the teacher and counting the phonemes heard. Each child participating in the game must have at least three 2-inch tagboard squares. These squares may be blank or each may have an alphabet letter written on it. Educators originally believed that letters confused children when teaching them to count phonemes in words; however, that assumption has been proven false. So you may choose to use either blank or lettered squares when playing the phoneme counting game. You should have the same number of squares that the students have, but your squares should be larger so all children in the classroom can see them. If you decide to use lettered squares then both the students and you must have the appropriate lettered squares for the words selected for the game.

Your squares should have cloth glued on the back of each so you can put them on a flannel board and move them as occasion requires. If a flannel board is not available, put masking tape on the back of each so they can be used on the chalkboard.

Introduce the game by placing three blank squares on the flannel board so that each square is in a line:

Say, "Listen to the sounds in the word *at*." As you say each phoneme in the word, move one square down about four inches. "/a/ /t/. How many sounds are in the word *at*?" Wait for a response. Say, "You say the word *at* with me and move down one of your squares for each sound you hear in the word. /a/ /t/." Wait for a response, then say, "How many squares did you move down?" The students respond. Say, "How many sounds are in the word *at*?" The students respond.

Continue the game using two-phoneme and three-phoneme words, such as the following examples. You will easily think of more.

Two-phoneme, two-grapheme words: *at, an, as, am, Ed, it, in, if, is, on.*

Two-phoneme, three-grapheme words: *toy, for, fur, jar, jaw, joy, say, saw, row, hay, her.*

If lettered squares are used in this game, the graphemes representing one sound should be written on one square. For example:

Three-phoneme, three-grapheme words: *web, wig, win, wet, wag, bus, bib, bed, bad, big, beg, bat, bag, bug, bun, but, bit, bet, sit, sob, sin, sad, set, sun, sat, fib, fan.*

Three-phoneme, four-grapheme words: *wait, wave, week, weed, wife, wood, beach, bead, bean, boil, book, boot, born, safe, sail, same, seat, soap, soon, south, face, fake, farm.*

Phoneme Matching Game

Children love riddles and guessing games. The phoneme matching game is a guessing game that requires children to match isolated phonemes with familiar words containing those phonemes.

The game can be played with half of the class competing with the other half, or it can be played in one group without the "friendly competition." If the game is played with all members of the class, children raise their hands when they think they have the answer to a riddle. You would then call upon various students to respond.

If class members enjoy competition, the classroom should be divided into two groups. Each group takes a turn trying to guess a riddle. The group gets only one guess. Each member of the group takes a turn responding for the group, but other members of the group may prompt the person responding if they believe they know the answer. If the team member responsible for responding for the group gives the correct answer, the team gets a point. If the answer is incorrect, no points are given.

Present a riddle by saying, "I am thinking of something that children ride. It has two wheels. It begins with the /bī/ sound (simple level)." Answer: *bike*. If the students are able to respond to a more difficult matching level task, then the teacher replaces the last sentence with, "It begins with the /b/ sound." Sample riddles follow.

Beginning Sounds.

I am thinking of a furry animal that dogs chase. Its name begins with the /ka/ sound (optional: the /k/ sound). Answer: *cat*

I am thinking of an animal that can fly and likes to swim. Its name begins with the /du/ sound (optional: the /d/ sound). Answer: *duck*

I am thinking of a something that goes high up in the sky. It has a string attached to it that I hold while it flies. It begins with the /kī)/ sound (optional: the /k/ sound). Answer: *kite*

I am thinking of something that shines in the sky. It begins with the /su/ sound (optional: the /s/ sound). Answer: *sun*

I am thinking of an animal that likes to eat cheese. Its name begins with the /mou/ sound (optional: the /m/ sound). Answer: *mouse*

I am thinking of something that we hit with a hammer. It begins with the /nā/ sound (optional: the /n/ sound). Answer: *nail*

I am thinking of an animal that has a curly tail. Its name begins with the /pi/ sound (optional: the /p/ sound). Answer: *pig*

I am thinking of something that I use when I take a bath. It begins with the /tu/ sound (optional: the /t/ sound). Answer: *tub*

I am thinking of something that policemen have. It begins with the /gu/ sound (optional: the /g/ sound). Answer: *gun*

I am thinking of something that lives in the water. Its name begins with the /fi/ sound (optional: the /f/ sound). Answer: *fish*

I am thinking of something that we see pictures of during Halloween. Its name begins with the /wi/ sound (optional: the /w/ sound). Answer: *witch*

I am thinking of something that needs a key. It begins with the /lo/ sound (optional: the /l/ sound). Answer: *lock*

I am thinking of something that grapes grow on. It begins with the /vī/ sound (optional: the /v/ sound). Answer: *vine*

I am thinking of something that we use to get the leaves off the ground. It begins with the /rā/ sound (optional: the /r/ sound). Answer: *rake*

I am thinking of something that we put on our heads. It begins with the /ha/ sound (optional: the /h/ sound). Answer: *hat*

I am thinking of something that we sometimes find on coats. It begins with the /zi/ sound (optional: the /z/ sound). Answer: *zipper*

I am thinking of another name for a penny. It begins with the /se/ sound (optional: the /s/ sound). Answer: *cent*

I am thinking of something good to eat. It begins with the /ja/ sound (optional: the /j/ sound). Answer: *jam*

I am thinking of something children do when they try to call to a friend down the street. It begins with the /ye/ sound (optional: the /y/ sound). Answer: *yell*

I am thinking of something that we put on a horse to ride. It begins with the /sa/ sound (optional: the /s/ sound). Answer: *saddle*

I am thinking of a piece of furniture. It begins with the /ch/ sound. Answer: *chair*

I am thinking of an animal. This animal was lost by Little Bo Peep. Its name begins with the /sh/ sound. Answer: *sheep*

I am thinking of something that is round. It is found on a bike. It begins with the /hw/ sound. Answer: *wheel*

I am thinking of something on a vine that hurts if you touch it. Its name begins with the /th/ sound. Answer: *thorn*

Ending Sounds. After children get the right answers to these riddles, ask them to repeat the word, then the ending sound. For example, "*Dad, /d/*."

I am thinking of something people usually eat with butter. It ends with the /d/ sound. Answer: *bread*

I am thinking of something that we use to throw on a fire to keep it burning. It ends with the /g/ sound. Answer: *log*

I am thinking of a very small animal with a tail. Its name ends with the /s/ sound. Answer: *mouse*

I am thinking of something a bear lives in sometimes. It ends with the /v/ sound. Answer: *cave*

I am thinking of an animal that has horns, and some people say eats cans. Its name ends with the /t/ sound. Answer: *goat*

I am thinking of something a spider walks on. It ends with the /b/ sound. Answer: *web*

I am thinking of a color. Its name ends with the /k/ sound. Answer: *black*

I am thinking of an animal that lives in the ground. Some people use it for fishing. Its name ends with the /m/ sound. Answer: *worm*

I am thinking of something that you throw. Its name ends with the /l/ sound. Answer: *ball*

I am thinking of something we generally use when we drink something warm. It ends with the /p/ sound. Answer: *cup*

I am thinking of something you see at night. Its name ends with the /n/ sound. Answer: *moon*

I am thinking of a number. Its name ends with the /ks/ sound. Answer: *six*

I am thinking of something that falls off trees in the fall. Its name ends with the /f/ sound. Answer: *leaf*

I am thinking of something you get when you win a contest. It ends with the /z/ sound. Answer: *prize*

I am thinking of something a policeman wears. Its name ends with the /j/ sound. Answer: *badge*

I am thinking of something you put on your finger. Its name ends with the /ng/ sound. Answer: *ring*

I am thinking of something that you put food on. Its name ends with the /sh/ sound. Answer: *dish*

I am thinking of a fruit. Its name ends with the /ch/ sound. Answer: *peach*

I am thinking of something you take when you get dirty. Its name ends with the /th/ sound. Answer: *bath*

Vowel Sounds. After children get the right answers to these riddles, ask them to repeat the word, then the vowel sound. For example, "*Top, /o/.*"

I am thinking of something that we wear on Halloween. Its name has an /a/ sound in the middle. Answer: *mask*

I am thinking of something that uses ink for writing. Its name has an /e/ sound in the middle. Answer: *pen*

I am thinking of a dessert that we eat on birthdays. Its name has an /ā/ sound in the middle. Answer: *cake*

I am thinking of something people wear on their heads when they don't have any hair. Its name has an /i̠/ sound in the middle. Answer: *wig*

I am thinking of a number. Its name has an /ī/ sound in the middle. Answer: *five*

I am thinking of a color. Its name has an /ē/ sound in the middle. Answer: *green*

I am thinking of something we put on the floor. We walk on it. Its name has an /u/ sound in the middle. Answer: *rug*

I am thinking of an animal that is something like a horse. Its name has a /ū/ sound in the middle. Answer: *mule*

I am thinking of something that we use to scrub floors. Its name has an /o/ sound in the middle. Answer: *mop*

I am thinking of a part of the face. Its name has an /ō/ sound in the middle. Answer: *nose*

I am thinking of something we use to carry money. Its name has an /ir/ sound in the middle. Answer: *purse*

I am thinking of something a dog does. It has an /ar/ sound in the middle of the word. Answer: *bark*

I am thinking of something we use when we eat. It has points on it. Its name has an /or/ sound in the middle. Answer: *fork*

I am thinking of something that is used to buy things. It is flat and round. Its name has an /oi/ sound in the middle. Answer: *coin*

I am thinking of something that we find in the sky. Its name has an /ou/ sound in the middle. Answer: *cloud*

I am thinking of something that growls and lives in caves. Its name ends with the /âr/ sound. Answer: *bear*

Phoneme Blending Game

The phoneme blending game is another guessing game. In this game you isolate phonemes, and the children mentally blend the phonemes to form words.

The phoneme blending game can be played with or without student competition. Group students for the game in the same manner as for the phoneme matching game. Tell the students that you are thinking of something that you will reveal through a secret code. Then tell them the word in your secret code. If the students understand the code they identify your word. For example, say, "I am thinking of a /k/ /a/ /t/. Can you tell me my word?" Wait for a correct response, which in this case is *cat*.

A variation of the game requires the use of a large bag of objects, much like the bag Santa Claus is supposed to carry. Reach into the bag, touch an object, and say, "I am touching a /k/ /a/ /n/. What am I touching?" The students then respond to your question, in this case saying *can*.

You can adjust the complexity of the game to meet the phonemic awareness levels of your students. At the simplest level, your secret code involves segmenting the word in two parts. The first part ends with the vowel, and the second part includes everything after the vowel: /ma/ /d/. At a more advanced level, the secret code also segments the word in two parts, but this time the first part is everything before the vowel, and the second part begins with the vowel and includes everything after it: /m/ /ad/. At the most advanced level, the secret code involves the segmentation of every phoneme in the word: /m/ /a/ /d/.

The following words, familiar to young children, are appropriate for use in the phoneme blending game. These words include most of the basic phonemes of speech: *bike, book, ball, dog, duck, dish, kite, key, king, six, sun, mouse, moon, match, nose, nine, nail, purse, pen, pig, tent, tail, tub, goat, gun, gate, five, fox, fish, wing, wall, witch, log, lock, lamp, vine, vest, van, rose, rake, ring, hook, hat, house, zest, jam, jet, queen, yarn, yell, sing, bed, head, can, nut, rain, jeep, soap, girl, coin, shout, fork, tooth, wig, chain.*

Phoneme Isolation Game

In the phoneme isolation game, the children play the teacher's role, isolating phonemes in words (saying words in a secret code) for other children to identify. The secret code they use depends upon their phonemic awareness level. Some children may isolate words in two parts, breaking the word after the vowel, such as /ju/ /j/ for the word *judge*. Others may be able to isolate the word in two parts, breaking the word before the vowel: /j/ /uj/. More advanced children might be able to isolate every phoneme in the word: /j/ /u/ /j/.

Students select words for this game that they are able to say in a "secret code." The game is enjoyed both by the students who can say the words in a secret code, and by those who try to identify them.

Using Literature Books to Enhance Phonemic Awareness

Teachers help children to understand that words are made up of sound elements by reading books to them that stress rhyming and alliteration. Other books can also be used to enhance children's phonemic awareness.

Literature books are meant to be enjoyed by children. In fact, the primary purposes for using them in classrooms are for enjoyment, learning, and enrichment. However, after children are well acquainted with specific books, teaching activities, using words or ideas from those books, are appropriate, and often extremely effective.

Creative teachers can find many ways to use the books children read to teach them all of the phonemic tasks described in this chapter. From them they may derive the raw materials for activities designed to develop word and syllabic awareness, and the words used in activities designed to help children hear and count phonemes. Furthermore, activities involving phoneme matching, blending, phoneme isolation, sound to symbol matching, and sound manipulation can all be developed from the themes, concepts, and/or words used in children's literature books. We close this chapter by illustrating three of the many ways in which children's books can be used to enhance phonemic awareness.

Example One: Phoneme Matching

In Steven Kellogg's book, *Can I Keep Him?* (Dial, 1971), a small boy wants to take all kinds of animals home and keep them. His mother explains why he can't. Dogs bark; cats have fur that affect people's allergies; deer have hooves and antlers that tear up furniture; bears smell; tigers eat too much; and pythons are messy because they shed their skins all over the house.

You could follow this story with a phoneme matching activity centered around other animals that do each of these things. You could, for example, use the following riddles:

I am thinking of another animal that barks. Its name begins with the /sē/ sound (optional: the /s/ sound). Answer: *seal*

I am thinking of another animal that causes allergies for some people. Its name begins with the /hor/ sound (optional: the /h/ sound). Answer: *horse*

I am thinking of another animal that has horns and feet that can destroy furniture. Its name begins with the /gō/ sound (optional: the /g/ sound). Answer: *goat*

I am thinking of another animal that smells. Its name begins with the /sku/ sound (optional: the /sk/ sound). Answer: *skunk*

I am thinking of another animal that eats a lot. Its name begins with the /pi/ sound (optional: the /p/ sound). Answer: *pig*

I am thinking of an animal that sometimes sheds fur all over the house. Its name begins with the /do/ sound (optional: the /d/ sound). Answer: *dog*

Example Two: Phoneme Matching

In Patricia Reilly Giff's book, *Today Was a Terrible Day,* illustrated by Susanna Natti (Puffin, 1984), a second-grade boy named Ronald Morgan couldn't do anything right until the end of the school day. By extracting sentences from that book and substituting a syntactically correct word for one of the words, you can provide phoneme matching activities for children (use a substitute word so that children cannot guess the word from memory). Read the sentence and say the first sound of the missing (substitute) word, and have the children guess the missing word. For example:

"Today was a terrible day.
It started when I dropped my [/bŏŏ/ or /b/]." Answer: *book*
"I tiptoed to the closet and ate a [/pē/ or /p/]." Answer: *peach*
"When lunchtime came, I had no money for [/ka/ or /k/]." Answer: *candy*

Example Three: Sound Substitution and Blending

In H. A. Rey's *Curious George* (Houghton Mifflin, 1969), a monkey named George gets into all sorts of trouble because of his curiosity. After reading the story, you might pick a few words from the story to do sound substitution and sound blending activities. For example, you might select the words: *had, man, hat, take, him, came, bag.*

When doing sound substitution and blending activities write the word on the chalkboard and say, "This word is *had.* Say the word *had* without the /h/ sound." The correct response would be *ad.* After the students respond appropriately, write *ad* underneath the word *had* so the children can visualize the sound–symbol connections, then say, "Say the /m/ sound and the /ad/ sound together and tell me what word you get." The students should respond with the word *mad.* When they respond correctly, write the word *mad* underneath the word *ad,* then say, "Replace the /m/ sound in *mad* with the /s/ sound and tell me the word you get." When the children respond with *sad,* write that word underneath the word *mad.* If this activity were to continue, you would create the following words by substituting and blending phonemes:

had	man	hat	take	came
ad	an	at	cake	name
mad	ran	rat	rake	tame
sad	tan	sat	sake	same
bad	can	cat	bake	fame
pad	pan	pat	make	game

Application Activities

1. Summarize, in writing, the stages of phonological awareness.
2. Use the "secret code" game with some preschool child. Use both compound and multisyllabic words in the game. Afterwards, see how well the child can respond to sound manipulation activities with these words. Write a paragraph describing your experience.
3. Use the phonemic awareness tasks outlined in this chapter and assess a child's level of phonemic awareness.
4. Create a game or song to enhance children's phonemic awareness.

Chapter 6

A Formal Phonemic Awareness Training Program

There are many ways to teach young children to hear and isolate phonemes, but perhaps none more effective than writing, especially if it is accompanied by brief periods of phonemic awareness training. Writing is essential in holistic classrooms. In fact, the amount of writing done by children is considered to be one of the indicators of holistic teaching. Holistic teachers recognize that reading and writing are reciprocal language processes, and that many children learn to read through their early writing experiences. They also recognize that writing is an effective vehicle to help young children develop an understanding of the alphabetic principle.

When children encode a word they use letters to represent its phonemes; however, if they can't hear phonemes, they can't spell accurately. Children cannot write effectively without some level of phonemic awareness. At the same time, phonemic awareness is enhanced through writing, especially when children are encouraged to write words according to their sounds, because they are constantly trying to isolate phonemes as they spell. Because of the reciprocal relationship between phonemic awareness and writing, young children should be encouraged to write, and teachers should concurrently provide them with relevant learning experiences to enhance their understanding of the alphabetic principle.

The formal phonemic awareness training program described in this chapter is designed to complement any writing program. The awareness training helps children spell words by sounds, and takes no more than ten minutes of daily classroom time to implement. Classroom studies indicate that children receiving this type of training write better, and move through the stages of invented spelling earlier, than children who do not receive it.

The Writing Process

Most writers, when producing publishable documents, follow in general a series of predictable steps: prewriting, drafting, revising, editing, and publishing. Educators now generally believe that children should learn these steps; that is, they should learn the process writers go through when they write. It is assumed that if children learn this process, they will become better writers.

In the first step, *prewriting*, authors get ideas, develop needed writing skills, obtain information about various subjects, and choose writing topics. This step takes considerable time for most authors.

After writers have selected their topics and prepared themselves to write about them, they begin *drafting* their document, putting all of their ideas related to the topic on paper. Their attention is on the content of the message at this time, not on the form or mechanics of writing.

After completing a draft, writers usually have other individuals read and critique it. They then use this critical feedback to *revise* and improve the written product.

During the fourth step, *editing*, writers closely examine the form and mechanics of their document. They ask themselves such questions as, "Are there any misspellings? Do I need to organize my message in a different way? Is my grammar usage proper? Is the written product attractive to the reader?"

After editing the written product, it is *published* so it can be shared with the intended audience.

Teachers who involve children in the writing process help them learn the steps through experience. Many teachers introduce the process to young children by *writing with them;* that is, teacher and children go through the steps together, jointly producing written documents. First, they spend time, often several days, pursuing an area of interest to the group. The teacher reads books aloud about the subject; they see films, filmstrips, and videos on the subject; they go on field trips related to it; they listen to guest speakers talk about it, and so on. At the conclusion of this step, the teacher and children jointly decide to write about some aspect of the subject.

After identifying a specific writing topic, the teacher and children select a title for the proposed product. Then, individual children dictate sentences about the topic. The teacher writes these on the chalkboard, then teacher and children read them together. After the chalkboard has been filled with children's sentences, the children read them all again with teacher assistance (see Chapter 9 on assisted reading strategies). They talk about the sentences and decide how to organize them. The teacher then numbers the sentences to identify the students' chosen sequence. Before erasing the chalkboard, the teacher makes a copy of the written draft.

The next day, the teacher projects a copy of the draft on a screen, through an overhead projector, so the children can watch as the teacher makes any revisions to the original document. Every line of print is double spaced on the draft copy so there is room to make revisions. With the teacher's assistance the children read the draft copy. Suggestions for improvement are elicited from the group, and revisions agreed upon by the majority of the students are made to the document.

The following day, the teacher projects a copy of the revised draft on the screen so the children can watch the editing phase. The teacher has purposely misspelled some simple words, and made a few simple punctuation errors on the revised draft. The teacher and students focus on the mechanics and form of the written product. The teacher asks the students to look for any misspelled words or punctuation errors so they can correct them.

The next day, the teacher distributes copies of the final version of the document to the children. A copy of the document is again projected on the screen. The children and the teacher read it several times. Children who desire to do so illustrate their individual copies of the document. The teacher encourages children to take their copy home and read it to their parents.

Students are then encouraged to go through the process by themselves. They choose their own writing topics after they have spent the prewriting time necessary. They make their own written drafts. During the drafting phase, the teacher encourages them to focus on the message they want to communicate and not to worry about spelling, allowing them to spell phonetically any words they are unsure of.

It is appropriate at this point to comment about spelling and grammar in children's writing. Most educators believe that the substance of children's writing is more important than its form during the initial stages of the writing process. Therefore, they tend to deemphasize spelling and grammar when children write drafts so they can focus on what they want to say. Most of these educators recognize that spelling and grammar knowledge greatly influences the quality of children's writing. Children who are able to organize sentences in meaningful ways tend to produce high-quality written products, and those who are not worried about spelling are free to focus their attention on the content of their messages. There is a time and a place to worry about spelling and grammar in children's written documents, however that time is not when children are trying to put their ideas on paper. Effective teachers do help children improve their syntax and spelling knowledge, but they do it in ways unobtrusive to the constructive thinking processes children are required to use during the initial phases of writing.

After the children complete their written drafts, they share them with classmates. Students form small groups for this purpose, and take turns reading their drafts to one another. After each reading, members of the group react to the draft, making positive comments about the author's work before they offer any suggestions for improvement. After the children receive this feedback, they make whatever revisions they want to make in their work.

After children revise their documents, they are encouraged to proofread and edit them for spelling, punctuation, and grammar. Other students then have the opportunity to proofread them. These students become "editors," and identify spelling, punctuation, and grammar problems. The authors of the documents make the needed corrections after the editors complete their work.

The final editor of children's work is the teacher. The teacher edits the documents after the author and two or three other students proofread them. The teacher writes the correct spelling above all misspellings the children did not find in small, but neat, handwriting. The student then makes a final copy of the document, illustrates it if desired, and makes it available for others to read. The final draft copy, containing the teacher's spelling corrections, is placed in the student's assessment portfolio.

The quantity and quality of children's writing are influenced by teachers. Teachers create a writing climate in the classroom; they provide relevant reasons for children to write; they motivate children to write; and they help children improve their writing abilities. One of the best ways to help *young* writers improve their writing is to provide them with phonemic awareness training.

Phonemic Awareness Training

Kindergarten children's early writing experiences often include, among other things, writing captions underneath their artwork. (The artwork might in fact be produced after the written document.) During "writing sharing time" students usually read their captions and display their artwork. Afterwards, each student's creation is made available for others to read and enjoy. Sharing time is important because students are motivated to do more writing when they have opportunities to share their work with others.

Teachers sometimes ask children to bring magazine or newspaper pictures to school so they can write captions for them. Many teachers collect newspapers and magazines so students not having access to them can participate in activities such as this one. Caption writing for single pictures eventually leads to caption writing for three or four related pictures. The short, captioned stories produced by children in this manner are usually interesting and creative, and the writing experience helps children view themselves as authors. Before long, they are writing and illustrating their own stories.

Teachers often use wordless picture books as tools for young children's writing. Children write simple stories for these books by creating captions for each picture in the book. These captions are loosely taped underneath each picture in the book while the children read their stories during the sharing time.

Some kindergarten teachers have children keep simple journals. Children write in their journals at the end of the school day, recording anything they want to about the day.

It is recommended that children continue to write throughout their kindergarten year. The simple writing products children create in the early part of the year will become more sophisticated as the year progresses.

Phonemic Awareness Activities

Phonemic awareness activities such as those presented in the rest of this chapter are an appropriate supplement to children's writing activities. These "sound to symbol" activities explicitly reveal to children the relationships existing between phonemes and the letters representing them. Once children perceive these relationships, they approach invented spelling with more confidence and their written products reflect a more sophisticated vocabulary.

The sound to symbol phonemic awareness activities described herein systematically teach children how to spell 41 of the 42 basic speech sounds in the English language. (Only 41 sounds are included since it is not practical to attempt to teach the /zh/ sound heard in the word *measure* to young children.)

As noted previously, these phonemic awareness activities should not take much classroom time; ten minutes a day is usually sufficient. If you choose to use the activities, however, you should use them daily. You will probably not complete the steps outlined in each phonemic activity in one ten-minute instructional period. The actual time needed to complete an individual activity will depend upon the developmental level of the children involved. For some groups, an activity can be completed in one or two days, but others may take longer. Short periods of instruction provided regularly will have a greater impact on children's learning than longer periods provided only once or twice a week. Therefore, I recommend that phonemic awareness activities be provided for young children throughout the year until they have been introduced to at least one spelling for each speech sound, and they are able to use invented spelling to spell any word they can say.

Materials Needed for Phonemic Awareness Activities. Teachers who choose to use the formal phonemic awareness activities should have the following items:

- a flannel board
- large flannel board replicas of the pictures and key words used for helping children associate phonemes with letters
- large flannel board letters and letter teams used for making words

Each child participating in the phonemic awareness training should be provided with the following:

- a personal copy of the picture and key word used for each lesson when it is introduced
- individual letter and letter team manipulatives needed for making words during the lesson

Activity 1: Phonemes /a/, /h/, and /t/. The picture and key word used for this activity:

h a t

Introduce the activity by placing the picture of the *hat* on the flannel board and the letters | h | a | t | underneath the picture. Say, "There are three sounds in the word *hat*. Watch while I touch the letters that make each sound." Touch each letter and isolate the sound of each as you do: /h/ /a/ /t/.

Say, "Tell me the sound of each letter as I touch it." Touch each letter and help the children respond with the appropriate sound: /h/ /a/ /t/. The children watch as you move each letter on the flannel board down a few inches, saying its sound as you do.

Move the letter [a] from the word *hat* and place it in the middle of the flannel board. Point to the letter and say, "Tell me the sound of this letter." After the children respond, touch the letter [t] and say, "Tell me the sound of this letter." After the children respond, place the letter [t] to the right of the letter [a] to make the word [a][t] . Point to the letter [a] and say, "Tell me the sound of this letter once more." After the children respond, point to the letter [t] and say, "Tell me the sound of this letter." After the appropriate response, point to the letters [a][t] and ask, "What new word did we make?" (You may need to help the students blend the /a/ and /t/ together so they can apprehend the word *at*.) After the students have identified the word, explain to them that spoken words are made up of sounds, and letters represent those sounds in written words. You might say, "We make written words by choosing letters to represent their sounds. When you make a word with letters, you put the letters that make the word's sounds in the right order."

Make the word [h][a][t] again and say, "Say the sounds in this word as I touch each letter out of order." Touch the [t], then the [h], and finally the [a]. After touching each letter, help the students to make the correct response.

Organize the children into groups of two and distribute the letters [h][a][t] to each team. Say, "Move your letters around so they no longer make the word *hat*." (Mix up the flannel board letters as the children respond to this direction.) Say, "Touch the letter that says /a/." The students are working in pairs so they can help each other. After the children have responded, touch the appropriate letter on the flannel board, and say, "This letter says /a/." Ask the children to touch the letter that says /h/, and then the letter that says /t/. The children respond after each direction. Reinforce their efforts by referring to the large flannel board letter representing the correct response.

Help the children make the word *hat* by walking them through the following steps:

1. "Find the letter that makes the /h/ sound and place it in front of you."
2. "Find the letter that makes the /a/ sound, and place it after the /h/ sound."

3. "Find the letter that makes the /t/ sound, and place it at the end of the word."
4. "Touch and sound each letter in the word, and then say the word."

After making words with the manipulatives, help children write words by sounds. For example, to help the children write the sounds of the word *at,* ask the students to (a) write the sound of /a/; and (b) write the sound of /t/ after the /a/ sound. After writing each word, ask the students to *touch and sound* each letter in the word before saying it.

The last step in this activity is to organize the children into groups of four and give them the opportunity to write words by sounds. They should not be restricted to the three phonemes used in this lesson as they write words by sounds. However, they should try to write as many words as they can think of containing these phonemes.

Activity 2: Phonemes / ā /,/r/, and /n/. The picture and key word used for this activity:

r ai n

This activity is introduced in the same manner as Activity 1. The new picture and key word are placed on the flannel board, and the letters representing the three sounds in the word *rain* are touched, sounded, and moved around.

When you and your students are ready for the "making new words" phase of the lesson, the picture and key word for Activity 1 are placed on the flannel board next to the picture and key word for this activity. The manipulatives h a t   r ai and n are used when making new words. You have the large flannel board version of the manipulatives, and each student pair has the desk-sized version. You can use these six manipulatives to make the following short words: *at, hat, rain, rat, an, ran, tan,* and *train.*

Move various manipulatives on the flannel board to form words. Point to each letter in a newly formed word and ask the students to say the sounds represented by each. The students then identify the words by their sounds.

Help the student teams make new words by asking them to find letters representing each word sound and by organizing those letters in proper sequence. After receiving each direction, the student teams use their desk-size manipulatives to respond. Reinforce their efforts by displaying the correct response on the flannel board. For example, to make the word *tan*, walk the students through the following steps:

1. "Find the letter that makes the /t/ sound and place it in front of you."
2. "Find the letter that makes the /a/ sound, and place it after the /t/ sound."
3. "Find the letter that makes the /n/ sound, and place it at the end of the word."
4. "Touch and sound each letter in the word, and then say the word."

After making words with manipulatives, help the children write words by sounds. For example, to help them write the sounds of the word *ran*, ask the students to first write the /r/ sound; then write the /a/ sound after the /r/ sound; and finally write the /n/ sound at the end of the word. After each word is written, ask the students to *touch and sound* each letter in the word before saying it.

Organize the children into groups of four so they can make words using the six manipulatives, and write words by sounds. Each student pair has a set of manipulatives, and each student should have a copy of the key words to help them as they make and write words. They make words with the manipulatives first. When children make new words using the six manipulatives, encourage them to think of the sounds of each letter or letter team available to them, and to put those sounds together to form words. After each student team makes a word they show it to the other team, who acknowledges the accomplishment and awards the team a point.

When children write words by sounds, they should not be restricted to the six phonemes used in this lesson. However, they should try to write as many words as they can think of containing these phonemes.

Activities 3 through 26 follow the same steps as those outlined for Activity 2.

Activity 3: Phonemes /o/, /l/, and /g/. The picture and key word used for this activity:

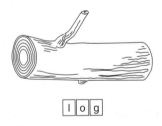

Step one. Touch and say the sounds of the letters under the key word on the flannel board. Ask the students to say the sounds of each letter as you touch them.

Step two. Make new words on the flannel board with the letters introduced in this lesson and all previous lessons. Point to the letters in the words formed and ask the students to say the sound represented by each. Ask the students to identify the words you form by their sounds.

Step three. Display all of the letter manipulatives in random order on the flannel board and ask the students to say the sounds of each.

Step four. Form students into groups of two and provide them with the desk-size manipulatives needed for the lesson. Help them form words by sounds. For example, "Find the letter that makes the /g/ sound and place it in front of you. Find the letter that makes the /o/ sound and place it after the /g/ sound. Find the letter that makes the /t/ sound and place it at the end of the word. Touch and sound each letter in the word, and then say the word."

Step five. Help the children write words by sounds. Follow the format outlined in step four, but adapt it for writing instead of moving manipulatives.

Step six. Form students into groups of four and give each pair of students the opportunity to create words with manipulatives and write words by sounds.

In this activity the nine manipulatives can be used to make the following short words: *at, hat, rain, rat, an, ran, tan, hag, gain, hail, tag, gag, lot, got, on, lag, hog, hot, tot, rag, rot, not, ant,* and *train.*

Activity 4: Phonemes /i/ and /w/. The picture and key word used for this activity:

w i g

In this activity the 11 manipulatives can be used to make the following short words: *at, hat, will, win, hit, it, in, wag, tin, hag, wait, rain, rat, an, ran, tan, gain, hail, tag, gag, lot, got, on, lag, hog, hot, tot, rag, rot, not, ant,* and *train.*

Activity 5: Phonemes /oy/ and /b/. The picture and key word used for this activity:

b oy

In this activity the 13 manipulatives can be used to make the following short words: *bag, big, bat, bit, bet, bill, bin, bait, gab, toy, bib, rob, nab, tab, at, hat, will, win, hit, it, in, wag, tin, hag, wait, rain, rat, an, ran, tan, gain, hail, tag, gag, lot, got, on, lag, hog, hot, tot, rag, rot, not, ant, blob, blot, brat, brag, grab, grin, grain, trot,* and *train.*

Activity 6: Phoneme /u/. The picture and key word used for this activity:

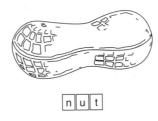

In this activity the 14 manipulatives can be used to make the following short words: *but, bug, bun, rug, rub, run, rut, lug, hut, hug, hub, tug, tub, bag, big, bat, bit, bet, bill, bin, bait, gab, toy, bib, rob, nab, tab, at, hat, will, win, hit, it, in, wag, tin, hag, wait, rain, rat, an, ran, tan, gain, hail, tag, gag, lot, got, on, lag, hog, hot, tot, rag, rot, not, ant, blob, blot, brat, brag, grab, grin, grain, trot, hunt, blunt, grunt,* and *train.*

Activity 7: Phonemes / ē/, /j/, and /p/. The picture and key word used for this activity:

In this activity the 17 manipulatives can be used to make the following short words: *weed, weep, job, jig, jug, jag, rip, nap, nip, lip, lap, gap, top, tip, tap, pig, pop, pan, pin, pot, pat, pit, but, bug, bun, rug, rub, run, rut, lug, hut, hug, hub, tug, tub, bag, big, bat, bit, bet, bill, bin, bait, gab, toy, bib, rob, nab, tab, at, hat, will, win, hit, it, in, wag, tin, hag, wait, rain, rat, an, ran, tan, gain, hail, tag, gag, lot, got, on, lag, hog, hot, tot, rag, rot, not, ant, blob, blot, brat, brag, grab, grin, grain, trot, hunt, blunt, grunt, plug, plot,* and *train.*

Activity 8: Phonemes /e/ and /d/. The picture and key word used for this activity:

In this activity the 19 manipulatives can be used to make the following short words: *web, wed, wet, bed, bad, bag, bud, did, dog, dad, dig, dip, dug, dot, den, jet, red, rid, rod, nod, net, led, lid, leg, get, ten, pod, pad, pen, pet, had, hid, hen, weed, weep, job, jig, jug, jag, rip, nap, nip, lip, lap, gap, top, tip, tap, pig, pop, pan, pin, pot, pat, pit, but, bug, bun, rug, rub, run, rut, lug, hut, hug, hub, tug, tub, bag, big, bat, bit, bet, bill, bin, bait, gab, toy, bib, rob, nab, tab, at, hat, will, win, hit, it, in, wag, tin, hag, wait, rain, rat, an, ran, tan, gain, hail, tag, gag, lot, got, on, lag, hog, hot, tot, rag, rot, not, ant, blob, blot, brat, brag, grab, grin, grain, trot, hunt, blunt, grunt, plot, plug, bled, pled, blond, bleed, breed, brand, tend, and, bend, end, lend, hand, land, bent, tent, blunt, tint, went, dent, rent, lent,* and *train.*

Activity 9: Phonemes /ō/ and /s/. The picture and key word used for this activity:

In addition to all of the words made in previous activities, the 21 manipulatives can be used to make these additional short words: *bus, sit, sob, sub, sin, sad, sag, set, sun, sap, sat, gas, sip, sail, soak, soap, road, roam, toad, coal, coat, spot, span, spat, sweet, sweep, stop, stab, stag, step, still, stunt, slap, sped, spell, spin, spit, speed, stub, stun, stand, stilt, sled, slid, slot, slob, slip, slug, pest, test, nest, slag, slit, slop, sleet, dust, past, snob, snub, snap, snip, snug, snag, swell, swept, list, rust, last, west, cost, rest, bust, best, lost, sent,* and *twist.*

Activity 10: Phoneme /k/ The picture and key word used for this activity:

| c | a | n |

In addition to all of the words made in previous activities, the 22 manipulatives can be used to make these additional short words: *can, cot, cub, cap, cad, cut, cup, cat, cog, cod, cab, clip, clan, clod, clog, clot, club, crop, crib, crab, crest, creel, creep,* and *coy.*

Activity 11: Phoneme /m/. The picture and key word used for this activity:

| m | a | s | k |

In addition to all of the words made in previous activities, the 23 manipulatives can be used to make these additional short words: *am, mad, mob, man, men, mud, map, mop, met, mat, jam, rim, hum, ham, hem, him, maid, mail, meet, roam, lump, lamp, jump, cramp, limp, dump, bump, camp, swam, swim, stem, stamp, stomp, stump, slim, slum, slam, slump, brim, plum, plump, clam, clamp, claim, glum, grim, grump, trim, drum, smog, smug, must, mist,* and *camp.*

Activity 12: Phonemes /or/ and /f/. (The letter *k* is also introduced as a representation of the /k/ sound). The picture and key word used for this activity:

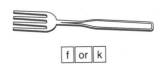

| f | or | k |

In addition to all of the words made in previous activities, the 26 manipulatives can be used to make these additional short words: *if, fee, fib, fan, fed, fun, fog, fad, fig, fat, fit, fail, feed, feel, feet, foam, form, fort, for, worn, born, sort, morn, peek, pork, cork, corn, kid, week,* and *soak.*

Activity 13: Phoneme /ir/. The picture and key word used for this activity:

g | ir | l

In addition to all of the words made in previous activities, the 27 manipulatives can be used to make these additional short words: *firm, dirt, bird, girl, first, twirl, swirl, flirt, skirt, fir, sir,* and *stir.*

Activity 14: Phonemes / o͞o / and /th/. The picture and key word used for this activity:

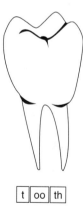

t | oo | th

In addition to all of the words made in previous activities, the 29 manipulatives can be used to make these additional short words: *fool, roof, proof, cool, drool, pool, spool, tool, bloom, boom, broom, gloom, loom, room, coon, croon, moon, noon, spoon, soon, coop, droop, hoop, loop, scoop, stoop, swoop, troop, boot, hoot, loot, toot, thin, thud, thug, thump, third, thirst, thorn, bath, broth, with, Beth, path, cloth, moth, math, booth, faith, teeth,* and *tooth.*

Activity 15: Phoneme /oo/. The picture and key word used for this activity:

b | oo | k

In addition to all of the words made in previous activities, the 30 manipulatives can be used to make these additional short words: *good, hood, stood, wood, book, brook, crook, hook, look,* and *took.*

Activity 16: Phoneme / ū /. The picture and key word used for this activity:

u | k | u | l | e | l | e

Children need a spelling for this phoneme for their invented spellings. However, there are few simple words where the letter *u* represents the / ū / sound. Sometimes the letter teams *ue* and *ew* represent the sound in simple words (e.g., *few* and *cue*). For this lesson, the teacher might use the manipulatives to attempt the construction of these words: *uniform, unit,* and *mule.*

Activity 17: Phonemes /ar/ and /y/. The picture and key word used for this activity:

y | ar | n

In addition to all of the words made in previous activities, the 33 manipulatives can be used to make these additional short words: *yes, yam, yet, yap, yelp, yell, yard, yarn, arm, art, ark, bar, car, far, jar, mar, scar, star, tar, mark, card, hard, bark, dark, lark, park, spark, farm, harm, barn, darn, yarn, harp, cart, part, smart, start, barb,* and *snarl.*

Activity 18: Phoneme / ī /. The picture and key word used for this activity:

t | ie

In addition to all of the words made in previous activities, the 34 manipulatives can be used to make these additional short words: *die, pie, lie, tie, died, tied, lied, cried, tried, spied,* and *dried.*

Activity 19: Phoneme /ou/. The picture and key word used for this activity:

t | r | ou | t

In addition to all of the words made in previous activities, the 35 manipulatives can be used to make these additional short words: *trout, cloud, loud, proud, bound, found, ground, hound, mound, pound, round, sound, count, mount, flour, our, scour, sour, blouse, house, louse, mouse, out, pout, scout, snout, spout, stout, noun,* and *foul.*

Activity 20: Phoneme /sh/. The picture and key word used for this activity:

In addition to all of the words made in previous activities, the 36 manipulatives can be used to make these additional short words: *shut, shop, sham, shag, shed, ship, shod, shot, shut, shelf, shift, shark, sharp, sheep, sheet, shirt, shoo, shook, shoot, short, shout, rush, cash, rash, blush, wish, flesh, gosh, brush, dish, fresh, sash, fish, clash, swish, slash, crush, crash, flush, splash, gush, dash, hush, flash, mush, smash, gash, trash, hash, lash, mash, ash,* and *harsh.*

Activity 21: Phoneme /ch/. The picture and key word used for this activity:

In addition to all of the words made in previous activities, the 37 manipulatives can be used to make these additional short words: *chop, chat, chap, chin, chip, chub, chug, chum, champ, chant, chest, chain, charm, chart, cheep, chirp, poach, pouch, coach, couch, crouch, grouch, slouch, speech, rich, such,* and *much.*

Activity 22: Phoneme /ng/. The picture and key word used for this activity:

In addition to all of the words made in previous activities, the 38 manipulatives can be used to make these additional short words: *long, sing, bang, bring, rang, rung, string, clang, song, cling, hung, slang, slung, fang, strong, ding, dong, lung, tang, sling, swing, gang, stung, sang, spring, hang, prong, king, sung, sprang, pong, swung, wing, ring,* and *sting.*

Activity 23: Phoneme /th/. The picture and key word used for this activity:

th	e	m

In addition to all of the words made in previous activities, the 39 manipulatives can be used to make these additional short words: *that, than, them, then,* and *this.*

Activity 24: Phoneme /v/. The picture and key word used for this activity:

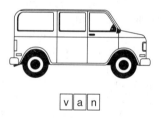

v	a	n

In addition to all of the words made in previous activities, the 40 manipulatives can be used to make these additional short words: *vest, van, vat, vent, vast, vouch,* and *vex.*

Activity 25: Phoneme /âr/. The picture and key word used for this activity:

b	ear

In addition to all of the words made in previous activities, the 41 manipulatives can be used to make these additional short words: *bear, pear, tear,* and *wear.*

Activity 26: Phoneme /z/. The picture and key word used for this activity:

| z | oo |

In addition to all of the words made in previous activities, the 42 manipulatives can be used to make these additional short words: *zap, zest, zip, zoo, zoom,* and *zing.*

Phonemic Awareness Training Research

My colleague, James Baird, and I in 1992 completed a phonemic awareness training study in Utah County, Utah, utilizing the strategies outlined in this chapter. The study compared the writing of 23 first-grade children who were provided phonemic awareness training in kindergarten with the writing of 26 first-grade children who were not provided training.

Samples of children's writing taken in February of their first-grade year indicated that the training provided for the experimental group was effective. The children in this group were significantly better writers than those in the control group. Their compositions revealed that they were at developmentally higher writing stages than children in the control group. On the average, they spelled more total words correctly in their compositions (51 vs. 36), and they spelled more unique or different words correctly (23 vs. 17). Both of these differences were statistically significant (.03 level).

The experimental students' compositions contained more words (72 vs. 48); more unique or different words (40 vs. 28); more difficult words (6 vs. 3); and more sentences (11 vs. 6) than the compositions of children in the control group. All of these differences were statistically significant (.03 to .002 level). The experimental children's holistic "quality of writing" scores were also significantly larger (36 vs. 21). The effect sizes on all of these measures were large. The results of this experiment suggest that teaching young children to spell words by sounds can be very effective.

Application Activities

1. Visit a kindergarten classroom and select a child, or locate a kindergarten-age child in your own circle of acquaintances. Obtain permission to try a phonemic awareness training lesson with this child. Use one of the early phonemic aware-

ness training lessons. Share the results of this experience with the parent or teacher involved, and with your colleagues.

2. Without the help of the text, see if you can identify the 42 sounds used in speech. Try to identify the various ways we "spell" each sound in the English language.

3. Develop a plan for implementing a writing program in either kindergarten, first, or second grade.

Chapter 7

Decoding Instruction in Holistic Classrooms:

Word Recognition, Analogy, and Context

Social Mediation and Scaffolding

Sociolinguists believe that language learning is a social process (Vygotsky, 1978, 1986). We live with and around people, and we use language to communicate with each other in a variety of different social settings. Even young children use the language to communicate and share experiences with others. All of us learn early in life that there is power in being able to use language. We use language so we can meet our needs, control other people's actions, acquire information, share information, and so on (Halliday, 1973). According to sociolinguists, we learn how to effectively use the language as we attempt to use it with other people.

Sociolinguists also believe that as adults interact with children, they systematically help them become increasingly more sophisticated language users. For example, Bruner (1978) claimed that parents contributed to children's language development by expanding and extending their talk. If a child said, "Leg hurt?" a parent might respond with, "Yes, Mother's leg hurts because she fell down." Bruner used the term *scaffold* to describe these parent interactions because they helped to move children to higher levels of language understanding, eventually raising their level of language development. Scaffolds are supports that mature language users provide for children to stimulate their language development to more complex levels. Any mature language user (parent, teacher, or older student) can provide scaffolds for children as they learn. Rosenshine and Meister (1992) offered the following definition: "Scaffolds are forms of support provided by the teacher (or another student) to help students bridge the gap between their current abilities and the intended goal. . . . Instead of providing explicit steps, one supports, or scaffolds, the students as they learn the skill" (p. 26).

Vygotsky (1978) used the term *zone of proximal development* to describe how children learn through their social interactions with adults. According to Vygotsky, the zone of proximal development is that level just beyond children's actual development. When mature language users, such as teachers, consistently help children perform language tasks at their zone of proximal development, where they cannot function independently, they eventually become able to perform at that level without support. Then, as teachers move children to a new zone of proximal development and work with them at that level, they "scaffold" them, leading them to a still higher level.

Social mediation is the term used to describe the scaffolding process mature language users use with children as they perform language tasks with them at their zone of proximal development. Teachers *mediate* students' learning in a *social* setting by helping them perform language tasks at their *zone of proximal development*, and then they *scaffold* them to higher language tasks when their language development level rises.

Social mediation involving the concept of scaffolding has been used effectively in both vocabulary (May, 1994) and comprehension (Pearson & Fielding, 1991) instruction. There is also a role for social mediation in informal and formal decoding instruction. The assisted reading strategies, the shared book experience, shared music and rhythm experiences, literature book activities, the Language Experience Approach, and writing activities described in Chapter 9 are all informal decoding strategies utilizing some form of social mediation. The formal phonics lessons presented in Chapter 10 also utilize social mediation. In both situations, children, in a "psychologically safe" environment, are assisted to perform tasks they cannot perform independently until they are able to perform those tasks without adult support.

Decoding Strategies

Decoding, the processes readers use to translate written text into either speech or inner speech, involves both a fast translation process called word *recognition,* and slower processes called word *identification.* Word recognition is the decoding process used by proficient readers. Word recognition implies an accurate, rapid, and automatic recognition of printed words. Utilization of various word identification strategies, along with some word recognition, is associated with less proficient readers. (See Chapter 2 for a fuller discussion of decoding.)

Words not recognized may be identified by readers through the use of strategies readers develop themselves, or through strategies teachers teach them to employ: (a) analogy, (b) context clues, (c) phonics, (d) morphemic analysis, and (e) syllabic analysis/phonics. Word identification strategies are considered interim strategies, employed only because word recognition abilities have not developed sufficiently for accurate, automatic, rapid decoding.

In this chapter, we will discuss three decoding strategies: (a) sight word recognition, (b) identifying words by analogy, and (c) using contextual information to identify words. In Chapter 8, we will discuss using phonics to identify single-syllable words, using morphemic analysis to identify words, and using phonics to identify polysyllabic words.

Sight Word Recognition

Sight word recognition is a near-instantaneous recognition of written words. It does not refer to a global, whole word recognition process, based upon word "shape," as some reading educators propose. It is the recognition of words based upon each word's unique sequence of letters.

Skilled readers have stored the written representations of many words in their lexical memories. When they see a particular letter sequence, the word associated with that letter sequence is immediately called to mind as inner speech, along with the meaning(s) previously attached to it. This is sight word recognition. It occurs very rapidly, enabling skilled readers to hold the inner speech obtained from word recognition in short term memory until they have apprehended complete sentences.

There are many different instructional approaches available to help readers develop the ability to recognize words by sight, both informal and formal. All approaches are built on the same basic principle: teachers must provide children with opportunities to see the written representation of words frequently enough for the letter sequences of those words to become firmly established in lexical memory.

Issues of Word Frequency

Estimates of the number of words existing in the English language vary from 500,000 to 750,000, depending on whether one includes inflected word forms and word variants. Some English words are considered *high-frequency words*, meaning that they are used frequently in both spoken and written discourse. The identification of high-frequency words was considered important in the past because both writers of basal readers and teachers had to determine which words should be taught as sight words. Identifying these words is considered important today because of their impact on children's reading fluency, and on word identification utilizing contextual information.

Over the past sixty years or so, many studies have been conducted to identify the most frequently used words in print (Horn, 1926; Dolch, 1936, 1948; Rinsland, 1945; Thorndike & Lorge, 1944; Kucera & Francis, 1967; Carroll, Davies, & Richman, 1971) and to assess the speaking and listening vocabularies of children (Wepman & Hass, 1969; Dale & O'Rourke, 1976; Hopkins, 1979; Moe, Hopkins, & Rush, 1982). Studies have also been conducted to identify those words "easy" for elementary school children to read so readability formulas could be developed (Dale & Chall, 1948; Harris & Sipay, 1980).

Word frequency research reveals that a relatively small number of English words account for most of the words children encounter in spoken and written discourse. Fry (1980) claimed that one-half of the written material available for children to read is composed of 100 words and their common variants. Walker (1979) claimed that his list of 1,000 high-frequency words, plus their variants and derivatives, accounted for about 85 percent of the more than 5 million words of running text analyzed in the Carroll, Davies, and Richman (1971) study.

The Carroll et al. study was one of the most extensive word frequency studies ever conducted. Words from 1,657 publications used in grades 3 through 9, covering a broad range of content areas, were counted, sorted, and listed in rank order by computer, and the results published in the *American Heritage Word Frequency Book*.

Walker's (1979) 1,000 high-frequency words were taken from this book. Walker combined the frequencies of a base word (e.g., *jump*) and all of its variants (e.g., *jumps, jumping, jumped*), whereas the book listed each word variant frequency separately. Walker (1979, p. 804) believed that the base word was the vital element in word recognition. This belief is interesting, and sounds reasonable, but needs to be substantiated by research. There is little doubt that the recognition of base words aids in the identification of words containing those elements. However, the vital element in word recognition, according to the most recent literature on the subject, is each word's unique letter sequence.

The rapid recognition of frequently used words is not the only factor related to fluent reading, but is essential. The instantaneous recognition of frequently used words is also essential for the identification of words through context. Readers must be able to recognize the words around the unfamiliar one to use the contextual information available for its identification. As Walker reasoned, " . . . if a student had instant recognition control of each of these thousand words, he or she would seldom meet a reading passage in which more than one word per sentence would need to be decoded by use of context and letter–sound association" (p. 804).

The Carroll et al. study analyzed word usage in a range of reading materials read by students in grades 3 through 9. Are the high-frequency words identified from these materials similar or different from those identified from young children's literature? In an attempt to answer the question here, I analyzed the words used in 235 primary-grade children's literature books. The books contained a total of 156,859 running words. Over 6,000 of the 156,859 words were names of people or characters, repeated many times. The 919 most frequently used words in these books comprised 85 percent of the running words analyzed. An examination of both studies suggests that while there are definite differences between the lists, there are also many similarities, particularly within the first 100 words on each list.

The first 100 words on the literature list comprised 55 percent of all the words used in the literature books analyzed. The first 300 words comprised 70.5 percent of all the words used. The literature book frequency list is presented in Appendix A for teachers interested in high-frequency words used in young children's books.

Recent editions of three first-grade basal programs (Ginn, McGraw-Hill, and Silver, Burdett & Ginn) were analyzed along with 231 literature books used in first-grade literature-based classrooms. These reading materials contained a total of 235,930 running words. From these words over 1,400 high-frequency words were identified. The 300 most frequently used words were each used over 100 times in these materials. They comprised 72 percent of all the words used in the books analyzed, and the instant recognition of these words by first-grade students should enable them to read and comprehend first-grade reading material. Thirty-six words comprised 39 percent of all the words analyzed in the study. Each of these 36 words was used over 1,000 times in the materials analyzed: *the, and, to, a, I, said, you, in, it, of, he, was, is, on, that, she, for, can, they, his, all, what, we, will, not, little, with, my, do, but, are, at, up, her, have,* and *out.* Thirty-nine of the 300 high frequency words are not found on the 300 instant word list Fry revised (1980) to incorporate the findings of the Carroll et al. study: *am, baby, bad, bear, bed, blue, can't, cat, cried, dark, didn't, dog, door, fast, frog, gave, heard, I'll, I'm, king, let's, looked, morning, Mr., Mrs., nothing, oh, rabbit, ran, red, sat, that's, toad, told, tree, witch, wizard, yes,* and *you're.*

THE ELDREDGE INSTANT WORD LIST
THE 300 MOST FREQUENTLY USED WORDS IN CHILDREN'S
LITERATURE BOOKS AND FIRST-GRADE BASAL READERS

a	brown	found	if
about	but	fox	in
after	by	friend	inside
again	called	friends	into
all	came	frog	is
along	can	from	it
always	can't	fun	it's
am	cat	garden	its
an	children	gave	jump
and	city	get	jumped
animals	come	girl	just
another	could	give	keep
any	couldn't	go	king
are	cried	going	know
around	dad	good	last
as	dark	got	left
asked	day	great	let
at	did	green	let's
ate	didn't	grow	like
away	do	had	little
baby	does	hand	live
back	dog	happy	long
bad	don't	has	look
ball	door	hat	looked
be	down	have	looking
bear	each	he	made
because	eat	head	make
bed	end	hear	man
been	even	heard	many
before	ever	help	may
began	every	hen	maybe
behind	everyone	her	me
best	eyes	here	mom
better	far	hill	more
big	fast	him	morning
bird	father	his	mother
birds	find	home	mouse
blue	fine	house	Mr.
book	first	how	Mrs.
books	fish	I	much
box	fly	I'll	must
boy	for	I'm	my

name	read	than	very
need	red	that	wait
never	ride	that's	walk
new	right	the	walked
next	road	their	want
nice	room	them	wanted
night	run	then	was
no	said	there	water
not	sat	these	way
nothing	saw	they	we
now	say	thing	well
of	school	things	went
off	sea	think	were
oh	see	this	what
old	she	thought	when
on	show	three	where
once	sister	through	while
one	sky	time	who
only	sleep	to	why
or	small	toad	will
other	so	together	wind
our	some	told	witch
out	something	too	with
over	soon	took	wizard
people	started	top	woman
picture	stay	tree	words
pig	still	truck	work
place	stop	try	would
play	stories	two	write
pulled	story	under	yes
put	sun	until	you
rabbit	take	up	you're
ran	tell	us	your

A knowledge of high- and low-frequency words is important to teachers. Teachers generally want to know if their students recognize high-frequency words since reading fluency and comprehension are directly related to this ability. Some teachers may want to create learning environments to help students instantaneously recognize high-frequency words. Others may want to evaluate their informal decoding activities in terms of their effect upon students' ability to recognize high-frequency words.

The ability to comprehend text material is also directly related to students' ability to recognize and understand low-frequency words, so teachers may want to identify difficult low-frequency words and preteach them, occasionally, prior to students' encountering them in specific text material. Knowledge about word frequencies is also important for informal and formal reading assessment since teachers generally want to know if students can fluently read and comprehend text material involving both high- and low-frequency words.

Regular and Irregular Graphophonic Word Patterns

Written languages based on alphabetic systems use letters to represent word sounds, even if the letters used to represent sounds are sometimes unpredictable. Technically speaking, all written words in English are regular because their sounds are represented by letters. However, teachers need labels to help them differentiate those English words spelled in predictable ways from those that are spelled in less predictable ways. Those words that are spelled in unpredictable ways will be referred to as *irregular* words in this book.

Some teaching strategies are more appropriate for teaching regular words while others are more appropriate for irregular ones. For example, phonics instruction is generally appropriate if a word's letter–sound relationships are predictable, while sight word instruction is more appropriate if those relationships are not 'so predictable. In both situations, however, children should be taught to associate a word's phonemes with its graphemes since words stored in lexical memory are best established in this fashion.

The term *graphophonics* is often used in place of the word *phonics*. The morpheme "graph" (a *morpheme* is a meaning unit in a word) refers to letters and the morpheme "phonics" refers to sounds. *Graphophonics* is often used specifically to refer to letter–sound relationships within words, rather than using the broader term *phonics.*

The letter–sound relationships in most words are predictable. For example, the words *up, can, step, branch, stretch,* and *trip* all contain predictable letter–sound sequences. They are all closed-syllable words (a *closed* syllable is one that ends in a consonant sound) and the vowel sound in each word is short. We will say more about predictable letter–sound sequences in Chapter 8.

A smaller percentage of English words contain letter–sound relationships that are not so predictable. For example, in the words *mind, most,* and *wild* the sound represented by the vowel letter in each word is unexpected, or occurs rarely. Since these words are closed-syllable words, short vowel sounds, rather than the long sounds observed in these words, generally occur in these syllable patterns.

Although the vowel sounds represented by the written words *mind, most,* and *wild* are unexpected, all of the other letter–sound relationships in the words *are* predictable. This is an important concept, and must not be passed by lightly. Research evidence suggests that readers store irregular words in lexical memory in the same manner as they store the regular ones (Gough & Walsh, 1991; Treiman & Baron, 1983; Lovett, 1987). That is, readers relate a word's letters with the sounds those letters represent as they store both regular and irregular words (Ehri, 1992). The predictable letter–sound relationships in regular words make this storage process easy, but the rare relationships slow it down. This reasoning is supported by research indicating that irregular words are not learned as quickly as are regular ones.

Sometimes the letter–sound relationships in words are difficult to predict. In these cases, the sound usually associated with a particular letter or letters is just different or unusual. For example, in the word *of* the letter *f* represents the /v/ sound rather than the /f/ sound usually associated with it. Other examples of words containing letters that are pronounced differently than expected are: m<u>a</u>ny, fr<u>o</u>nt, w<u>or</u>k.

Children learn to recognize many high-frequency words, both regular and irregular, through the use of the informal decoding strategies discussed in Chapter 9. Repeated exposures to high-frequency words in meaningful reading activities may eventually lead students to recognize those words by sight. If they do not learn high-frequency words through informal decoding strategies, explicit phonics instruction and/or sight word instruction will address students' needs.

Brief but meaningful phonics instruction will help children learn how speech sounds normally map onto print. Brief but meaningful sight word instruction will help children learn to recognize graphophonically irregular words not learned through informal decoding activities. Such instruction will therefore complement the decoding knowledge students acquire through informal decoding strategies, and may give students insights into the alphabetic principle and unusual letter–sound relationships not always perceived by students using informal, holistic strategies.

Some teachers may want help determining whether students are learning irregular words through the use of informal decoding strategies. Appendix B contains 275 high-frequency irregular words drawn from the 919 high-frequency words derived from children's literature books. This list can be used by teachers to determine if students are able to instantaneously recognize graphophonically irregular high-frequency words after extensive involvement in the informal decoding activities described in Chapter 9, and also to determine which words need to be explicitly taught when the time for such instruction seems appropriate.

The list in Appendix B comprises about 30 percent (29.9) of the high-frequency words from which it was drawn, which does not reflect the true proportion of irregular to regular words in the language. The percentage is inflated for two reasons. First, the number of irregular words occurs proportionately more in the first 300 high-frequency words than anywhere else. Second, there are many words with recognizable letter–sound patterns on the lists that some researchers would consider consistent enough to be considered regular. For example, the letter *a* generally represents the vowel sound heard at the beginning of the word *all* when it is followed by an *l* or *r*, and when preceded by a *w*. Words on irregular word lists consistent with this pattern include *water, called, also, small, warm, tall, talking, walrus, wants,* and *watching.*

Other graphophonics patterns on the lists that some researchers consider regular are: the phonogram *ome* frequently says /um/—*some, come, something, sometimes, comes, coming, someone, becomes, become, somebody;* when *or* is preceded by a *w, or* represents the /ir/ sound—*words, work, word, world, working, works;* the *o* in the phonogram *old* represents the long *o* sound—*old, told, cold, hold, gold, sold, holding;* and the letters *oul* represent the same sound as the letters *oo* in the word *wood*—*would, could, should, couldn't, wouldn't.*

Teaching Sight Words

When you determine that explicit sight word instruction is needed for any student or group of students, you may want to teach brief sight word lessons according to the following model. Such lessons should take no more than 10 minutes of classroom time, and are based upon the following principles:

1. Children will more likely remember the words taught to them if those words are meaningful to them.
2. Children will more likely retain words if they focus on the words' letter sequences along with the sounds represented by those letter sequences.
3. The likelihood that children will remember words will be enhanced if they see each word taught at least six times during the lesson.
4. Children will more likely remember words if teachers explicitly emphasize any unusual letter–sound relationships.
5. Children will more likely retain words if they see them in context.
6. The likelihood that children will remember specific words will be enhanced if teachers involve their senses of touch, sight, and sound while learning each word's letter–sound sequences.

Model Lesson.

Step 1: Select three or four words students need to learn from the irregular word list or from some other source (example: *any, come, move*). Write each word in manuscript form on the chalkboard. Read each word as you write it. Distribute three blank tagboard cards for each student or student team to use to make word cards. Ask the students to write each word on one of the cards provided for that purpose. Supervise this process carefully, making sure that students spell each word correctly.

Step 2: Point to the first word on the chalkboard (example: *any*). Read the word. Ask the students to read the word. Ask them to find the card on their desks that has the same word written on it and hold it up so you can see it. Repeat this process with the other two words.

Step 3: Ask the students to create several sentences using the three target words. As the students dictate the sentences, write each in manuscript form on the chalkboard. Help students who have difficulty thinking of sentences.

After dictating each sentence, ask the students to read it while you point to each word. When you come to the new words, underline them (example: I don't have <u>any</u> crayons in my desk).

Step 4: Ask the students to trace each letter on the *any* card with their fingers, naming each letter as they trace it. When they finish tracing the last letter, ask them to say the word once more. Repeat this process with the other two words.

Step 5: Ask the students to write the target words in manuscript form on a piece of paper. (Remind them not to look at the words on the chalkboard or on their desks.)

After writing, have them check the words against their word cards for accuracy.

Step 6: Ask the students to read the sentences on the chalkboard again. Help them with any words they may have forgotten. However, they should be able to read the underlined words without any help.

Step 7: Ask the students to copy each sentence in manuscript form in a special notebook or on a sheet of paper for reading to their parents or some other person that day. Have them save the sentences so they can read them periodically.

Step 8: Refer to the words on the chalkboard again. Point out the distinguishing characteristics of each word. (For example, the word *come* is a word that looks like it should be pronounced /kōm/. However, the letter *o* in the word represents the /u/ sound rather than the /ō/ sound.) Say the sounds of each word as you point to the letters representing those sounds. (For example, for the word *come*, say /k/ /u/ /m/ as you point to the letters c o me.). Ask the students to say the sounds of each word as you point to the letters representing those sounds.

Step 9: Ask the students to place their word cards in front of them. Do not let them see the written word. As you say each word, the students should pick up the appropriate card and hold it up for you to see. Go through the word cards several times.

When you finish this step, ask the students to file their word cards in a special container (a recipe box works well) to be used later to construct sentences, to use in word games, or to review.

Identifying Words by Analogy

When children encounter unknown words they often identify them by analogy, associating word parts in the unfamiliar words with word parts in familiar words. For example, the unfamiliar word *tame* might be identified by associating it with the familiar word *name*. Then by substituting the *n* in *name* with *t*, the new word can be identified. After associating the ending analogs in *tame* and *name,* some children might even associate the sound represented by the letters *ta* in the word *tame* with those found in the word *tape*. Ending analogies (*rimes*) seem to be easiest for children to access. However, it appears that readers of all ages associate patterns whether at the beginning (**ba**ck, **ba**t), middle (p**ea**ch, t**ea**m), or end (p**oach**, c**oach**) when identifying unknown words by analogy.

Interesting reciprocal relationships seem to exist among various decoding abilities. Children are able to identify words by analogy only when they have fairly large sight vocabularies since they must be able to find patterns in known words to associate with those found in unknown words. However, subsequent sight word recognition is enhanced when readers begin to recognize familiar analogs in unknown words; these words need fewer exposures before they become stored in lexical memory. Finally, phonics knowledge seems to be necessary for both word recognition (Ehri & Wilce, 1983, 1985) and word identification by analogy (Ehri & Robbins, 1992). While it is likely that word identification activities emphasizing onsets (**t**ap) and rimes (t**ap**) also enhance phonics knowledge, that issue needs further study. Phonics instruction helps students learn the regular graphophonic patterns found in the written language because its focus of instruction is on letter–sound sequences. As students become consciously aware of basic sequences, they are able to recognize analogs.

Several researchers have suggested that reading by analogy does not develop until after first or second grade (Marsh, Friedman, Desberg, & Saterdahl, 1981; Marsh, Friedman, Welch, & Desberg, 1981; Manis, Szeszulski, Howell, & Horn, 1986; Zinna, Liberman, & Shankweiler, 1986). However, it appears that even young children can identify words by analogy if they have a sufficient store of familiar words in memory (Ehri & Robbins, 1992; Goswami, 1986, 1988).

Analogy Identification Activities

The letter substitution activities, frequently found in teaching materials written by implicit phonics advocates, help students identify common rimes students frequently access for the identification of unknown words by analogy. Furthermore, these activities also help teach and reinforce letter–sound relationships found in the initial position of words.

Begin letter substitution activities by writing a word containing a common word ending (rime) on the chalkboard: *cake.* Then write *_ake* under the word *cake.* For example,

cake
_ake

Pointing to the word cake, say, "This word is *cake.* Tell me what letter I need to write in the blank space below the word *cake* to make the word *rake.*" This activity is continued using the following words: *bake, fake, lake, make, sake, take, wake,* and *quake.*

Using Contextual Information to Identify Words

If students' word recognition abilities are fairly substantial, and if they have been taught that reading should make sense to them, they may not need to recognize every word in a sentence in order to understand the message the author intends to convey. Furthermore, those few words children do not recognize may be identified by deriving contextual information from the sentences containing them.

When using contextual information for word identification, students are not technically unlocking the alphabetic code. Instead, they are identifying words by making "intelligent guesses." Those guesses are based upon readers' knowledge of syntax, graphophonics, and semantics. Syntax refers to the structure of the sentence, and each word's function in the sentence. Graphophonics refers to words' letter–sound relationships. Semantics refers to word meanings. The process children employ to identify unfamiliar words by using these three language cueing systems is called contextual analysis.

Effective readers use contextual information to determine the unfamiliar word's function. Is the unfamiliar word a naming word, a describing word, or an action word? Sentence cues suggest the word's function. For example, "The young man took off his shoes and socks, rolled up his pant legs, and went wading in the____." The missing word names some place where the young man went wading, and is therefore a naming word.

Readers also use graphophonics information; they look at the initial letter in an unfamiliar word, think of the sound associated with that letter, and think of words beginning with that sound. Readers also use semantic information along with the graphophonic information obtained. If students know the meanings of all the other words used in the sentence, they can use that information to eliminate word options that begin with the "right sound," but just don't make sense in a particular sentence.

Readers use whatever information they can acquire to make intelligent guesses at unknown words in specific sentences. They do not retrieve information in any particular sequence, nor are they always able to retrieve information from all three cueing systems. However, the thinking processes involved, when using contextual analysis, communicate to students that reading involves meaning, plus these thinking processes help students identify unfamiliar words quickly, much quicker than when using phonics.

Read the following sentence: "The young man took off his shoes and socks, rolled up his pant legs, and went wading in the l_____." Effective readers could use their syntax knowledge to conclude that the unknown word is a noun or naming word. They could use their graphophonics knowledge to conclude that the unknown word begins with the /l/ sound, and they could use their semantics or vocabulary knowledge to make sure that the word selected makes sense in the sentence. They might ask themselves, "What 'naming' word, beginning with the letter *l*, would make sense in this sentence?"

Contextual analysis has been called the "supervisor" of all of the other word identification strategies because its major focus is on meaning. Readers should verify all words identified using other strategies (analogy, phonics, morphemic analysis, or syllabic analysis with phonics) by asking the question, "Does the word make sense in this sentence?"

Teaching Children to Use Contextual Information

If children have difficulty identifying words in context, you may want to consider teaching them how to make logical word guesses from contextual information available in sentences. The most important of the three text clues available for word identification is the semantic, or vocabulary, clue since contextual analysis is based on logic and meaning. Therefore, the first question you will want to help students ask themselves about an unfamiliar word is as stated previously: "What word would make sense in this sentence and the rest of the text?"

The syntax clue helps students identify those semantically appropriate options that make sense in a particular sentence, for example, whether the unknown word is a noun (naming word) or a verb (action word) or an adjective or adverb (describing word). You will want to help students extend their original question to, "What naming (or describing or action) word would make sense in this sentence and the rest of the text?"

There might be many appropriate options for a particular unknown word. Because of this, you should also teach students to use graphophonic clues to ensure a better guess. For example, consider the logical word options for the following sentence: "Maria went boating in the_____." The words *ocean, lake, water, river,* and *pond* are all naming words, and all of them make sense in the sentence. However, if students learn to consider the sound of the first letter of the unknown word, then they reduce the number of acceptable options. Encourage your students to ask themselves a question that focuses on all three language cueing systems. For example, in the sentence above, if the unknown word began with the letter *o*, you would encourage students to ask themselves, "What naming word beginning with the letter *o* would make sense in this sentence and the rest of the text?"

Context clues, of course, have limitations. First, students must be able to recognize all of the words around the unknown word they are trying to identify. If students' sight vocabulary skills are limited, contextual analysis becomes an ineffective strategy, as they will be unable to derive the information needed to use it. Second, sometimes more than one word fits the syntactic, semantic, and graphophonic clues in the text. For example, consider the options for the following sentence: "The young man took off his shoes and socks, rolled up his pant legs, and went wading in the p_____." The words *pond, pool,* and *puddle* are all nouns, they all make sense, and they all begin with the letter *p*.

Because of the limitations of contextual analysis, you should also teach students phonics strategies to supplement it. Effective phonics strategies will help students both sound out words and speed up their word recognition development.

In spite of its limitations, contextual analysis is effective, and it is efficient. A *modified cloze activity* is an excellent way to help children learn to use the three language cueing systems necessary for the identification of unfamiliar words. The following modified cloze activity was adapted from the children's book, *I Will Not Go To Market Today,* by Harry Allard, illustrated by James Marshall (Dial, 1981). In the activity, key words found in the original story (*looked* and *blizzard*) have been substituted with synonyms (*gazed* and *storm*) for two reasons. First, the activity should *not* replace children's experiences with the story. The story should be read and enjoyed by children before introducing the modified cloze activity. By using synonyms, the children will not be able to identify the omitted words from memory. Second, since children may remember the original words used in the story, the activity will also enhance children's vocabulary abilities by helping them associate words with similar meanings.

Introduce the modified cloze activity to students as a total-class activity. Enlarge and display the portion of the story used so that you and your students can read it together. When the group comes to a blank space they should be taught to say "blank" and then read the rest of the sentence. After reading the sentence, model the questioning strategy you hope students will eventually adopt when reading by themselves. For example, as a group, read the first three sentences as they are written. Read the fourth sentence as, "Fenimore B. Buttercrunch 'blanked' out the window." Then say, "What action word beginning with the letter *g* would make sense in this sentence?" Help students use the semantic information, "out the window," to help them identify the word *gazed*. (Students might use *gl* as a graphophonic clue to select the word *glanced*. If they do, compliment them for their reasoning, and tell them to identify a word that begins with the single consonant g.)

After students have learned how to ask the right questions, provide them with modified cloze activities that they can complete in small cooperative learning groups (two or three students).

I Will Not Go To Market Today

Fenimore B. Buttercrunch awoke one morning to find there was no jam for his morning toast and tea. "No jam!" he said. "I must go to market today."

Fenimore B. Buttercrunch g_____ out the window. There was a
(verb)

st_____ raging. "I cannot go to market today," he said.
(noun)

Application Activities

1. The 36 alphabetized words that follow are considered to be the most frequently used words in young children's books: *a, all, and, are, at, but, can, do, for, have, he, her, his, I, in, is, it, little, my, not, of, on, out, said, she, that, the, they, to, up, was, we, will, what, with*, and *you*. Analyze one or two pages in any children's book to determine how often these words occur.

2. Use the word list in Appendix B and assess a first- or second-grade child's irregular word sight vocabulary. Ask the child to read the words on the list as quickly as he or she can. If any word is not instantly recognized (within a second or less), count the word wrong. When the child misses a total of five words, stop. How far into the list did the child go before making five errors?

3. Identify a first- or second-grade child who needs sight word instruction. Following the nine steps outlined in this chapter, teach four high-frequency irregular sight words to this child.

4. The ability to use analogy as a decoding strategy is dependent upon a child's word recognition vocabulary. Visit an elementary classroom. Ask the teacher to identify an "excellent" reader and a "poor" reader. Perform the following analogy activity with each child:
   a) Write the word *deep* on the chalkboard. Say, "This word is deep."
   b) Write the word *keep* underneath the word *deep*. Say, "What is this word?"
   c) Repeat the step b using the following words: *peep, weep, creep, sheep, sleep, sweep,* and *steep*.
   Write a paragraph describing what you have concluded from this experience about word identification by analogy.

Chapter 8

Decoding Instruction in Holistic Classrooms:

Phonics, Morphemic Analysis, and Syllabic Analysis

Phonics

Traditional Phonics

Phonics has traditionally been perceived as a set of "skills" that should be taught to children. These skills are usually organized in a certain order, and then integrated into an instructional program for children from kindergarten through grade three or beyond. Explicit phonics programs are generally completed before grade three, while many implicit programs extend into grade six. "Scope and sequence charts" outline the skills to be taught, and the grades in which they are to be introduced, reinforced, and mastered. Traditional phonics instruction consists of teachers teaching children some phonics skill followed up by activities designed to help them practice or "reinforce" the skill. Worksheets or ditto sheets are the most popular vehicles used to practice skills.

Phonics rules are often taught to children so they can determine when to associate specific sounds with letters or letter clusters, even though there is little evidence that children apply those rules to improve their reading performance. In explicit phonics basals, children are taught how to "say" the sounds of letters, and how to blend those sounds together so unfamiliar written words can be identified by "sounding them out." In implicit phonics basals, children are taught how to associate sounds with letters so they can use that knowledge to identify unfamiliar words through context.

In many traditional phonics programs, only the children who can read are able to do the phonics lessons. In these situations, it is difficult to justify taking valuable classroom time for phonics lessons. For example, a teacher, using one implicit phonics program, taught children the two sounds represented by the letters *ea*. The children were told that the *ea* vowel team represented either the vowel sound heard in the word *teach* or the vowel sound heard in the word *bread*. Children were then given examples of words, each containing one sound or the other. After the examples, various words were written on the chalkboard and read for the children. The children were asked to identify whether the vowel sound in each word was like the sound heard in *teach* or *bread*. They were shown how to place marks over the vowels to differentiate between the two vowel sounds (a breve to designate the short sound of *e,* and a macron to designate its long sound).

When the teaching part of the lesson was finished, the children were given a worksheet to complete. The worksheet contained about 15 words. Each word contained an *ea* vowel team. The students were instructed to read the words, listen to the vowel sound in each word, and identify whether it was the sound heard in *teach* or *bread*. They were asked to write a breve over the *e* if the vowel sound in the word was like the one heard in the word *bread* and a macron over the *e* if the vowel sound was like the one heard in the word *teach*.

The phonics lesson just described is representative of traditional phonics programs; it is not atypical. It was designed to help children associate specific sounds with the *ea* vowel team. While one may not want to argue about the lesson's intent, it is certainly justifiable to argue about the effectiveness of the lesson design. The lesson, in fact, proved to be ineffective for both good and poor readers.

Only the good readers were able to successfully complete the worksheet. The other children could not read the words, so they could not identify the vowel sounds in each word, which made it impossible for them to complete the culminating assignment. Remember that phonics knowledge is supposed to help children "sound out" words when words are not recognized, and it is also supposed to help them improve their word recognition abilities. For the children who could already read the words on the worksheet, the lesson was a waste of time. There was no need to help them "sound out" or recognize words they could already read. For the children who could not do the culminating activity, the lesson did not help them "sound out" unfamiliar words containing the *ea* vowel team, nor did it teach them to recognize the words containing those elements.

At no time in the *ea* vowel team lesson just described, did the teacher either isolate (segment) the vowel sounds for children or teach children to isolate them. Furthermore, children were never taught to blend sounds so they could use phonics to identify unfamiliar words. Yet, there is overwhelming evidence indicating that children must master segmentation and blending before the results of phonics instruction are transferable to the reading of unfamiliar words (Jeffrey & Samuels, 1967; Jenkins, Bausell, & Jenkins, 1972; Muller, 1973; Fox & Routh, 1976), and there is strong evidence indicating that explicit phonics instruction, incorporating segmentation and blending, enhances word recognition (Adams, 1990).

Problems with Phoneme Distortion

Although research evidence tends to favor explicit phonics approaches over implicit ones (Anderson, Hiebert, Scott, & Wilkinson, 1985), these approaches are not without problems. As Anderson et al., writing for the Reading Commission, demonstrate, one of the problems with explicit phonics programs is the distortion of phonemes that occurs when children attempt to isolate and blend them for word identification: ". . . a problem with explicit phonics is that both teachers and children have a difficult time saying pure speech sounds in isolation. The *b* sound becomes /buh/, for instance. When figuring out a new word, the child who has been taught the sounds of letters in isolation may produce /buh-ah-tuh/ and never recognize that the word is *bat*" (1985, p. 41). It should be pointed out that the Reading Commission followed this quoted comment with a statement indicating that they were uncertain about whether the distortion problem was hypothetical or real (Anderson et al., 1985, p. 41). However, the evidence reviewed in previous chapters suggests that phoneme distortion is a problem for children. It makes the development of phonemic awareness difficult, and the application of phonics knowledge for word identification awkward.

As discussed previously, words are comprised of "coarticulated (overlapped or merged) phonemes. (A few words, however, are single phoneme words, such as *I* and *a*.) Coarticulated phonemes are not discrete language units that children can easily hear or reproduce. Coarticulation is an advantage for speech because it enables people to create thousands of words, each distinguished from all other words by its unique sequence of phonemes, and it enables individuals to speak words rapidly. Coarticulation is a disadvantage for reading, however, because phonemes and words become distorted when readers try to isolate and blend coarticulated phonemes. This problem is particularly acute when isolating certain voiced consonant sounds. For example, when sounding out the word *dog*, the reader gets /du/ /o/ /g/, which is a distorted version of /dog/.

It is possible, however, to eliminate the phoneme distortion problem in phonics instruction and application. Furthermore, the connection between the oral and written language is more visible to young children when those distortions are eliminated. The key to the solution of the distortion problem lies in a rethinking of the syllable structure. The popular way to view syllables is to view them as comprising both an onset and a rime. In the word *dime,* the onset is the *d* and the rime is *ime.* When pronouncing onsets and rimes there is no sound distortion in the rime, but there is frequently a distortion in the onset. For example, /bu/ oks/ for *box,* and /du/ /īm/ for *dime.*

There is another way to view the structure of the syllable. Every syllable, and hence every single-syllable word, contains one vowel sound. Vowels are voiced sounds and can be articulated without any distortion. Every consonant element preceding that vowel is coarticulated with it, and can be said as a unit without any sound distortion. Furthermore, the consonant sound(s) following the vowel can be isolated without any distortion. Ending consonant sounds are said no differently when isolated from, or coarticulated with, the vowel preceding it. (This is not true with beginning consonant sounds.) Therefore, all single-syllable words can be said in two parts without distorting either part, if the first isolated part ends with the vowel sound. For example, the word *box* could be said in two parts (/bo/ /ks/) without sound distortions in either part. Consider all of the following examples: *beach* = /bē / /ch/; *church* = /chur/ /ch/; *dog* = /do/ /g/; *stand* = /sta / /nd/; *strap* = /stra / /p/; *rain* = /rā / /n/; *shrub* = /shru/ /b/; and *bird* = /bir/ /d/.

The vowel is the key element in a syllable. In fact, *syllable* is defined as a word, or part of a word, containing one vowel sound. The first part of a syllable can be viewed as *the vowel and everything in front of it,* and the second part as *everything after the vowel.*

Viewing syllables as being comprised of onsets and rimes may be useful for rhyming and other related activities. However, viewing syllables as onsets and rimes distorts the relationship between the spoken and written forms of the language when those parts are pronounced. The relationship between the spoken word *brick* and its written representation is more visible when pronouncing the syllable parts as /bri/ /k/ than when pronouncing them /bu/ /ru/ /ik/ or /bru/ /ik/. Furthermore, the former pronunciations of the syllable parts do not distort any of the phonemes in the syllable, while the latter ones do. Finally, when viewing syllable parts in the manner described herein, the letters in written words more nearly represent actual speech, rather than an abstraction.

Using Phonics to Identify Single-Syllable Words

Teaching a Phonics Strategy Students Can Use. Unless students can use their phonics knowledge to improve their reading performance, there is little reason to teach it. Fortunately, readers can so use phonics knowledge in two distinctively different ways. First, they may use it to help identify words through context, and, second, they may use it to sound out words.

When phonics knowledge is combined with syntax and semantic knowledge, children can use contextual information to identify unfamiliar words. A knowledge of letter–sound relationships is sufficient for students when using phonics in this manner since the sound represented by the initial letter in the word is the best graphophonic clue to use when identifying words in context. However, when using phonics knowledge to sound out words, this level of phonics knowledge is insufficient. Children must also learn how to segment letter sounds and how to blend them to identify words by their sounds.

As stated, using phonics knowledge to identify unfamiliar words in context is totally ineffective when children possess weak word recognition abilities; they just cannot recognize enough words to obtain the information needed for analysis. Furthermore, when identifying words through context, students do not focus attention on the letter sequences of words sufficiently to store them in lexical memory. Hence, future word recognition is delayed unless teachers supplement contextual analysis instruction with phonics instruction requiring students to address all of the letters within words.

Children need a word identification strategy to help them when their word recognition skills are limited. Phonics meets that need. The phonics strategy described herein was developed in the early 1980s and has been field tested in many classrooms since then. Research suggests that it helps students sound out unfamiliar words, and increases their ability to store written words in lexical memory (Eldredge and Butterfield, 1986; Eldredge, 1991).

Children learn to use the following steps when using phonics to identify unfamiliar words:

1. Determine the vowel sound in the word, and isolate that sound.
2. Blend all of the consonant sounds in front of the vowel sound with the vowel sound.
3. Isolate the consonant sound(s) after the vowel sound.
4. Blend the two parts of the word together so the word can be identified.

The following examples demonstrate the application of this process to various types of written words:

Example 1: *dog*. First step: /o/. Second step: /do/. Third step: /g/. Fourth step: /dog/.

Example 2: *stop*. First step: /o/. Second step: /sto/. Third step: /p/. Fourth step: /stop/.

Example 3: *bend*. First step: /e/. Second step: /be/. Third step: /nd/. Fourth step: /bend/.

Example 4: *soap*. First step: /ō/ Second step: /sō/. Third step: /p/. Fourth step: /sōp/.

Example 5: *bark*. First step: /ar/. Second step: /bar/. Third step: /k/. Fourth step: /bark/.

Example 6: *shrub*. First step: /u/. Second step: /shru/. Third step: /b/. Fourth step: /shrub/.

The phonics strategy determines the phonics elements to be taught. The first step requires students to determine the vowel sound in words. Therefore, children should be taught how to identify vowel sounds in words according to the pattern or structure of the syllable. The second step requires students to blend all of the consonants occurring before the vowel sound with the vowel. There are four different consonant–vowel patterns children could encounter in this step: (a) a single consonant preceding a vowel (*time*); (b) a consonant blend preceding a vowel (*strap*); (c) a consonant digraph preceding a vowel (*shine*); and (d) a consonant digraph/consonant combination preceding a vowel (*throat*). Therefore, children should be taught to associate the appropriate sounds with these consonant elements, and to blend them with the vowel sounds following them. The third step requires students to isolate the consonant sound(s) after the vowel. The same four consonant patterns occur in step three: (a) a single consonant (*job*); (b) a consonant blend (*send*); (c) a consonant digraph (*wish*); and (d) a consonant/consonant digraph combination (*lunch*). Therefore, children should be taught to isolate these sounds at the end of words.

Phonics Elements. The phonics elements used in the strategy are single vowels, vowel teams (including regular and irregular vowel digraphs, vowel diphthongs, and murmur diphthongs), single consonants, consonant digraphs, consonant blends, and *y* as a vowel and consonant. These phonics elements comprise written words, and are used to represent all of the phonemes utilized in the spoken language.

Much could be said about the relationships existing between phonics elements and phonemes, particularly those found in graphophonically irregular words. However, the position taken in this book is that graphophonically irregular words, if not learned through informal decoding strategies, are best taught by explicit sight word instruction. The unusual, rare, unpredictable, or low-frequency letter–sound relationships found in graphophonically irregular words are called to children's attention through the sight word approach, so there is little need to devote space to discuss them here. However, if the reader is interested in low-frequency letter–sound relationships, see Appendix C.

Graphophonically regular words, on the other hand, are best learned through phonics. Predictable letter–sound relationships are emphasized in phonics instruction so children can quickly apprehend them. The speed at which children learn to recognize new words is directly related to children's familiarity with predictable letter–sound relationships. However, whether children learn words through phonics, sight word instruction, or any other strategy, they will store and retrieve them from lexical memory more accurately and efficiently if they learn to associate each word's graphemes with its phonemes. Poor readers read by partial letter cues, focusing on only a few of the letters in a word to help them remember it, and therefore, do not decode accurately and efficiently.

Vowel Phonemes. Vowel phonemes are voiced sounds that vibrate the human larynx when produced. Single vowels and various vowel teams represent these phonemes in written words. The syllable or word pattern containing single vowels letters (*a, e, i, o, u,* and *y*) indicates the sounds those letters represent in written text, while the sounds represented by vowel teams (*ai, ay, ea, ee, aw, au, oa, igh, ow, ew, ue, oo, oi, oy, ou, or, ar, ir, er, ur, air, are, ere*) remain fairly constant. There are 18 English vowel phonemes represented by vowel graphemes:

/a/	*at*	/e/	*edge, bread*
/ā/	*ate, raid, say, ba.con*	/ē/	*eve, feet, eat, me*
/i/	*it*	/o/	*off, saw, fraud, ball*
/ī/	*ice, ci.der, high*	/ō/	*so, oak, ode, show*
/u/	*up*	/oo/	*book, put*
/ū/	*use, few, cue, u.nite*	/ōō/	*moon, rude, blue, grew*
/ir/	*bird, fur, fern*	/ar/	*car*
/or/	*for*	/oi/	*boy, oil*
/ou/	*cow, found*	/âr/	*hair, care, there, bear*

Single vowels are said to represent either long (*bone, so*) or short (*top*) vowel sounds. Vowel teams also represent vowel sounds. Vowel teams can be either a regular vowel digraph (*soap*), an irregular vowel digraph (*dead*), a vowel diphthong (*out*), or a murmur diphthong (*dirt*).

A *vowel digraph* is a vowel team (two or more letters) representing one vowel sound. A vowel digraph is regular when the first vowel in the vowel team represents its long sound or letter name (*pain*). A vowel digraph is irregular when the first vowel in the vowel team represents a sound other than its long sound (*moon, book, saw, fraud, bread, blue, grew*). An inconsistent vowel team rule often taught by phonics programs is, "When there are two vowels in the word, the first vowel does the talking (says its own name), and the second one does the walking (is silent)." This rule describes regular vowel digraphs, but doesn't work with any of the other vowel teams.

A *vowel diphthong* is a gliding vowel sound. There are two vowel diphthong sounds, both of which are heard in the word *cowboy*. Two graphemes represent the first diphthong sound (*plow* and **out**), and two represent the second (*toy* and **coin**).

A *murmur diphthong* is a vowel followed by the letter *r*. The vowel and the *r* should be viewed as a single unit. Some phonics teachers try to separate the sounds in a murmur diphthong. However, murmur diphthongs each represent one gliding, "murmuring" vowel phoneme, and teachers and children should never attempt to separate them into two sounds. Three murmur diphthongs represent the same sound (*fir, fur, fern*). These three vowel teams are often called the /ir/ triplets. The murmur diphthong *ar* represents the sound heard in the word *car*, and the murmur diphthong *or* represents the sound heard in the word *fork*.

There are 20 vowel teams that consistently represent certain sounds and occur frequently in written words:

ir as in *sir*	*au* as in *cause*
er as in *herd*	*aw* as in *lawn*
ur as in *burn*	*ai* as in *aim*
ar as in *cart*	*ay* as in *stay*
or as in *sort*	*ee* as in *feet*
oi as in *join*	*oa* as in *coat*
oy as in *joy*	*oo* as in *spoon* and *look*
ea as in *seat* and *bread*	*ew* as in *blew* and *few*
ou as in *trout*	*ue* as in *glue* and *cue*
ow as in *now* and *crow*	*igh* as in *fight*

Consonant Phonemes. Consonant phonemes can be either voiced or voiceless. Voiced sounds vibrate the larynx while voiceless sounds are produced by forcing air through the mouth in various ways. When words beginning with consonant phonemes are pronounced, those phonemes, both voiced and voiceless, are coarticulated with the vowel sounds that follow them. If teachers and children try to isolate these phonemes, particularly the voiced consonants, phoneme distortion often results. The consonant phonemes that end syllables and words, however, can be isolated without distortion. There are 24 consonant phonemes, represented by the following graphemes:

/b/	*bat*	/v/	*voice*
/f/	*fish*	/y/	*yes*
/h/	*had*	/sh/	*shoe*
/k/	*kiss, cat, kick*	/th/	*the*
/m/	*man*	/ng/	*sing*
/p/	*pan*	/d/	*dog*
/s/	*sun, cent, geese*	/g/	*go*

/j/	*jump, gem, rage, fudge*		/w/	*watch*
/l/	*lamp*		/z/	*zoo, dogs, rose*
/n/	*no*		/ch/	*church*
/r/	*run*		/th/	*thing*
/t/	*teeth*		/zh/	*measure*

Consonant elements are either single consonants, consonant digraphs, or consonant blends. The following *single consonant* letters are used to represent consonant phonemes: *b, c, d, f, g, h, j, k, l, m, n, p, q, r, s, t, v, w, x, y,* and *z.* The letters *c* and *x* have no sounds of their own. The letter *c* represents the /s/ sound when it is followed by an *e, i,* or *y* (*cent, fence, cycle, city*). At all other times the letter *c* represents the /k/ sound (*crack, cap, cup, cod, car, coat,* etc.). The letter *x* represents the /ks/ sound at the end of words (*six, fox*). At the end of syllables, the letter *x* sometimes represents the /gz/ sound (*exam, exit*), and sometimes the /ks/ sound (*express, explode, export*).

The letter *g* has its own sound (*go*), but when it is followed by an *e, i,* or *y* it may represent either the /j/ sound (*gem, ginger, gym*), or its own sound (*get, gift, gynecology*). However, when the letter *g* is followed by an *e* at the end of words, it always represents the /j/ sound (*huge, badge*). Also notice that the letter combinations *ge* and *dge* represent the same sound. When the vowel letter in the word represents the long sound, the /j/ sound is spelled *ge,* and when the vowel letter represents the short sound, the /j/ sound is spelled *dge.*

The letter *q* is always followed by a *u* in English words, and the *qu* represents the /kw/ sound (*quiet, quit, question*). The /k/ phoneme is represented by the letters *ck* when it follows short vowel sounds (*back, pick, sock, deck, duck*). However, when the /k/ sound is preceded by long or other vowel sounds, it is represented by the letter *k* (*take, took, bike, oak*). English words do not end with the letter *v.* Therefore, an *e* is always placed after a word ending with the /v/ phoneme (*live, have*).

The letter *y* represents a consonant sound when it is used to begin a word (*yes*) or a syllable (*canyon*). At all other times it is used to represent vowel sounds (*myth, cry, rhyme*).

Based on physiological data regarding children's speech development and the frequency at which various consonant letters are found in words, consonant letter–sound relationships should be taught in the following order: *m, p, s, b, t, d, f, l, r, n, w, h, c/k/, k, j, g, g/j/, c/s/, y, v, z, qu.*

Consonant digraphs are two or more consonant letters representing one consonant sound (*peach, shop, thing*). The following consonant digraphs are used to begin words or syllables: *shine, chirp, when, then, thing, phone.* With the exception of the *ph* digraph, all of the other digraphs represent unique sounds. The letters *gh* are a digraph in words such as *laugh* and *cough.* However, the few words containing this digraph are best taught as sight words. Most of the time when *gh* is used in words, it is a part of a vowel (*sigh, right,* etc.). The *wh* digraph represents the /hw/ sound heard at the beginning of the words *white, while, which,* etc.; however, because of lazy speech habits over the years many individuals are now pronouncing these words the same way they pronounce words beginning with *w* (*wine, wine, was,* etc.).

The following consonant digraphs are used to end words or syllables: *teach, catch, wish, sing, with, bathe.* The *ch* and *tch* digraphs represent the same sound, but the spelling of the sound is usually *ch* when it follows long, or other vowel sounds (*reach, couch, roach*), and *tch* when it follows short vowel sounds (*stitch, batch, stretch*). There are five words that are exceptions to this spelling pattern: *much, such, rich, which, touch.* The letters *nk* found at the end of syllables or words represent a combination of the /ng/ and /k/ sounds (*bank, sink, honk*). The only difference between the pronunciations of the words *sing* /sing/ and *sink* /singk/ is the /k/ phoneme at the end of the word *sink.*

Instead of representing one sound, *consonant blends* are clusters of consonant letters representing blended consonant phonemes (**stop, bend, strap, first**). While each consonant in a consonant blend represents its own sound, it is blended with the other consonants in the cluster. Because consonant blends are blended consonant sounds, teachers and children can take them apart and put them back together when sounding out words. For example, when using the phonics strategy to identify the word *stop*, the first step would be to determine the vowel sound in the word. The sound of the letter *o* in the word *stop* is /o/ (we will discuss how to determine vowel sounds in the next section). The next step would be to blend all of the consonants in front of the vowel with the vowel. The sounds represented by the letters *st* when blended with the /o/ sound result in /sto/. However, children could blend the sound represented by the letter *t* with /o/ first, and get /to/, and then blend the sound represented by the letter *s* with /to/ to get /sto/. The third step in the strategy would be to isolate the sound represented by the letter *p*, which is /p/; and the final step would be to blend /sto/ with /p/ to get /stop/.

Consonant blends can be separated and blended back together, if children cannot initially recall the sound represented by the entire consonant cluster; however, consonant digraphs cannot be separated in this fashion. For example, if children tried to sound out the word *shop* by /o/ /ho/ /s/ /ho/ /p/, the end result would be /s/ /hop/ rather than /shop/.

Phonics Patterns. Written words are structured by patterns, and syllables within words are structured by patterns. Furthermore, many word parts (letter combinations within words) are organized in patterns. Letter, syllable, and word patterns occur repeatedly in the written language, and successful readers, consciously or subconsciously, recognize them and associate them with predictable sounds.

A knowledge of phonics patterns is important in decoding. The pattern of the syllable, or word, tells readers whether the vowel letter in the syllable, or word, is long or short. Furthermore, readers see certain letter combination patterns within words and associate specific sounds with them. Vowel digraphs, vowel diphthongs, murmur diphthongs, and consonant digraphs are examples of letter patterns. Other letter patterns, such as *wa* (**water, want, wall**), *wor* (**work, world, worm**), and *al* (**call, already, also**) are also associated with predictable sounds.

There are about 3,000 single-syllable words in an unabridged dictionary. They are familiar to most adults. An analysis of these words reveals that there are 74 distinct syllable patterns among them. The most common pattern is the consonant-vowel-consonant-consonant pattern (CVCC) represented by such words as *just, send,* and *tell.* A little over 17 percent of all single-syllable words fall into this pattern.

Forty-three of the 74 patterns each represent less than 10 words; 37 represent less than 5 words; and 19 are represented by only 1 word—therefore, there are only 31 predominant single-syllable word patterns. A close analysis of these 31 distinct patterns reveals that many of them are variations of the same basic group. For example, all of the patterns containing only one vowel and ending in one or more consonants belong to the same group. After analyzing the 31 patterns in this manner, it was concluded that there are only 4 basic single-syllable word patterns in the English language.

The most frequently occurring word pattern is what is commonly referred to as the *closed* syllable: there is one vowel in the syllable and the syllable ends with a consonant sound. There are thirteen variations of this pattern, and 45 percent of the words analyzed belonged to this group. The variations of the pattern are listed, according to frequency of occurrence, in descending order:

Pattern	*Example*
CVCC	*sand*
CVC	*cup*
CCVCC	*trash*
CCVC	*slip*
CVCCC	*witch*
CVCCe	*badge*
CCVCCC	*crutch*
CCVCCe	*grudge*
CCCVCC	*script*
VCC	*add*
VC	*up*
CCCVC	*scrap*
VCCC	*inch*

The vowel letters in closed syllable patterns generally represent short sounds. Good readers either consciously or subconsciously make this association. They may also begin to realize that short vowel sounds occur more frequently in words than long vowel sounds.

The second most frequently occurring word pattern is the *vowel team* pattern. About 37.5 percent of the words analyzed fell into this group. Words containing the 20 vowel teams (vowel digraphs, vowel diphthongs, and murmur diphthongs) discussed earlier in the chapter belong to this group. There are 12 variations of the pattern, given here according to frequency of occurrence, in descending order:

Pattern	*Example(s)*
CVVC	*seat, bird*
CCVVC	*train, stork*
CVVCC	*peach, march*
CVV	*day, car*

CCVV	*clay, scar*
CVVCe	*leave, force*
CCVVCC	*bleach, thirst*
CCVVCe	*freeze, charge*
CCCVVC	*sprain*
VVC	*air, ark*
VVCC	*each, arch*
CCCVV	*three*

About 15.8 percent of the words analyzed fell into the vowel-consonant-silent *e* pattern. There were only four variations of this pattern. They are, according to frequency of occurrence, in descending order:

Pattern	*Example*
CVCe	*nice*
CCVCe	*slave*
CCCVCe	*stride*
VCe	*ace*

The letter *e* in these word patterns does not represent any sound. It does, however, signal to the reader that the first vowel letter in the word represents its long sound.

The last syllable pattern group is commonly referred to as the *open* syllable. There is only one vowel letter in the syllable, and the syllable ends with the vowel's sound. Words in this pattern represent only about 1.5 percent of the single-syllable words in the language. Since the pattern occurs so infrequently one might wonder why it should be mentioned at all. If the pattern occurred only in single-syllable words, this concern would be valid. However, the pattern occurs frequently in polysyllabic words, and children need to become familiar with it so they can associate the appropriate vowel sound with the letters found in the pattern. There are two variations of the pattern:

Pattern	*Example*
CCV	*she*
CV	*he*

The four syllable patterns just discussed occur in both single-syllable and polysyllabic words. Since the syllable pattern helps readers predict the vowel sound represented by the vowel letters in the pattern, this knowledge is important for readers when attempting to identify both types of words. The knowledge also facilitates readers' sight word recognition and their ability to identify words by analogy.

Phonics Scope and Sequence. Phonics can be taught as a strategy beginning with the first lesson, if teachers help students perform those tasks they are unable to perform by themselves. The phonics elements and phonics patterns can be taught as they are needed in the strategy. Since short vowel sounds are the most frequently occurring vowel sounds in English words, it is recommended that the phonics elements and patterns be taught as follows:

1. Teach children the five short vowel sounds while teaching the strategy.
2. Teach children the sounds represented by the consonant letters *m, p, s, b, t, d, f, l, r, n, w, h, c/k/, k, j, g, g/j/, c/s/, y, v, z, qu,* and teach them how to blend these consonants with any vowel sound following them.
3. Teach children that syllable patterns help readers predict whether the vowel in the syllable is long or short. Teach them how to identify vowel sounds in closed, open, and vowel-consonant-*e* syllable patterns.
4. Teach children the sounds associated with the 20 vowel teams most frequently used in English words: *ir, er, ur, ar, or, au, aw, ai, ay, ee, oa, oi, oy, ea, ou, ow, oo, ew, ue,* and *igh.*
5. Teach children to isolate the consonant sounds ending words, represented by the following consonant letters: *p, b, x, f, n, ck, k, t, m, l, d, g, ge, s, z, ve,* and *ce.*
6. Teach children the sounds associated with consonant digraphs (*sh, ch, th, tch, wh, ng,* and *nk*), and help them blend the sounds represented by beginning consonant digraphs with the vowel sounds following them, and isolate those that occur at the ending of words.
7. Teach children the sounds associated with consonant blends, and teach them to blend those that begin words with the vowel sounds following them, and isolate those that occur at the ending of words. The beginning consonant blends are *st, sk, sl, bl, br, pl, cl, cr, gl, gr, pr, tr, fr, dr, fl, sm, sn, sw, sp, sc, str, scr, spr, thr, spl, shr,* and *tw.* The ending consonant blends are *st, sk, mp, nt, nd, nk, lt, ft, ct, pt, sp, nge, nce, nse, nch,* and *dge.*
8. Teach children the vowel sounds represented by the letter *y,* and teach them how to determine those sounds by syllable pattern.

Morphemic Analysis

Using Morphemic Analysis to Identify Words

Morphemes are meaning units. For example, in the word *unwise,* "un" is a morpheme meaning "not," and "wise" is a morpheme meaning "having or using good judgment." Root words, prefixes, suffixes, and inflectional meanings are morphemes. Root words with prefixes and/or suffixes are called word *derivatives.* Root words with inflectional endings are called word *variants. Inflectional meanings* are endings added to root words to deal with meaning issues related to the syntax of the language. These endings are used to communicate (a) plurality, (b) possession, (c) tense, (d) person, or (e) comparison. For example:

The boy**s** went to the store. (Plurality)

The boy**'s** shirt was torn. (Possession)

I walk**ed** to school yesterday. (Past tense)

I walk to school every day. She walk**s** to school on Fridays. (Second person)

He runs fast**er** than Brad. (Comparison)

Sometimes children do not immediately recognize word derivatives or word variants, but are able to identify a familiar morpheme within the word that facilitates full identification. When children recognize familiar roots, prefixes, suffixes, or inflectional endings and identify words from those elements they are using morphemic analysis. Because children have been known to use their knowledge of morphemic elements to identify written words, teachers occasionally engage them in activities where they are required to identify those elements in written text.

Syllabic Analysis

Using Phonics to Identify Polysyllabic Words

When children use phonics to sound out single-syllable words, they isolate and blend letter sounds. This task is not too difficult for children who have been taught to do it. However, the key to successful phonetic decoding (often called *recoding*) is knowing how to identify the vowel sound in the word before trying to sound it out. The sounds represented by consonants are fairly predictable, so identifying these sounds beforehand is not necessary, but the sounds represented by vowels vary from word to word. The right vowel sound must be determined before blending a word's sounds. For example, say a child started to sound out the word *scrap* by isolating the letter sounds in the word. The child begins by saying, "/s/ /k/ /ru/ . . ." and then pauses to determine the vowel sound. The vowel letter *a* represents three sounds, so the child sounds out the three possibilities, "/ā/ /ä/ /a/." When the child interrupts the blending process to determine which vowel sound was appropriate for the word, the entire process breaks down. It's like standing in line to buy a ticket to a cultural or sporting event and not checking to see if you have enough money before you get to the cashier's window. Some things have to be determined beforehand or you will never reach your goal. Therefore, readers must be helped to determine vowel sounds in words by the structure of the syllable, before they attempt to sound out words.

Phonics knowledge is indispensable to sounding out single-syllable words. In a very real sense, phonics is a study of letter–sound relationships within syllable patterns. A knowledge of the four basic syllable patterns described in this chapter helps readers identify *appropriate* sounds to associate with letters when there is more than one possibility. So when children see an unfamiliar word like *map*, they identify the appropriate vowel sound with the letter *a* (/a/ in this case) because they know that vowel letters represent short sounds in closed syllables.

Phonics knowledge, however, is not so valuable to children when they encounter unfamiliar polysyllabic words. If they can't identify the syllable boundaries in polysyllabic words, they won't know the syllable's pattern and the appropriate vowel sound to associate with the vowel letter in the syllable. For example, children might encounter an unfamiliar word such as *maple*, and associate the first part of it with the word *map*. If they view the first syllable in *maple* as *map* and the second one as *le* they will sound the word out as /map/ /ul/ rather than /mā/ /pul/. Children often associate inappropriate sounds with vowel letters in words such as this, simply because they don't know where the first syllable in the word ends and the second one begins. The problem is compounded in words of three or more syllables. In short, phonics as a word identification strategy breaks down for many children when they encounter unfamiliar polysyllabic words, simply because they can't perceive the syllable patterns within each word.

In order to use phonics to identify such unfamiliar words, children must be able to identify the syllable boundaries within words so they can determine the correct vowel sound in each syllable. After vowel sounds in syllables have been determined, the rest of the blending process is fairly simple.

In the past, the teaching of syllabication has been a "can of worms." Children were taught rules for breaking words into syllables and rules for accenting them. Many children and teachers found the experience difficult and confusing. Furthermore, there is little or no evidence that the information taught was ever used by children, or ever improved their reading performance. Teachers need a simple syllabication strategy to help young children identify syllable boundaries in unfamiliar multisyllabic words so they can use their phonics knowledge to sound them out.

Syllabication. The key to syllabication is the vowel. As stated, each syllable contains one vowel sound. For example, *me, box, bone, stretch, seed, boat,* and *bird* are all single-syllable words containing one vowel sound. The words *paper, complete, discharge,* and *yesterday* are polysyllabic words containing more than one vowel sound. However, since not all vowels in words represent sounds, the number of vowel letters in a word is not equivalent to the number of vowel sounds in the word. For example, the emphasized letters in each of the sample words listed represent vowel sounds while the others do not. After examining each of the four syllable patterns, one can quickly see that the vowel-consonant-*e* syllable and the vowel team syllable each contain more vowel letters than vowel sounds. In the open and closed syllable patterns, however, there is one vowel letter representing one vowel sound in each syllable.

Since each syllable contains only one vowel sound, if children can identify the number of sounding vowels in a word they automatically identify the number of syllables in the word. Furthermore, they also identify a part of a syllable since each grapheme representing a vowel sound is a part of a syllable. Therefore, a beginning point for the identification of syllable boundaries is to locate the vowels in a word that represent vowel sounds. This process is relatively easy for children if they are familiar with phonics elements and patterns. They will know that vowel teams represent only one vowel sound, that the letters *ge* at the end of words represent a consonant sound (/j/) rather than a vowel sound, and that the *e* at the end of vowel-consonant-*e* syllables is silent. See if you can identify the letters representing vowel sounds in the following words: *complete, merchant, misjudge, cabin, certain, discharge*.

Once children can identify the vowel letters representing sounds in polysyllabic words, they are ready to discover some basic linguistic patterns related to syllabication. Consider the words listed in the following two columns:

Column 1	*Column 2*
letter	*tiger*
except	*pilot*
complete	*fever*
athlete	
enchant	*bacon*
discharge	*cabin*
harmful	*robin*

Identify the vowel letters representing vowel sounds in each word, in both columns. How many vowel sounds are in each word? How many syllables are in each word? How are all of the words in both columns alike?

The words in column 1 are different and alike in several ways. Some of them contain consonant blends while others do not, some contain consonant digraphs while others do not, and so on. Some linguists have developed syllabication rules to account for the differences noted in the words. Would you be surprised to know that some linguists have developed a different syllabication rule for each of the seven words listed in column 1?

All of the words in column 1 contain two syllables, but they are also alike in another way. What other common feature do you notice about these words?

The words in column 2 are also both different and alike. The differences among the words in this column, however, are not as great as those found in the first column.

Each of the words in column 2 contains two syllables, but they are also like each other in another respect. Do you notice another feature common to all of the words in column 2?

Consider the number of consonant letters between the sounding vowels in each word in both columns. The difference between the number of consonant letters between sounding vowels in the words is what separates the words in column 1 from those listed in column 2.

The words in both columns deliberately contain only two syllables. The linguistic patterns affecting syllabication can be perceived easier in two-syllable words, and once perceived, the knowledge acquired can be applied to all types of polysyllabic words.

All polysyllabic words (words ending with *le* are a special case discussed shortly) have either one consonant unit separating the letters representing vowel sounds (see column 2), or two or more consonant units separating those sounds (see column 1). A *consonant unit* is either a single consonant or a consonant digraph. For example, in the word *fiber*, there is only one consonant unit between the two vowel sounds, a single consonant *b*. In the word *ether*, there is only one consonant unit between the two vowel sounds, a *th* consonant digraph.

When two or more consonant units separate vowel sounds, the first syllable is closed (i.e., the first syllable ends with the first consonant unit), and the second syllable begins with whatever consonant units are left:

let-ter

ex-cept

com-plete

ath-lete

en-chant

dis-charge

harm-ful

In most polysyllabic words there are two or more consonant letters between two sounding vowels, as in the words in column 1. Children eventually learn that the first vowel in these situations represents its short sound. Notice that all of the vowels in the list represent their short sounds except the words *complete* and *harmful*. If the vowel doesn't represent its short sound in closed syllables, it is because the vowel is a vowel team (*ar* in *harmful*), or the syllable is unaccented (*com* in *complete*). In unaccented syllables, the vowel letter represents the /u/ sound regardless of the letter(s) representing the sound (*alone, lemon, pencil open, circus, certain, famous*). This situation occurs in all English words. In two-syllable words, the second syllable is usually the one unaccented, unless the first syllable is a prefix. Prefixes are usually unaccented.

When only one consonant unit separates vowel sounds, the first syllable either ends with the vowel (see column A) or ends with the consonant after the vowel (see column B):

A	*B*
ti-ger	*bac-on*
pi-lot	*cab-in*
fe-ver	*rob-in*

An analysis of words with only one consonant unit between sounding vowels suggests that in 55 percent of the words we find pattern A, and in 45 percent we find pattern B. If the first syllable ends with a vowel (pattern A) the vowel letter represents its long sound (open syllable pattern). If the first syllable ends with the consonant (pattern B), the vowel letter represents its short sound (closed syllable pattern). When children encounter unfamiliar polysyllabic words where vowel sounds are separated by one consonant unit, they quickly learn to say the first syllable using the long sound of the vowel first. If that strategy doesn't work, they say the first syllable using the short sound.

A special linguistic pattern involves the use of *le* at the end of multisyllabic words, for example, *maple, candle, babble, bottle, able,* and *bugle*. In these situations, the *le* stands for the /ul/ sound and the first syllable ends before the consonant letter preceding the *le: ma-ple, can-dle, bab-ble, bot-tle, a-ble*, and *bu-gle*. When the first syllable is open, the vowel letter represents its long sound (*ma-ple, a-ble, bu-gle*), and when the first syllable is closed, the vowel letter represents its short sound (*can-dle, bab-ble, bot-tle*).

The Decoding "Path of Least Resistance"

Students should be helped to decode words efficiently. The most efficient of all decoding processes is sight word recognition. Accurate, automatic, fluent sight word recognition is one of the hallmarks of a good reader, and is the objective and focus of this book. Identification strategies (analogy, context, phonics, morphemic analysis, and syllabic analysis/phonics) are only a means to this goal. Identification strategies are important for readers to learn, however, if their word recognition abilities are inadequate for successful independent reading. These strategies help students decode when sight vocabularies are underdeveloped. Furthermore, when children learn those identification strategies that focus their attention on the letter–sound sequences of words, word recognition is enhanced.

When students' word recognition abilities are weak or underdeveloped, they should be provided with many holistic reading experiences where they are assisted to read books they cannot read by themselves (shared book experience, dyad reading, group assisted reading, taped assisted reading, etc.). We discuss these strategies in Chapter 9.

When reading independently, some identification strategies are more efficient for students to employ than are others. It is hoped that children will learn to choose the most efficient identification strategy available so they spend less time and focus on decoding and more time and focus on meaning while they read. To help students identify words as quickly as possible, encourage them to use the identification strategies as follows:

1. First, try to identify the unknown word by analogy. This is a quick identification process. If the unknown word can't be identified by analogy,
2. try to identify the unknown word using contextual analysis. This is also a fairly quick process. If contextual analysis doesn't work,
3. use phonics to sound out the word if it is a single-syllable word. If the unknown word is a polysyllabic word,
4. look at the word to see if it contains a familiar root word, prefix, suffix, or inflectional ending. The recognition of familiar morphemes may help in the identification of the word. If morphemic analysis doesn't work,
5. locate the word's syllable boundaries and sound out the word.

Application Activities

1. Single vowel letters, regular vowel digraphs, irregular vowel digraphs, vowel diphthongs, murmur diphthongs, single consonant letters, consonant digraphs, and consonant blends comprise the elements of phonics. Analyze a page of text and identify and label each of the phonics elements contained in the words on that page.

2. Consonant sounds are either voiced or voiceless. Sometimes the only difference in the speech mechanisms used to produce two consonant sounds is whether the voice is used. For example, /b/ and /p/ are produced with the tongue, teeth, and lips in the same position, but when producing /b/ the larynx is vibrated, and when producing /p/ air is forced from the mouth. Because the only difference in the production of these two consonant sounds is whether they are voiced or voiceless, we say that /b/ and /p/ are *voiced* and *voiceless complements*. Experiment with the consonant sounds identified in this chapter to see how many voiced and voiceless complements you can find.

3. Analyze the single-syllable words on a page or two of any text and identify those words that are graphophonically regular and those that are graphophonically irregular. Classify the graphophonically regular words by syllable pattern. What percentage of those words represent the closed syllable pattern? What percentage represent the vowel team pattern? What percentage represent the vowel-consonant-*e* pattern? What percentage represent the open syllable pattern?

4. Analyze the polysyllabic words on a page or two of any text and identify those words that are graphophonically regular and those that are graphophonically irregular. Using the syllabication principles taught in this chapter, analyze the graphophonically regular words. How many of them have two or more consonants between sounding vowels? How many of them have only one consonant unit between sounding vowels? In what percentage of the words having only one consonant unit between sounding vowels did you find the first syllable ending with the vowel sound?

5. Visit an elementary school. Listen to several children, at different grade levels, read. Try to identify the decoding strategies they use. Were most of them using word recognition? When children could not recognize words, what strategies did they use? How many of them had developed strategies for identifying words they could not recognize? Were the strategies effective? Were you able to help students by suggesting strategies for them to use?

Chapter 9

Teaching Decoding Informally Through Reading and Writing Activities

Over the past four decades, educators have experimented with various strategies designed to help poor readers cope with comprehension difficulties created by decoding deficiencies. Much of what has been learned about informal, holistic decoding strategies has come from analyses of these experimental efforts.

Poor decoding ability means poor comprehension. The ability to decode written words will not ensure good reading comprehension, but comprehension will not occur without it. Certainly one cannot create meaning from printed text without a knowledge of the words used by the author. However, the translation of words alone is not sufficient for reading comprehension. Readers must also be able to hold the words decoded in short term memory long enough to apprehend sentences. Decoding speed affects this process. If a sentence is read too slowly—say, one word every five seconds—its structure collapses and what remains is a string of words producing little meaning. Many teachers have observed "word-by-word readers" who took so much time to decode that they seemed to have forgotten the words that began a sentence by the time they got to the end.

The speed at which one hears words or decodes them affects listening (McNeill, 1968) and reading comprehension. Smith (1975) believes that one must read close to 250 words per minute for good comprehension. Yet, a common characteristic of poor readers is that they tend to read word by word, rather than fluently. Slow, halted reading limits the number of words readers can focus on within relevant time periods, which, in turn, affects the meaning they are able to construct from text. This conclusion is supported by research indicating that fluent readers perceive phrases while reading whereas less able, word-by-word readers do not (Kowal, O'Connell, O'Brian, & Bryant, 1975).

The theory of automatic information processing proposed by LaBerge and Samuels (1974) supports the proposition that reading fluency affects reading comprehension. LaBerge and Samuels believe that good comprehenders decode fluently, and automatically as well. That is, good readers decode rapidly, and do so without being consciously aware that decoding is even taking place. Because good readers decode text automatically, they are able to give full attention to text comprehension. Beginning and word-by-word readers, on the other hand, are nonautomatic in their decoding, and because most of their attention is on decoding, comprehension suffers.

LaBerge and Samuels's theory of automaticity is based on "attention" research suggesting that the brain acts as a single-channel processor; that is, it normally processes only one source of information at a time. Yet readers must process two sources of information simultaneously: they must be able to translate the written text into inner speech, and they must be able to process the message. According to the theory, the brain is able to process both sources of information simultaneously only if one of them (decoding) is brought to the level of automaticity. The analogy of driving a "stick-shift" car is often made to this reading issue. This task, like reading, requires the brain to process two sources of information at one time. When individuals first learn to drive a car with a manual transmission, they have to focus both on the task of shifting the car, and on moving the car safely down the road. They usually master shifting before driving on public roads since the safety of the people around them is affected by this mastery: if too much of the drivers' attention is on shifting, not enough is left for safe driving.

According to LaBerge and Samuels, beginning and immature readers have to give competing attention to both decoding and comprehension tasks because decoding is not automatic. Mature readers, however, possess large "sight" vocabularies, so decoding no longer requires conscious attention, and they can give full attention to the message of the text. Samuels (1976) stated that "to have both fluent reading and good comprehension, the student must be brought beyond accuracy to automaticity in decoding" (p. 323).

Assisted Reading Strategies

Various assisted reading strategies have been used with poor readers since the early 1950s to remove the "decoding burdens" hindering their reading comprehension. All of them possess common characteristics supporting the notions that reading abilities can be improved by reading, and that children's decoding abilities can be improved when mature readers help them read material they can't read by themselves.

Historical Use of Assisted Reading Strategies

The Neurological Impress Method. Heckelman seems to have been the first to remediate reading handicaps by helping poor readers get involved with reading natural text. Heckelman (1962, 1966, 1968, 1969) developed in the early 1950s the *neurological impress method,* a technique of impressing mature reading behaviors upon students with severe reading disabilities.

The method was a system of unison reading whereby the student and the teacher read aloud, simultaneously, at a rapid rate. The disabled reader was placed slightly to the front of the teacher with the student and the teacher holding the book jointly. As the student and teacher read the material in unison, the voice of the teacher was directed into the ear of the student at close range. The teacher tracked the words on the page with a finger as they were being spoken. At times the instructor read louder and faster than the student and at other times read softer and slower than the student. The goal was to cover as many pages of reading material as possible within the time available.

Heckelman (1969) worked over a 6-week period with 24 remedial secondary students with severe reading handicaps in selected schools in Merced, California. All of them had reading levels that were at least 3 years below grade level, and all had IQ scores of 90 or above on the WISC. At the end of the treatment period, he reported a range in achievement gains from 0 grade levels to 5.9 grade levels. Many studies using the neurological impress method produced similar achievement results (Cook, Nolan, & Zanotti, 1965; Gardner, 1963; Gardner, 1965; Embrey, 1968; Miller, 1969; Langford, Slade, & Barnett, 1974; Robin, 1977; Stinner, 1979; Cook, Nolan, & Zanotti, 1980). Three studies failed to find significant achievement differences (Arnold, 1972; Gibbs & Proctor, 1977; Lorenz & Vockell, 1979).

Gardner (1965) believed that some reading disabilities were due to an interruption of synaptic transmissions in the brain brought on by anxiety (Smith & Carrigan, 1959). He believed that anxiety raised the circuit-breaking effect of two body chemicals interacting with each other: cholinestraerase (CHE) and acetylcholise (ACH). He suggested that the neurological impress method (NIM) lowered student anxiety as they read because they were freed from the failure experiences they encountered using traditional methods of reading instruction.

Hoskisson's Assisted Reading. Smith (1971, 1973, 1976) argued that children learned to read by reading, and a teacher's prime task was to do as much reading as was necessary for them until they could go on their own. Influenced by Smith, Hoskisson (1974) proposed a technique for parents to use to help their children learn to read. He called this technique *assisted reading.* Assisted reading was based on the premise that if children saw written words, heard them pronounced, and followed their patterning in sentences, they would learn to read. He stated (1975a) that children could learn to read by reading, much as they learned to talk by talking, claiming (1975b) that children would discover the orthographic patterns in written language if they were provided with enough assisted reading practice. Using Hoskisson's method, a parent moved one finger slowly under the line of print being read to get the child to begin to focus on the words. After repeated visual exposures to words as they were pronounced by the parent, the child was eventually able to read the book.

Hoskisson and others (Hoskisson, Sherman, & Smith, 1974) reported both qualitative and quantitative data suggesting that the strategy was effective with preschoolers and poor readers in the elementary grades. Krohm (Hoskisson & Krohm, 1974) implemented assisted reading strategies in her second-grade classroom as a supplement to her regular reading program. She taped stories, prepared from supplemental reading texts, that were on or just above her students' reading level. Students read the stories while listening to the prepared tapes. They shared the stories they read with their classmates. Krohm reported that the students enjoyed the experience, poor readers became more confident, and overall student achievement was improved.

The Method of Repeated Readings. Dahl and Samuels (1974) developed the *method of repeated readings* to increase the automaticity of poor readers' word recognition skills. Unskilled readers, they claimed, could access meaning by rereading a passage several times. They believed the first few readings would bring the written material to the phonological level as if the students were "listening" to it rather than reading it.

The method involved the use of short selections (50–200 words), taken from interesting stories selected by students, which were marked off for reading practice (Samuels, 1979). Students read a selection to an assistant, or into a tape, and immediately afterward their reading speed and number of recognition errors were calculated and recorded on a graph. The students then reread the selection, which was again timed, and a new word error count calculated. The procedure was repeated until the student reached an 85 word per minute (wpm) criterion rate (the speed at which student comprehension was defined as successful for the study; Dahl [1974] set the original criterion rate at 100 wpm). Then the student went on to the next selection.

Samuels (1979) found that as a student's reading rate increased, word recognition errors decreased, and reading comprehension improved, observing also that reading comprehension improved with each additional rereading. He reasoned that improvement resulted because the decoding barrier to comprehension was gradually overcome. Gonzales and Elijah (1975) studied the effects of repeated readings on informal reading inventory (IRI) performance. They found that when a student read material at a "frustrational reading level" twice, the difficulty of the material on the second reading moved to "instructional level."

The method of repeated readings could be implemented with or without audio support. With audio support, the student initially would read the passage silently while listening to the recorded narration over earphones. It was believed that the key to the success of the method, with or without taped support, was practice. Samuels (1976) concluded that students would learn to read fluently only if they practiced reading. Recent research has substantiated the positive benefits of repeated readings on both decoding and reading comprehension (Herman, 1985; Taylor, Wade, & Yekovich, 1985; Amlund, Kardash, & Kulhavy, 1986; Dowhower, 1987).

Dyad Reading. Eldredge and Butterfield (1986) modified the neurological impress method so it could be used in the regular classroom, renaming it *dyad reading*. Among the modifications made in the original technique, a "lead reader," a student in the classroom, replaced the teacher. The "assisted reader," a student who could not read well, worked with a different lead reader each week. (The terms *lead reader*, and *assisted reader* in this text refer to the dyad member who can read the book, and the dyad member who cannot read it, respectively. These terms should *not* be used as labels for children in the classroom. In the classroom, lead readers should be referred to as *team leaders*, and assisted readers as *team members*.) In dyad reading, the difficulty level of the reading material was ignored, whereas Heckelman had controlled it. As long as a book could be read by the lead reader and was of interest to both the lead reader and the assisted reader, it was appropriate for use in dyad reading.

The first study of dyad reading was conducted in fifty Utah second-grade classrooms (Eldredge & Butterfield, 1986). Poor readers in experimental classrooms were placed in dyad groups where they read grade-level, or above grade-level, material with lead readers, while poor readers in control classrooms were grouped according to their reading levels and read below grade-level material appropriate for individual reading. The students in the dyads sat side by side, reading aloud from the same book. The lead reader touched each word as it was read, while the assisted reader read along with the lead reader. The lead reader read the book at a normal oral reading speed, avoiding word-by-word reading. Over a period of time, the assisted readers were able to read the regular school material without any assistance. At the end of the school year, children in the experimental classrooms obtained significantly higher scores in both reading achievement and reading attitudes than those in the control classrooms. These findings were supported by a follow-up study conducted in two Utah school districts (Eldredge, 1990b).

The dyad reading groups in both studies provided poor readers with holistic reading experiences in "frustrational level" reading material. The findings seemed to contradict the generally accepted notion that children should be taught to read in "instructional level" materials. A third study (Eldredge & Quinn, 1988) also examined whether poor readers make better reading achievement gains when they are helped to read "frustrational level" material than when they are given "instructional level" material to read without any help. Poor readers in dyads made greater achievement gains on all reading outcomes than their matched controls in this study. At the end of the year, 27 out of 32 experimental students (84%) scored at or above grade level, while only 6 out of 32 control students (19%) achieved this level. Poor readers in the experimental group outperformed the poor readers in the control situation by an average of 49 percentile points.

These results indicate that (a) children do not have to be taught to read with relatively easy "instructional level" text; (b) poor readers can significantly improve their decoding and reading comprehension abilities when helped to read material too difficult for them to read by themselves; and (c) children who are assisted to read difficult material in dyad groups for a period of time become able to read difficult material independently.

Group Assisted Reading. *Group assisted reading* is a strategy intended to adapt dyad reading to groups of children who could not individually read grade-level material (Eldredge, 1990a). A study of group-assissted reading involved a teacher as the lead reader and a small group of students as assisted readers. The teacher read the text material along with the students, modeling correct phrasing, intonation, and pitch. As the students read the material in unison with the teacher, they tracked the words in the text with a finger.

The students receiving the assisted reading treatment read eight paperback books with the teacher over an 8-week period. The books selected were drawn from the literature books supplied in each third-grade classroom as a part of their literature-based reading program. They were selected because the experimental students were interested in the books, but could not read them without help. During the assisted reading period, the students were grouped in dyads, and each dyad had one copy of the day's text. The teacher also had a copy. The teacher and the students read the story together orally. The teacher set the pace for reading and provided the expressive model, reading the story in phrase units, emphasizing correct stress, pitch, and juncture. The students in the dyads tracked each word on the page nearest them with a finger as it was being read. Both students kept their eyes on the words in the text while reading. They read the story several times so they could read it expressively without teacher assistance. At the end of the period, the students in the dyads read a part of the story together orally without teacher assistance.

The students receiving the unassisted reading treatment read literature books silently during this same period of time. The same eight books used by the assisted reading group were provided for students to read if they chose. However, these students did not select them because they were more difficult than other books that were available. The children used "trial and error" procedures until they found books they could read. They read their books silently during the 15-minute reading period while the teacher made herself available to help them read unfamiliar words.

The students in the unassisted group made no achievement gains over the 8-week period while the average total reading achievement gain for the students in the assisted group was 10 raw score points on the Gates MacGinitie Reading Test. The difference was significant, and the size of the effect large. The poor readers in the group assisted reading experiment outgained the poor readers in the control situation by an average of 26 percentile points.

These results clearly indicate that (a) teachers can assist children, in groups, to read material that is too difficult for them to read by themselves; (b) when poor readers are assisted to read difficult material, their decoding and reading comprehension abilities improve; and (c) poor readers who are assisted to read difficult material achieve better than poor readers who independently read interesting, but simple, material matched to their "instructional reading levels."

Using Group Assisted Reading with First-grade Students. We have successfully used group assisted reading activities with first-grade children in three elementary classrooms in Utah (Eldredge, 1991). Ten-minute daily phonics lessons (see Chapter 10) accompanied the group assisted reading activities, as did writing and other activities consonant with holistic classroom practices. The effects of the holistic practices on the reading attitudes and achievement of these first-grade children were compared with those obtained in three first-grade basal classrooms.

Students involved in the holistic program made significantly greater vocabulary, comprehension, total reading, and phonics gains than students involved in the basal program. The average total reading achievement on the Gates MacGinitie Reading Test, Level A, Form 1, for the basal group at the end of the year was 59. The average score for the holistic group was 70. An analysis of covariance indicated a significant treatment effect, $F = 40.33$, df = 1, 102, $p < .0001$. In addition, we noted significant reading attitude differences in favor of the holistic group.

Taped Assisted Reading. William Jordan popularized the combined use of audio tapes and written text to help poor readers become more meaningfully involved in reading. Adapting Heckelman's neurological impress method, Jordan (1965, 1966, 1967) in the mid 1960s developed Prime-O-Tec, a combination visual-audio-tactile-kinesthetic-motor input form of reading instruction (Meyer, 1982). Learners used teacher-made prerecorded tapes and headphones. They were instructed to listen to a tape, follow the print with a finger, and finally to read along with the tape. The listening, seeing, saying, and touching was all done in unison.

Railsback (1969) and Hollingsworth (1970, 1978) conducted studies using audiotaped programs similar to Jordan's. Railsback reported that his subjects gained a half year or more in test scores per instructional month involved. Hollingsworth (1970) did not find significant achievement gains in his first study. He repeated his study (1978) several years later, doubling his previous treatment time, and found significant achievement differences. The experimental group gained 1 year's growth while the control group gained only .04 of a year.

Chomsky (1976, 1978) reported a successful experiment using tapes with five slow readers in the third grade. Chomsky recorded two dozen storybooks ranging from second- to fifth-grade reading level, most of which were 20 to 30 pages long. The students selected the books they wanted to read, listened to the tapes, read along with the tapes, and tried to memorize each book before moving on to another.

Chomsky (1976) said, "Mechanical as the idea of memorization may seem in itself, it gives these children practice in reading connected discourse, and it put them in touch with a variety of books. They had a feeling of success right from the start, and a sense of progress as book after book was added to their repertoire" (p. 296). Chomsky reported that the students' passivity about reading declined dramatically over the 15 weeks they were involved in the experiment. Their confidence also increased and they began to pick up new books of their own choosing. Pretest and posttest scores on several reading tests showed encouraging gains. Children averaged 5 months' gain on the Wide Range Achievement Test (WRAT) reading subtest, and several months' to one-year gains in oral speed on the Durrell Analysis of Reading Difficulty.

Carbo (1978) taped stories with correct phrasing for eight average intelligent learning-disabled students in grades 2 and 6 to listen to and mimic. She recorded entire books and parts of books, varying the reading rate and phrase length depending on the reading ability of the student. Students usually listened to their individual tapes three or four times and then read the passage aloud. The students were able to read the stories with fluency and expression. In her uncontrolled study she reported impressive gains for all eight students in word recognition, comprehension, and attitudes toward reading. Carbo's students had memory problems, attention difficulties, and auditory perception difficulties. She believed that the taped assisted reading method worked because it possessed the following characteristics:

- It was multisensory and helped compensate for the students' perception deficits.
- It was interesting and held the students' attention.

- It removed the decoding burden so students were able to attend to comprehension.
- It was highly structured so steady growth and feelings of security were obtained.
- It was fail-safe, so self-concept was not weakened.
- It provided the repetition the students needed to overcome their deficiencies in memory.

Common Characteristics of Assisted Reading Strategies

All of the assisted reading strategies we have reviewed here were designed to help students with immature decoding abilities have better experiences with written text. When the method of repeated readings was accompanied by audiotape support, all strategies shared the following characteristics:

1. All were "psychologically safe" strategies. No student could fail when employing the strategies, and students were able to learn from errors without embarrassment.
2. All involved students in reading experiences they could not participate in by themselves. That is, students were helped to read material that they could not individually read.
3. All strategies involved students in reading activities where they "saw" written words while simultaneously "hearing" the pronunciations of those words, providing students with sight word recognition "drill," naturally, subconsciously, and painlessly.
4. All provided students with multiple exposures to the most frequently used words in the English language (see Chapter 7).
5. All involved students in holistic, connected reading experiences. The phrase and sentence reading made the reading experience more meaningful for them, and students were able to focus their attention on text messages rather than on the words conveying those messages.
6. All strategies provided students with language and thinking experiences that enhance reading comprehension: background knowledge experience; vocabulary experience; syntax experience; experience with narrative and expository discourse structures; opportunities for inferencing and imagery; and opportunities to engage in metacognitive processes.
7. All utilized the principle of scaffolding: once individual performance levels were established, students moved to higher-performance tasks and were provided the necessary assistance needed to perform those higher-level tasks.
8. All provided a vehicle for involving students in personally interesting reading material, which can potentially improve students' attitudes toward reading and motivate them to read more.

Poor and/or immature readers cannot direct enough of their attention on text messages because they have to concentrate so heavily on decoding tasks. All the assisted reading strategies discussed free readers from their decoding burdens so they can give needed attention to text messages. The method of repeated readings, without taped support, eventually brings the printed material to the phonological level as if the students were "listening" to it rather than reading it.

Helping students read interesting material in phrases and sentences helps them (especially word-by-word readers) realize that reading is a meaningful process. Helping students read interesting books extensively can improve their schemata, vocabulary knowledge, syntax knowledge, discourse knowledge, inferencing and imagery, and metacognitive processing. Assisted reading strategies also help poor and/or immature readers decode better by providing them with extensive experiences seeing written words while simultaneously hearing them pronounced. These repeated visual/auditory word exposures improve students' sight word recognition abilities which, in turn, improve reading comprehension.

Students' reading abilities, then, can be improved by reading, and *decoding can be taught informally* when mature readers help immature readers read material they can't read by themselves.

Using Assisted Reading Strategies in the Classroom

Dyad Reading. Dyad reading is an effective instructional tool to use with students who are unable to read books they want or need to read. It is also an effective tool for improving the oral reading abilities of those students who serve as lead readers. When lead readers read books with students unable to read them, they should do so with the intent of practicing their own oral reading skills rather than "tutoring" other students. The major focus of dyad reading is to improve the oral reading abilities of *both* members of the dyad team, while the secondary focus is on the tracking of the print being read.

You can offer dyad reading to students as an option, or may institute dyad reading as an integral part of the regular classroom program. In the former situation, give students willing to serve as lead readers instruction and practice in oral reading and "tracking print" with their fingers as they read. Periodically, let them practice oral reading while other students read along with them. In the latter situation, give all students in the classroom oral reading instruction and opportunities to practice their oral reading skills. In either situation, allow frequent practice for all students needing reading assistance.

Dyad reading involves the following steps and guidelines:

1. *Identify the students who could benefit from the strategy.* If you use the strategy in a first-grade classroom, probably all of your students will qualify as candidates for assistance. If it is used at higher grade levels, you can either ask students needing help to identify themselves, or identify those needing help by observing students read.

    To identify students who need help, ask all of the children, at the same time, to orally read a book they have been assigned or have chosen to read, in quiet but audible voices. Since everyone reads aloud at the same time, students are preoccupied with their own performance rather than the performance of others, and no one is embarrassed by the activity. As you move around the classroom listening to students read, you can easily identify those with decoding problems.

2. *Identify lead readers.* Lead readers do not have to be gifted readers. They must, however, be able to read the material that assisted readers cannot read by themselves. If dyad reading is used in the first grade, you might recruit older students in the upper grades as lead readers. Both groups of students should benefit from the experience. You may also ask parents or other volunteers to be lead readers instead of classmates or older students.

3. *Match lead readers with assisted readers.* A lead reader and an assisted reader form a dyad team for a specified time, usually no longer than four or five days. New dyads are formed as old ones are eliminated. This is done so lead readers are not involved in a steady diet of oral reading.

4. *Encourage dyad teams to read both expository and narrative text.* When using basal readers, science, social studies, or other school texts for dyad reading, the text material is predetermined. However, it is good practice to allow dyad teams to select books they want to read from the school or classroom library.

5. *Dyad members share one book.* Members of a dyad sit side by side sharing one book between them. The lead reader sets the reading pace. The lead reader touches each word as it is read while the assisted reader tries to read aloud with the lead reader. It is important that the assisted reader look at each word as it is touched and read. However, the lead reader should read in a natural, fluent manner so that both readers are able to get involved in the content of the book and forget about the individual words being read. There should be no deliberate, word-by-word reading.

6. *Lead readers should be able to read the books selected or assigned.* If a word appears in the book that the lead reader does not recognize or cannot identify, they may skip it and simply move on. If they miss too many words, however, the material may be too difficult for the team.

7. *It is important for children to read extensively.* The goal of dyad reading is to get both members of the team to read as many pages of interesting reading material as possible in the time available to them without causing physical discomfort on the part of either student, such as dryness of mouth or fatigue of voice.

8. *Scaffolding should be a part of the dyad reading experience.* As assisted readers gain word recognition skill they need opportunities to silently read materials on their own. They also need opportunities occasionally to read out loud to mature readers (a parent, volunteer, teacher, older student, etc.) who will silently read along with them checking their word recognition accuracy and fluency. In these situations, the mature reader should read aloud those words the assisted reader hesitates on, so the assisted reader can repeat them and move on. It is important that this type of reading experience flow naturally so students can maintain their interest.

Group Assisted Reading. Group assisted reading is an effective strategy to use with all of the children in first-grade classrooms. It is also an effective strategy to use with small groups of children, in grades two through six, who are unable to read books they want or need to read.

Group assisted reading involves the following steps:

1. *The text material to be read must be visible to all students participating in the activity.* A big book, transparencies, charts, or one book for every two students in the classroom will satisfy this requirement.
2. *Teachers and students read the story or text together out loud.* You are the lead reader and all students in the classroom or in a smaller group are the assisted readers. Read each book at a normal, or slightly slower than normal speed, modeling correct phrasing and logical expression.
3. *Teachers touch each word in the text as it is read.* Encourage the children to read along, and to look at each word as you touch and read it. If using basal readers or textbooks, organize the children into dyads and give each dyad one copy of the book used. As you and your students read the book out loud together, students in each dyad track the print on the side of the text nearest to them.

Taped Assisted Reading. Taped assisted reading is also an effective strategy to use with books students find difficult to read by themselves. It is important that the story or text material on the tape be read at the proper speed. Teacher-made tapes are generally best; commercial tapes are generally read too fast. Children who listen to tapes while reading should be taught to track the print of the text with a finger while it is being read, and to try to read along with the tape rather than just listen to it.

Taped assisted reading works particularly well when two students, each wearing earphones connected to a tape recorder or tape junction box, share one book while reading the story along with the tape. As they listen to the tape recording of the story, each student tracks the print on the side of the text nearest to her/him as they read. Using taped text support in this manner, each student is able to keep on the print "tracking" task.

The Shared Book Experience. Holdaway (1979) believed strongly in the benefits preschool children derive from the book sharing experiences they have with their parents. From his beliefs he developed the *shared book experience* for primary-grade teachers. The term implies an experience with books that goes beyond the "reading aloud" activities school children normally experience. Holdaway wanted children to see the written text and the book's pictures while hearing a story read, just as children sitting on their parents' laps do. He developed "big books" so children and teachers could jointly "share" the pictures and text while reading the book aloud.

In many homes, parents read stories to children regularly. After a period of time, children select "favorites" and ask parents to read them repeatedly. In fact, preschool children enjoy certain books so much that they often "exhaust" parents with requests to read them. Holdaway believed that children should have these kinds of recreational experiences with books in the school. He encouraged teachers to create a "homelike" environment in their classrooms that would expose children to good literature, and give them opportunities to have favorite stories read over and over again.

When you are using the shared book experience with a big book, glide your hands under the words as you read them so students have a sense of print going from the left to the right and from top to bottom. As words are tracked children begin to develop a concept of written word boundaries. After reading a story once, invite students to read along with you when they feel ready.

When the stories you read to children contain "predictable" elements, children are able to read those elements along with you when encouraged to do so. As you read the stories repeatedly, children begin to memorize them. Many children are then able to read all, or parts, of the story without help. Many children also begin to match written words with spoken ones, and begin to develop their decoding abilities.

Shared Music and Rhythm Experiences. The concept of shared reading can also be applied to music and poetry. During whole-class singing or poetry reading, place at the front of the room a large chart containing the song's or poem's words. Track the words with a pointer, finger, or pencil as you and the children sing or say them. In addition to songs and poetry, raps and other language-play activities can be read using this procedure.

Motivating Children to Read

Informal decoding strategies work because children develop word recognition through practice. The more children read the more proficient they will become at reading. In Chapter 2 we stated that there are both qualitative and quantitative dimensions to word recognition practice. The qualitative dimension focuses on the alphabetic principle. When teachers help students see how the letters in written words relate to the sounds in spoken words, they are emphasizing qualitative word recognition practice. The quantitative dimension involves the amount of practice students receive—the number of experiences students have associating written words with spoken words. When teachers provide students with many reading experiences that reinforce written–spoken word associations, they are emphasizing quantitative word recognition practice. All of the informal decoding strategies discussed so far emphasize this quantitative dimension. Teachers who wish to improve students' decoding abilities through these informal strategies must find ways to help them get lots of reading practice; that is, they have to engage them extensively in various "assisted" reading experiences. In addition, since reading is improved by reading, teachers will need to motivate children to read extensively on their own.

Motivation occurs within people. It is a feeling inside that influences them to behave in certain ways. Sometimes individuals might be concerned about an undesirable consequence they perceive might follow a behavior and therefore avoid it. Some individuals behave in certain ways because they perceive that something they want will follow the behavior. At still other times, people might be motivated to do things for others because they love them. These and other sources of influence on human behavior are referred to as *motivation variables*. The major motivation variables are concern, positive or negative feelings associated with tasks, interest, feedback, success, positive or negative consequences associated with behaviors (rewards or punishment), love, values, and perceptions. Teachers can use these sources of influence to encourage students to behave in specific ways. However, they cannot "force" or "control" students. No one really motivates anyone else in the sense that they *make them* "do things." All teachers, or anyone else for that matter, can do is *influence* individuals and hope for the best.

The most important sources of influence for literacy teachers to use are the motivational variables of feelings, success, feedback, interest, and reward. Children who do not read much have negative attitudes toward reading, and have a history of unsuccessful experiences with it (Quandt & Selznick, 1984). Children will want to read if (a) they have learned to associate positive feelings with reading; (b) are successful at reading; (c) receive feedback to reinforce those feelings of success; and (d) find reading personally interesting and rewarding. All of the informal decoding strategies discussed incorporate these motivational variables. Teachers using these informal strategies assist children to read until they experience success in independent reading, minimizing negative experiences generally associated with reading failure and enhancing feelings of success. Students have holistic, connected reading experiences with relevant text material so reading is interesting and rewarding to them.

The quality of the reading material provided for students is critical to motivation. Students will want to participate in reading activities if the content of those activities is relevant, interesting, and meaningful to them. It is important both to select appropriate material when reading with students, and to make available the very best books for children to choose to read by themselves.

Children's Literature

Selecting Books for Children to Read

Teachers have an important role to play in stocking classrooms with books easy enough for children to read independently. However, readability, while important, is not the primary criterion to use for book selection. The most important question to ask is, "Will children enjoy reading this book?" Books are meant to be read, and children find it difficult to stay away from books that are interesting and appealing to them.

Among the characteristics of a book that make it interesting and appealing to children are the type of book (mystery, humorous, informational, etc.), its content (dinosaurs, circus clowns, rocks, etc.), and its focus (conflict with other people, conflict with nature, etc.). Children have a variety of interests, and what is appealing to one child may not be appealing to another. If teachers stock their classrooms with books, dealing with a range of topics, they will more likely meet the diverse needs and interests of their students.

Other obvious aspects of books appeal to children besides type, content, and focus. For example, the physical features of a book—its cover and illustrations—are important to children. The book's characters, its plot, and the author's writing style are important as well. Authors of the best books use plot, characterization, setting, theme, style, and point of view to create stories that children will want to read many times. You will want to consult with librarians, children's literature specialists, and the list of children's book choices published yearly in *The Reading Teacher* to identify some of these special books.

A list of 235 books frequently used by primary-grade teachers is provided in Appendix D. The list is only an example, and is not meant to be either ideal or exhaustive. Readability estimates appear with each title. These estimates provide helpful information for teachers, but should never be viewed as sacred, infallible, or even as necessarily valid. In fact, educators should constantly remind themselves that all readability estimates from traditional formulas share three characteristics that render their credibility suspect: (a) they are based upon early notions about what makes a text difficult to read (word difficulty and sentence difficulty); (b) they do not include information about those reader variables (interest, background knowledge, motivation, etc.) that influence a reader's ability to comprehend text material; and (c) they are subject to the usual flaws associated with traditional methods of determining difficult words and sentences within the book.

Readability estimates obtained from traditional formulas may be inflated by unusual situations, such as the one found in Wendy Watson's *Lollipop* (Viking), whose readability estimate is 13.3. This is a delightful picture book that young children enjoy and find rather easy to read. A close examination reveals that the entire 25-page book is one sentence long. Each page contains a picture and a line of text. Each line of text contains a clause (sometimes two clauses) that the reader is able to read like a sentence (remember that clauses contain subjects and predicates). Each line of text, other than the first line, begins with the words *and, so,* or *but.* If a period is inserted after each line of text, the readability estimate obtained is 1.29, which more nearly reflects the difficulty of the text. If teachers know that estimates are based on sentence length and word difficulty they can visually scan books with questionable estimates to determine if and why those estimates might be "out of line."

Because of these limitations, each book on the list was also analyzed to determine the ratio of unique words to total words used in the book. For example, *Lollipop* contains 151 words, but there are only 62 unique words used in the entire book: *a, and, asked, asleep, began, bunny, but, cry, dark, did, door, down, finally, fell, for, gave, he, hear, heard, her, him, his, in, it, kept, kissed, let, lollipop, lollipops, mom, no, one, out, penny, piggybank, ran, said, sat, saw, she, so, someone, spanked, still, store, street, the, this, time, to, told, took, up, wanted, wanting, was, were, when, where, woke, worried,* and *you.* Some of these words are repeated multiple times. If the total words used in the book are divided by the number of unique words used, a ratio of unique words to total words is found. That ratio for *Lollipop* is 1:2.4, which means that if each unique word was repeated the same number of times as every other unique word used in the story, each word would be repeated an average of 2.4 times. Difficulty level is not only affected by the percentage of difficult words and average sentence length, but also by the number of unique words, the difficulty of those words, and the number of times they are repeated. For example, in *Lollipop*, 52 of the 62 unique words (84%) are easy words, according to the Spache and Dall Chall readability formulas. (Only the words *asked, kissed, lollipop, lollipops, mom, piggybank, spanked, wanted, wanting*, and *worried* were considered difficult.)

Readability estimates plus unique-to-total-word-ratio data, when combined, give teachers more insight into the difficulty level of books. For example, the books *Daniel's Duck,* *"Quack," Said the Billy Goat, Q Is For Duck, Wet Cats*, and *This Is Bear* all have readability estimates of 1.0. However, the unique-to-total word ratios for those books are 1:4, 1:1.55, 1:2.65, 1:1.85, and 1:2.18, respectively. The ratio differences are significant, and are probably important readability factors. Word repetitions are particularly important when using assisted reading strategies; the more often readers see words while hearing them pronounced, the more quickly they store their letter sequences in lexical memory.

Decoding Is Improved by Reading Good Literature

The amount of time children spend reading may be the most important factor in reading achievement. Children who read extensively become better readers and decoders than children who do not read much. Once basic letter–sound relationships have been taught, students need repeated opportunities to read to increase their familiarity with written words so they can be recognized rapidly and automatically. Students' decoding abilities are improved through reading practice, and the evidence for this proposition is convincing (Reitsma, 1988; Barron, 1986; Gough & Hillinger, 1980; Perfetti, 1985; Reitsma, 1983; Seidenberg, 1985). Therefore, one of the most effective ways to improve students' decoding abilities is to stock the classroom with interesting books, allow students to select books they want to read, provide time for them to read, encourage them to read, and provide opportunities for them to share what they have read with others.

Reading provides enjoyment, adventure, excitement, knowledge, and therapy. It helps children cope with the problems they face in life because they can read about others who have problems similar to their own and vicariously share in the solutions to those problems. Reading helps children learn about the human condition because they are able to objectively examine the consequences of people's moral and amoral actions through books. Literature transmits knowledge in a powerful way. It nurtures and expands children's imaginations, and it stimulates their language, personality, social, and cognitive growth. When teachers make good literature available for children, and help them discover the treasures waiting to be found therein, reading will become a lifetime habit for them.

Relating Phonics Instruction to Holistic Literature Experiences

You can relate your phonics instruction to children's holistic reading activities in several ways. Phonics instruction may involve the book's title only, or may incorporate many of the words found in the book. All lessons should take no more than 10 minutes of classroom time.

The following principles are important to remember:

1. Phonics instruction should be process or strategy oriented instead of skills oriented; you should teach it to students so they can use the knowledge acquired to identify unfamiliar written words.
2. Instruction should help students associate graphemes with the phonemes they represent.
3. Students should learn to isolate sounds represented by graphemes without distorting them.
4. Phonics instruction should help students blend word sounds without distorting them so they may identify written words by a sensible sounding-out process.

Using Book Titles for Phonics Activities. After you and your students share an enjoyable encounter with a book (through either a group assisted reading or shared book experience), you may use the title of the book to teach or reinforce phonics knowledge.

Model Lesson. Literature book: *The Very Hungry Caterpillar,* by Eric Carle (Puffin Books, 1985). Grouping format: Dyads.
Materials needed:

1. Eleven 1-inch blank paper squares for each student team (dyad). You may prepare these squares in advance or give students a sheet of paper and show them how to fold it and cut (or tear) it as needed.
2. Eleven lettered squares containing the following letters:

c a t e r p i l l a r

These squares must be large enough for all of the children in the classroom to see. They may be magnetic letters that stick to a magnet board, tagboard squares with tape on the back to stick on the chalkboard, or squares made from a transparency to place on an overhead projector and projected on a screen.
Approach:

1. Form student dyads.
2. Distribute eleven blank paper squares to each student team or distribute blank sheets and have students make the squares.
3. Write the word *caterpillar* on the chalkboard.
4. Read the word to the children if they cannot read it themselves. Ask them to write each letter in the word on one of their squares.
5. After lettering the squares, ask each student team to put the squares together to spell the word *caterpillar.* Spell the word with your lettered squares so the students can check their work against your model.
6. Ask the student teams to take a letter out of the word that stands for the /a/ sound. After each team responds, display the *a* square to reinforce their correct responses, or to help those teams self-correct who may have made an error.
7. Ask the student teams to take a letter out of the word that stands for the /t/ sound, and to put it with the letter *a* to make the word *at.* After each team responds, place your *t* after the *a* to make the word *at.*

8. Continue this activity, moving and replacing letters, to make the following words:

cat	*cell*	*ape*	*eat*
rat	*call*	*car*	*treat*
rate	*tall*	*cart*	
ate	*all*	*part*	*pal*
late	*ail*	*tart*	
plate	*pail*	*tar*	*lip*
pat	*tail*	*art*	*tip*
pit	*rail*	*rare*	*rip*
pet	*trail*	*care*	*trip*
let	*lap*		
lit	*tap*	*pear*	
it	*rap*		
ill	*trap*	*pie*	
pill	*cap*	*tie*	
till	*cape*	*lie*	
tell	*tape*		

Using Words in Literature Books for Phonics Instruction. After you and your students read a book together, you may also tie your phonics lessons to the words used in the book. Again, these lessons should be brief, occupying no more than 10 minutes of classroom time.

There seemingly is no end to the phonics lesson possibilities available from just one literature book, as most if not all of the phonics elements and patterns described in Chapter 8 are found naturally in children's literature. If you elect to teach students the phonics knowledge they need to be effective readers and writers through the books you read with them, you should follow some systematic approach. The following sequence is recommended for teachers who have not developed a systematic plan for the teaching of phonics elements and patterns: short vowel sounds, initial consonant sounds, syllable patterns affecting vowel sounds, vowel team sounds, final consonant sounds, consonant digraph sounds, consonant blends, and *y* as a vowel (see Chapter 8).

Model Lesson. We use here Harry Allard's *I Will Not Go to Market Today* (Dial, 1992) to demonstrate the phonics lesson possibilities contained in just one children's literature book. The book contains words that include the following sounds:

Short Vowel Sounds

a   *am, an, and, as, ask, at, jam, had, last, that, bag, bath*
e   *bed, fell, get, leg, next, rest, well, went*
i   *him, his, if, it, in, did, six, will, with*
o   *fog, hot, not, off, stop*
u   *but, just, must, run, up, luck*

Initial Consonant Sounds

b   *bag, bath, bed, but, by*
d   *day, did, down*
f   *fell, fibbed, fog, foot, for, forced, found*
g   *get, go, good*
h   *had, he, heat, him, his, home, hot, house*
j   *jam, jar, just*
l   *laid, last, late, leg, like, looked, luck*
m   *made, mean, must, my*
n   *next, night, nine, no, not*
r   *rest, right, road, run*
s   *seem, six, so*
t   *tea, teeth, toast, too*
w   *wave, well, went, will, with*

Syllable Patterns Affecting Vowel Sounds

Closed Syllable

bag, bath, bed, did, but, fell, will, fog, him, jam, leg, next, run, with, get, his, just, luck, not, six, had, hot, last, must, rest, well

Open Syllable

go, no, so, he, my, by

Vowel-Consonant-*e*

made, wave, time, home, nine, late, like, shake, stile

Vowel Team Sounds

oa   *coast, road, toast*
ea   *heat, mean, tea, screamed*
ea   *heavy, weather, weatherman*
ee   *seem, teeth, peeked*
or   *for, forced,*
ou   *found, house, out*
ow   *down, however*
igh   *night, night's, right*
ar   *jar, yard*
oo   *foot, good, looked, tootsies*
oo   *too*
ay   *day*
ai   *laid*
er   *clerk, perfect*

Final Consonant Sounds

m   *am, him, jam, seem, time*
n   *an, in, mean, mine, nine, run*

t	*at, but, foot, get, it, late*
g	*bag, fog, leg*
d	*bed, did, good, had, laid, made, road, yard*
l	*fell, well, will, stile*
t	*heat, hot, not, out*
f	*if, off*
x	*six*
p	*stop, up*

Consonant Digraph Sounds

tch	*kitchen*
ng	*sang*
th	*with, bath, teeth*
th	*that, this*

Consonant Blends

bl	*blew, blocks, blizzard*
br	*broke, brushed*
cl	*clear, clerk*
dr	*dreaming*
fr	*from, front*
st	*steps, stop, stile*
tr	*traffic*
ck	*luck*
nd	*and*
nt	*front, went*
st	*just, last, must, rest*
xt	*next*

Y as a Vowel

by, my

The following sample lesson uses those words containing the short vowel sound /a/.

1. Write the following words on the chalkboard: *am, an, and, as, ask, at, jam, had, last, that, bag, bath.* Say, "These words were used in the story, *I Will Not Go To Market Today.* Notice that all of the words contain the vowel letter *a.*" Touch the letter *a* in each of the words.
2. Focus the children's attention on the first six words (those that begin with the vowel sound): *am, an, and, as, ask, at.* Say, "Let's read the first six words." Touch each word as you read it with the students.
3. Underline the *a* in each of the first six words. Say, "Can you hear the /a/ sound at the beginning of each of these words? Listen for the /a/ sound as I read them again." Read the words again, and as you read each one touch the letter *a* and isolate the vowel sound /a/ before you add the sounds represented by the consonant(s) that follow it. Say, "Did you notice that the sounds in each of these

words are represented by letters? In the word *am* the letter *a* stands for the /a/ sound and the letter *m* stands for the /m/ sound. Say the sounds in each of these words with me as I touch the letters that stand for those sounds." Say the sounds in each word with the students as you touch the appropriate letters.

4. Say, "Notice that the letter *a* in each of these words is followed by one or more consonant sounds. When this happens the sound represented by the letter *a* will usually be /a/."

5. Say, "If you don't recognize written words or cannot identify them using context clues, you can use your phonics knowledge to sound them out. When you sound out words, follow these steps:
   a. Look at the vowel in the word, identify its sound, and say it.
   b. Blend the consonant sounds that come before the vowel with the vowel sound.
   c. Isolate the consonant sound(s) that follow the vowel.
   d. Blend all of the sounds together so the word can be identified.
   Let's use that process to sound out the other six words used in our story." Focus the students' attention on the last six words: *jam, had, last, that, bag, bath.* Point to the letter *a* in the word *jam.* Say, "What is the sound of this letter?" Wait for a response. Say, "When we blend the letter *j* with the /a/ sound, we get /ja/." Point to the letters *ja* in the word *jam.* "Say /ja/." Wait for a response. Say, "The letter *m* in the word (point to the letter) stands for the /m/ sound. Say /m/." Wait for a response. Say, "Blend /ja/ and /m/ together and identify the word." Wait for a response. Repeat this process with the remaining five words: *had, last, that, bag, bath.*

6. Write the following sentences on the chalkboard: *But Fenimore <u>had</u> not gone two blocks before he found himself caught in a <u>traffic</u> <u>jam</u>. "This isn't the <u>jam</u> I <u>had</u> in mind,"* *he said.* Say, "These sentences are taken from the story we read today. Notice that the underlined words contain the letter *a.* Let's read these sentences together and when we get to the underlined words, let's identify them by their sounds." Read the sentences with the students and have them sound out the underlined words.

Note: Since students at this age would probably be unfamiliar with syllabication, sound out the first syllable in the word *traffic,* and say the second one with or for them. It helps students begin to grasp syllabication principles if you rewrite the word *traffic,* placing a hyphen within the word to separate the two syllables: *traf-fic.*

The Language Experience Approach (LEA)

The Language Experience Approach (LEA) to reading has been used effectively in classrooms for years. This strategy can be traced to the old sentence and story methods popular in the middle of the nineteenth century, the experience story material in the progressive education movement of the 1930s, and the work of Roach Van Allen in the late 1950s (Hall, 1981).

The rationale behind LEA is that what children say can be written down and read. It uses children's oral language productions to help them bridge oral and written language. Since vocabulary, syntax patterns, and schema all originate from the child when using this approach, the written material produced is considered easier for children to read and comprehend than text material produced by someone else. As children see the words they speak written, they are able to focus on each word's letter sequences, a task necessary for word recognition. As they read their written compositions, and study the words used in those compositions, word recognition abilities are further enhanced.

Follow the listed steps when using the LEA with a group of children:

1. *Provide a common experience for the group.* Examples: read a story to them, take them on a trip to the bakery, or have a cooking experience in the classroom.

2. *Talk, write, and read about the experience with the group.* Example:
   a. Ask questions about the experience. (After reading the story, *The Stonecutter*, you might ask, "Why do you think the stonecutter trembled at the end of the story?")
   b. The students respond to your questions, and you write the statements made by individual children on a large sheet of paper that can be read by the entire class. Write each child's statement with a different color of chalk or felt-tipped pen so students can remember who said what. Another approach is to begin each statement with the speaker's name: "Michelle said. . . ."
   c. Read each sentence after it is written and ask the child who dictated the sentence to read it.
   d. After writing all student statements, read the story aloud once or twice to the children, emphasizing left-to-right progression using a sweeping hand movement. After reading the story, ask questions to individual children, such as, "Whose sentence is the blue one? Nicole, can you read it?" Children take turns reading the story, a line at a time, or even the entire story in some cases. Help with the rereading as much as needed.

3. *Study individual words in the story.* Write separately on the chalkboard words used in the dictated story to study so the children can eventually recognize them in isolation; or make devices to frame individual words in the story for study, while blocking out other words that might provide contextual clues.

4. *Make tagboard word cards, phrase cards, and sentence cards for children to study.* Provide individual children, or student teams, with cards containing story words, phrases or sentences to be matched with those found in the story. Copy the individual story sentences on sentence strips for children to reassemble in proper order.

5. *Make copies of the story.* Type the story, using a primary typewriter, or computer. (When typing the story on the computer, select a large font.) Make enough copies of the story so each child has a copy from which to work. Ask children to illustrate the story and encourage them to read their illustrated stories to others (students, other teachers, or parents). As children read their copies of the story, ask them to underline the words they are able to recognize by sight. Have each child print each word underlined on a small card, to be filed in an

individual word bank for use in building sentences, playing word games, or phonics instruction later on.

Using the LEA with Individual Children

After students have worked in groups for a time, you may wish to give them opportunities to dictate their individual stories or experiences. The motivation for these written records or stories will come from family trips or vacations, a pet, a gift, a holiday, or a reaction to a movie or TV show.

During dictation, you may ask leading questions, but should be careful not to structure children's written work. After children dictate their stories or experiences, read aloud what you have written. Later the documents will be read, with adult help, by the children who dictated them. Eventually, the children should be able to read their own compositions without assistance.

Because of the time involved in transcribing individual work, you may wish to use aides, parent volunteers, or older children to transcribe children's compositions.

The Writing Process

Writing is considered to be an integral component of "holistic" classrooms. Children write daily for intrinsic purposes, on personally relevant topics. Since content is considered more important than form, teachers encourage children to write anything they can say even when they don't know how to spell the words they want to use. If children are unsure about a word's spelling, they try to spell it by its sounds, using invented spelling. When children attempt to spell words as they write, they are constantly reflecting on the relationships between word sounds and letters. These kinds of writing experiences contribute significantly to an understanding of the relationships between spoken and written language, which improves students' decoding abilities. Researchers have found writing to have a positive influence on the word recognition ability of young children, especially when they were encouraged to write using invented spelling (Clarke, 1988; Tierney & Shanahan, 1991).

Some level of phonemic awareness and phonics knowledge is necessary before children can begin to write with invented spellings. Then, as children continue to write words they can't spell, segmenting them into phonemes and assigning letters to those phonemes, their phonemic awareness abilities, phonics knowledge, and word recognition increase through the experience (see Chapter 3).

Will children's normal exposures to the written language in both their home and school environments be sufficient for them to develop the phonemic awareness and phonics knowledge needed to begin writing with invented spellings naturally, or should teachers help students write words by sounds? Although educators are presently divided on this issue, the more popular position seems to be that the ability to use invented spelling develops naturally in most children. Proponents present evidence to support their position from studies of children's early writing indicating that many children go through predictable writing stages.

Children come to school with varying degrees of knowledge about the written language, knowledge they have acquired through their exposures to print in the home and community. Many of them have already experimented with writing by the time they enter school. These early preschool experiences are immediately followed by writing experiences in school, since writing is a normal part of the daily curriculum in most kindergarten and first-grade classrooms. Researchers studying children's early writing (from prekindergarten through grade two) have concluded that most of them pass through predictable writing stages that reflect varying levels of understanding of the alphabetic principle. Different researchers have given these stages different labels, but the descriptions of those stages are fairly consistent.

The term *invented spelling* describes children's spellings before they learn the orthographic (spelling) system of the language. The first writing stage, the *precommunicative* or *prephonemic* stage, is characterized by the random use of letters. At this stage, children string letters together so their writing looks something like it should, but the letters do not relate in any way to the sounds they represent. Children at this stage are generally always nonreaders, but they know that words are represented by letters.

During the second stage, the *semiphonetic* or *early phonemic* stage, children begin to realize the connection between letters in written words and sounds in spoken ones. However, at this stage they write letters for only one or two sounds in a word, either the beginning, or the beginning and ending. For example, the word *dog* might be spelled *d,* or *dg.*

During the third writing stage, the *phonetic, phonemic,* or *letter-name* stage, vowels begin to appear in children's invented spellings. It is at this stage that children consistently try to break words into their phonemes and represent them with letters. Children often choose letters to represent phonemes on the basis of their letter-name sounds. They try to match each phoneme in a word with one alphabet letter, perceiving a one-to-one match between word sounds and letters.

The letter-name spelling stage is a time when children's concept of a written word is beginning to stabilize:

> Children who produce letter-name spelling have developed a system of spelling that can be read by others who understand the system. Letter-name spelling represents the high-water mark of children's intuitive spelling development, and their spellings during this period are their most original. From this point on, children will become increasingly aware of the details of standard spelling, and their spelling will grow closer to that of adults.
>
> Most children become letter-name spellers by Thanksgiving in first grade. Some begin sooner, and several may wait until late first grade to start using the letter-name strategy. Letter-name spellings will persist into second grade, though most second graders will use transitional strategies, especially in the second half of the year. (Temple, Nathan, Temple, & Burris, 1993, p. 113)

Children begin letter-name spelling before they begin to recode words since they acquire the ability to spell words by sounds before they are able to read words by sounds (Bryant & Bradley, 1980; Huxford, Terrell, & Bradley, 1991). Evidently the ability to segment sounds in words and match them with letters is easier for children than blending sounds in written words. However, phonemic spelling seems to be an indicator that children will profit from recoding instruction.

During the fourth, or *transitional*, writing stage, children abandon the habit of trying to match each phoneme in a word with one letter. They recognize that sometimes word sounds are represented by chunks of letters. They begin to include silent letters, and incorporate spelling patterns in their spellings (silent *e* to represent long vowel sounds, etc.), but not consistently. Words with irregular spellings are often misspelled. Children at the transitional stage are readers.

The last stage is called the *correct* or *conventional* stage. Even though children at this stage misspell words, they have learned enough about English orthography to spell a large number of words correctly, even many of the irregularly spelled ones.

Do all children invent spelling? Probably not. "If every child spontaneously wrote out invented spelling at the kitchen table, the phenomenon would be as widely known a writing behavior as baby talk is a speech behavior. But they don't and it's not. Many children do not explore writing before they enter school, and there they usually practice writing only words they have memorized" (Temple et al., 1993, p. 79).

Although we know much about children's writing stages, there is still much to learn. Many questions are unanswered about the factors influencing children's writing development. What causes children to move from one developmental stage to another? Can teachers help children move through developmental stages by using intervention strategies? If so, what kinds of intervention strategies are most effective?

Application Activities

1. Find a reader who does not decode well. Identify a book this reader wants to read, but cannot read independently. Using the dyad reading strategy described in this chapter, read the book with the student for 20 minutes a day, over 5 or 6 days. Discuss and evaluate the experience with the student when the activity is completed.

2. Suppose four literature books had unique-to-total word ratios of 1:4, 1:8, 1:2.5, and 1:1, respectively. In which book would the words used be repeated most frequently? Which book would be best suited for group assisted reading? Why?

3. How many words can you make from the letters used in the title, *Make Way for Ducklings*?

4. Analyze a preschool or kindergarten child's written composition. Which writing stage is the child in?
   a. precommunicative or prephonemic
   b. semiphonetic or early phonemic
   c. phonetic, phonemic, or letter-name
   d. transitional
   e. correct or conventional
   Justify your conclusion.

Chapter 10

Teaching Phonics in Ten Minutes a Day

In the previous chapter, we discussed strategies for teaching phonics in the context of children's meaningful reading experiences. In this chapter, we present strategies for teaching phonics as a brief, but separate and isolated, activity. Although the present sentiment among some educators is against teaching phonics "out of context," there are legitimate reasons for ignoring that censure. Critics of isolated phonics instruction argue that it is ineffective and meaningless to children, and that children dislike it, but offer little evidence against "out of context" phonics instruction other than personal reasoning generated from a whole language philosophical perspective. On the other hand, research findings (Eldredge & Butterfield, 1986; Eldredge, 1988–1989; Eldredge, 1991) reveal that brief, isolated phonics instruction in an otherwise predominantly holistic environment improves children's reading achievement; helps them understand how print and speech are related; and is associated with positive attitudes toward reading rather than negative ones. In fact, "out of context" phonics instruction may actually make it possible for children to have better experiences with literature, since their experience is not encumbered with a phonics component. However, making the decision to teach phonics in or out of context is a choice that, as a teacher, you must make for yourself. We describe both approaches in this book. The features of effective phonics instruction noted in Chapter 4 are more important to successful instruction than whether you teach phonics in or out of "context."

Effective phonics instruction does not need to absorb much classroom time. You can teach each of the lesson models presented in this chapter to large or small groups of children in no more than 10 minutes. Many holistic teachers presently using them teach one lesson per day (short vowel lessons excepted) to all of the children at one time, and complete their instruction in about 7 minutes.

Young children need two types of experiences with written language to become fully literate individuals. They need personally relevant reasons to use it, and they need to be involved in metalinguistic awareness activities to help them understand how it works. Children need to be involved in holistic reading and writing experiences, and they need to understand the spelling–sound system that underlies these experiences. Effective phonics instruction provides the metalinguistic experiences children need to become literate individuals.

The 10-minute phonics lessons described in this chapter support the efforts of holistic teachers by helping them teach children how the alphabetic system works. Using these lessons, holistic teachers may allocate more classroom time for children to enjoy other reading and writing activities:

1. engage in shared book experiences, taped assisted reading, dyad reading, and group assisted reading
2. write on topics relevant to them
3. read extensively (magazines, books, and other text material)
4. explore topics of interest
5. engage in other practices consistent with holistic classrooms (see Chapter 1)

Phonics Lessons

The phonics elements and patterns described in Chapter 8 are taught in the lessons presented in this chapter. In keeping with this text's intent to teach phonics as a strategy for children to use rather than skills for them to learn, the following lessons are designed to help students develop and use a strategy for "sounding out" words. However, as important as word identification strategies are to nonfluent readers, the major benefits young readers will reap from these lessons will be increased understanding of how the spoken language maps onto the written language, and increased ability to access written words into lexical memory (see Chapter 4).

When teaching these lessons, you will utilize the principles of social mediation and scaffolding discussed in Chapter 7. You will be interacting with the children, acting as mediators for them, when needed, as they interact with the written text. In the initial lessons, you will do the majority of the lesson tasks with children, while they do only a small number of tasks independently. In the later lessons they will need less assistance.

All of the lessons are "strategy oriented." Phonics elements and patterns are introduced systematically, in the following order:

1. short vowel sounds
2. initial consonant sounds
3. vowel principles (determining vowel sounds by syllable pattern)
4. vowel teams (determining vowel sounds by letter clusters)
5. final consonant sounds
6. consonant digraph sounds
7. consonant blends (two alternate approaches)
8. the letter *y* as a vowel

The lessons progress in the following steps. While every lesson does not contain all steps, the steps for each lesson follow the same order:

1. association
2. synthesizing
3. application (sentences)
4. word formation

5. word discrimination
6. dictation
7. advanced synthesizing

> *Note:* In each step of a lesson, except dictation, you are asked to write something on the chalkboard needed for that step. We have organized the lessons this way to help you better visualize how what you say in the lesson step relates to what you write on the chalkboard. When teaching the lessons to children, however, you should write on the board everything needed for all of the lesson steps before you begin each lesson.

Word lists for all of the phonics lessons are found in Appendix E.

Short Vowel Sounds

The six steps in a short vowel lesson are designed to help students (a) learn to associate the appropriate sounds with specific vowel letters, and (b) learn to identify written words by sounds.

Association. Write the words *am, at, an,* and *add* on the chalkboard. Underline the letter *a* in each of the words, and say, "Notice that each word I have written on the chalkboard begins with the same letter. Each word also begins with the same sound. Listen carefully to the words as I read them to see if you can hear the /a/ sound at the beginning of each one." As you read each word point to the letter *a* and emphasize the /a/ sound.

Point to the word *am.* Say, "Listen as I say the two sounds in the word *am.*" Point to the appropriate letters as you say the two sounds, and then glide your finger under both letters as you say the word: "/a/ /m/—/am/." Say the two sounds in the word *am,* pointing to the appropriate letters: "/a/ /m/—/am/." Say, "The letter *a* (point to the letter) in the word *am* stands for the /a/ sound." Keep pointing to the letter *a* in the word *am.* "Say /a/." Wait for a response. Point to the appropriate letters as you continue. "Say /a/ /m/—/am/." Wait for a response. Repeat this process with the words *at, an,* and *add.*

Synthesizing. Write the words *ask, and,* and *ant* on the chalkboard. Point to the letter *a* in each of the words. Say, "You know the sound of this letter. We are going to identify each of these words by their sounds. You say the sound of the letter *a* in each of the words, and I will say the sounds after the letter *a.* After you hear all of the sounds in a word, blend them together quickly in your mind, and tell me what the word is."

Point to the letter *a* in the word *ask.* Say, "Say the sound of this letter." Wait for a response. Say, "The last two letters in the word (point to the letters *sk*) stand for the /sk/ sound. What is the word?" Wait for a response. Repeat the process above with the words *and* and *ant.*

Application (Sentences). Write the following sentence on the chalkboard: *That man can dance fast.* Say, "I taught you to isolate the /a/ sound at the beginning of words because it's easier to hear it there. However, most of the time the /a/ sound will be found in the middle of words." Point to the letter *a* in each of the words in the sentence on the chalkboard. Say, "If you do not recognize written words, and if you cannot identify them using context clues, then you can sound them out by doing the following:

1. Say the vowel sound of the word.
2. Blend the sound of the letter or letters before the vowel *with* the vowel sound.
3. Say the sound of the letter or letters after the vowel.
4. Put all of the sounds together to identify the word."

Say, "Let's see if we can sound out the words in this sentence." Point to the letter *a* in the word *That*. "What is the sound of this letter?" Wait for the students to respond with the appropriate sound. Point to the letters *Tha* in the word *That*. Say, "In this word the letters *T, h, a* say /tha/." Point to the letter *t* at the end of the word. Say, "In this word the letter *t* comes after the vowel and the sound of *t* is /t/." Say, "When you blend the sounds /tha/ and /t/ together, what word do you get?" Wait for a response. Continue this process with all of the words in the sentence, and then ask the students to read the entire sequence as quickly as they can.

Word Formation. Write the following on the chalkboard: _*n*. Run your finger under the _ and the *n* while you say, "This word is /a/ /n/. What sound is missing?" Wait for a response. "What letter is missing?" Wait for a response. Repeat this process with _*m*, _*dd*, _*ct*.

Word Discrimination. Write the following on the chalkboard:

> *at*
> *it*

Point to the letter *t* in both *at* and *it*. Say, "What letter is the same in these two words?" Wait for a response. Point to the letters *i* and *a* in *it* and *at*. Say, "What letters are different?" Wait for a response. Say, "What sounds are different?" Point to the letter *a* in the word *at*. Wait for the students to say /a/. Point to the letter *i* in the word *it*. "The sound of this letter is /i/." Point to *a*. Say, "Say /a/." Wait for a response. Point to *i*. Say, "Say /i/." Wait for a response. "The ending sound in these words is /t/. What is the first word?" Wait for a response. "What is the second word?" Wait for a response. Repeat this process with other word pairs: *an, on; add, odd,* and so on.

Dictation. Provide the students with "magic" slate boards, small chalkboards, or scrap paper to write on. Say, "Write the letter that stands for the /a/ sound that you hear at the beginning of the word /a/ /sk/. At the count of three hold up what you have written. one . . . two . . . three." Scan the room to assess the accuracy of individual responses. Write the letter *a* on the chalkboard. Say, "Most of you have written the letter *a* on your paper. The letter *a* stands for the /a/ sound we hear at the beginning of the word *ask*." Write the letters *sk* after the *a* as you say the word *ask*. Repeat this process with the words *at, add,* and *am*.

Beginning Consonant Sounds

The seven steps in a beginning consonant lesson are designed to help students (a) learn to associate the appropriate sounds with specific consonant letters; (b) learn to blend beginning consonant sounds in words with the vowel sounds that follow them; and (c) learn to identify words by sounds.

Association. Write the words *wax, with, west,* and *wish* on the chalkboard. Underline the letter *w* in each of the words, and say, "Notice that each word I have written on the chalkboard begins with the same letter. Each word also begins with the same sound. Listen carefully to the words as I read them to see if you can hear how they sound alike at the beginning." As you read each word, point to the letter *w*.

Point to the letter *a* in the word *wax*. Say, "You know the /a/ sound in the word *wax*. When you blend the /w/ sound with the /a/ sound you get /wa/. Listen as I say the word *wax* in two parts." Point to the appropriate letters as you say the sounds, and then glide your finger under all the letters as you say, "/wa/ /ks/— /waks/. Say the word *wax* in two parts." Point to the appropriate letters. "/wa/ ks/—/waks/. The letters *w* and *a* in the word *wax* stand for the /wa/ sound." Point to the letters. Keep pointing to the letters *wa* in the word *wax*. Say, "Say /wa/." Wait for a response. Point to the appropriate letters as you continue. "Say /wa/ /ks/— /waks/." Wait for a response. Repeat this process with the words *with, west,* and *wish*.

Synthesizing. Write the words *wag, win, web,* and *wind* on the chalkboard. Say, "We are going to identify these words by their sounds." Point to the vowel letters in each word and say, "You know the vowel sounds in each of these words. Say the vowel sound in each word first. Then blend the sound of *w* with the vowel sound, and then I will say the sound or sounds after the vowel. After you hear all of the sounds in the word, blend them together quickly in your mind, and tell me what the word is."

Point to the letter *a* in the word *wag*. "Say the sound of this letter." Wait for a response. Point to the letters *wa* in the word *wag*. "Say the sound of the first two letters." Wait for a response. Point to the letter *g*. "The last letter in the word says /g/. What is the word?" Wait for a response. Repeat the process above with the words *win, web,* and *wind*.

Application (Sentences). Write the following sentence on the chalkboard: *The witch of the west wept.* Say, "We will read the underlined words in this sentence and sound out the words that are not underlined." Point to the first word and read it with the students. Point to the letter *i* in the word *witch*. Say, "Say the sound of this letter." Wait for a response. Point to the letters *wi* in the word *witch*. "Say the sound of the first two letters." Wait for a response. Point to the letters *tch*. Say, "The last three letters in the word say /ch/. What is the word?" Wait for a response. Continue this process with all of the words in the sentence, and then ask the students to read the entire sentence as quickly as they can.

Word Formation. Write the following on the chalkboard: _ _*pt*. Run your finger under the _ _ and the *pt* while you say, " This word is /we/ /pt/. What sound is missing?" Wait for a response. "What letters are missing?" Wait for a response. Repeat this process using the words: *wish, west, web,* and *witch*.

Word Discrimination. Write the following on the chalkboard:

west

test

Point to the letters *est* in both *west* and *test*. Say, "What letters are alike in these two words?" Wait for a response. Point to the letters *w* and *t* in *west* and *test*. Say, "What letters are different?" Wait for a response. "What sounds are different?" Point to the letters *we* in the word *west*. Wait for the students to say /we/. Point to the letters *te* in the word *test*. Say, "These letter sounds are /te/." Point to *we*, then to *te*. Say, "Say /we/ and /te/." Wait for a response. "The ending sound in these words is /st/. What is the first word?" Wait for a response. "What is the second word?" Wait for a response. Repeat this process with word pairs: *will, hill; wept, kept; wed, bed*.

Dictation. Provide the students with "magic" slate boards, small chalkboards, or scrap paper to write on. Say, "Write the two letters that stand for the /wi/ sound that you hear at the beginning of the word /wi/ /th/. At the count of three hold up what you have written. One . . . two . . . three." Scan the room to assess the accuracy of individual responses. Write the letters *wi* on the chalkboard. Say, "Most of you have written the letters *w* and *i* on your paper. The letters *w* and *i* stand for the /wi/ sound we hear at the beginning of the word *with*." Write the letters *th* after the *wi* as you say the word *with*. Repeat this process with the words *wept* and *wish*.

Advanced Synthesizing. Write the word *wade* on the chalkboard. Point to the letter *a* in the word *wade*. Say, "In this word this letter says /ā/." Glide your finger under the letters *wa* in the word *wade*. Say, "What is the sound of the first two letters?" Wait for a response. Point to the letters *de* in the word *wade*. Say, "The last two letters say /d/. What is the word?" Wait for a response. Continue this process with the words *waist, wait, wake, wave, way, we, weak, week, weed, weep, wide, wife, wipe, wood, wool*.

Vowel Principles

Write the words *jump* and *robin* on the chalkboard. Point to the *u* in the word *jump*. Say, "Words that have one vowel sound are one-syllable words." Point to the letters *o* and *i* in the word *robin*. Say, "Words that have two vowel sounds are two-syllable words." Rewrite the word *robin*, adding a space between the syllables: *rob in*. Point to the *rob*, and then point to the *in*. Say, "A syllable is the part of the word that contains one vowel sound. The word *robin* is a two-syllable word." Point to *rob*. "This syllable says /rob/." Point to *in*. "This syllable says /un/."

Write the word *men* on the chalkboard. Point to the letter *e* in the word *men*. "The vowel sound in the word *men* is /e/. Whenever a single vowel word or syllable ends with consonant letters, the vowel says its short sound. Another way of saying this principle is, if a vowel letter is followed by one or more consonants that vowel is 'protected' and says its calm short sound—the sound you have already learned."

Write the word *me* on the chalkboard right under the word *men*. Point to the letter *e* in the word *me*. Say, "Whenever a single vowel word or syllable does not end with consonant letters, the vowel says its long sound. Another way of saying this principle is, if a vowel letter is not followed by consonant letters that vowel is 'unprotected' and says its long sound. The vowel's long sound is its own name. For example, the long sound of *a* is /ā/. Unprotected vowels yell out in frustration and say their own names because they are not protected by consonants." Point to the letter *e* in the word *me*. Say, "In this word the vowel sound is /ē/ and the word is *me*."

Continue this discussion of open (unprotected) vowels and closed (protected) vowels and syllables using the following words:

on	*it*	*at*	*up*
so	*pi-lot*	*ba-con*	*fu-ture*

Write the word *cap* on the chalkboard. Point to the letter *a* in the word *cap*. Say, "What is the vowel sound in this word?" Wait for a response. "The vowel letter *a* says /a/ because it is a protected vowel."

Write the word *cape* on the chalkboard underneath the word *cap*. Point to the letter *a* in the word *cape*. Say, "The vowel letter *a* in the word *cape* has a consonant (point to the *p*) after it to protect it, but the vowel letter *e* (point to the letter) has no protector. Guess what happens in these types of words? The letter *a* cries out and says his own name /ā/ because it is worried about his vowel friend *e*. His friend *e* doesn't say anything. We call this syllable a lonely *e* syllable. Whenever you see a vowel in a lonely *e* word or syllable, give the vowel its long sound."

Continue this discussion of closed syllables and vowel-consonant-*e* syllables using the following words:

us	*it*	*end*	*odd*
use	*ice*	*eve*	*ode*

Write the words *not, no,* and *note* on the chalkboard. Say, "Let me summarize what we have learned today. There are three types of word or syllable patterns." Point to the word *not*. "There is the protected vowel syllable." Point to the word *no*. "There is the unprotected vowel syllable." Point to the word *note*. "There is the lonely *e* syllable." Point to the vowel in the word *not*. "Protected vowels say their short sounds." Point to the vowel in the word *no*. "Unprotected vowels and (point to the vowel in the word *note*) vowels in lonely *e* syllables say their long sounds."

Synthesizing. Ask students to say the vowel sounds in the following words, tell you why they chose the sounds they chose, and identify the words by sounds. When blending sounds in polysyllabic words, ask students to sound out the first syllable only. You sound out the second syllable for them.

ate, ba-by, bake, back, ba-sic, ape, came, fame, age, ba-con, cap, cape, fan, da-ta, cat, cage, fa-vor, fat, fate, la-ter, face, fast, la-dy, safe, sat, la-bor, eve, be-came, he, hen, be-gan, wed, we, fete, ce-dar, tweed, fled, flee, get, ce-ment, beg, bee, e-ven, trend, tree, fe-ver, bed, be, hem, he, yet, ye, fret, free, she, shed, gee, spree, three, thresh, when, whee, ice, ci-der, bite, bit, wife, di-ver, bike, line, fi-ber, lid, time, i-cy, wide, size, li-lac, sit, side, bone, bo-ny, owe, cone, co-bra, rock, rope, do-nate, sob, so, fo-cus, poke, ho-ly, pond, pop, lo-cal, doze, dog, lo-cate, go, got, log, lo, fro, frost, pro, prod, tho, use, hu-mor, cut, cute, mu-sic, mule, mud, pu-pil, fuse, fuss, u-nit, ute, fume, fun

Note: Six phonograms violate the closed (protected) vowel principle: *ost, old, oll, olt, ind,* and *ild.* We call these phonograms "foolers."

ost	old	oll	olt	ind	ild
post	bold	toll	bolt	bind	wild
most	cold	roll	colt	wind	mild
ghost	told	poll	jolt	mind	child
host	sold	stroll		rind	
	mold	troll		hind	
	gold			kind	
	hold			find	
	fold			grind	

Vowel Teams

The six steps outlined below are to be followed when teaching any of the vowel teams. However, you will need to modify your word formation and dictation steps when teaching vowels represented by more than one vowel team. For example, the vowel team *oi* represents the same sound as the vowel team *oy.* If you ask students to write the letters that stand for the /oi/ sound in a particular word they could logically give either spelling. Therefore, if you ask the students to write the letters that stand for the /oi/ sound in the word *boy* and they write *oi,* ask them to write the other two letters that also represent the /oi/ sound, and explain to them that the /oi/ sound in the word *boy* is spelled *oy.*

Association. Write the words *arm, art, arch,* and *ark* on the chalkboard. Underline the letters *ar* in each of the words and say, "Notice that each word I have written on the chalkboard begins with the same two letters. Each word also begins with the same sound. Listen carefully to the words as I read them to see if you can hear how they sound alike at the beginning." As you read each word point to the letters *ar* and emphasize the /ar/ sound.

Point to the letters *ar* in the word *arm.* Say, "This word says *arm.* Listen to the /ar/ and the /m/ sounds in the word /ar m/." Repeat the word, isolating the /ar/ and the /m/ sounds so the students can hear them. "Say the sounds of each part of the word as I underline the parts: /ar/ /m/." Wait for a response. Point to the letters *a* and *r.* Say, "The letters *a, r* in the word *arm* stand for the /ar/ sound. Say /ar/ /m/—/arm/." Wait for a response. Repeat this process with the words *art, arch,* and *ark.*

Synthesizing. Write the words *barn, start, shark,* and *march* on the chalkboard. Say, "We are going to identify these words by their sounds." Point to the letters *ar* in the word *barn.* "Say the sound of these letters." Wait for a response. Draw a line under the letters *bar* in the word *barn.* Say, "Say the sound of these first three letters." Wait for a response. Draw a line under the letter *n* in the word *barn.* Say, "Say the sound of the last letter." Wait for a response. Ask, "What is the word?" Wait for a response. Repeat the above process with the words *start, shark,* and *march.*

Application (Sentences). Write the following sentence on the chalkboard: *March the large cow out of the yard and put her in the barn.* Say, "We will read the underlined words in this sentence and sound out the words that are not underlined." Underline the letters *ar* in the word *March.* Say, "Say the sound of these letters." Wait for a response. Draw a line under the letters *Mar* in the word *March.* Say, "Say the sound of the first three letters." Wait for a response. Draw a line under the letters *ch* in the word *March.* "Say the sound of the last two letters." Wait for a response. Help the students with the /ch/ sound if necessary. Ask, "What is the word?" Wait for a response. Continue this process with all of the words in the sentence, and then ask the students to read the sentence as quickly as they can.

Word Formation. Write the following on the chalkboard: *sh_ _k.* Run your finger under *sh_ _* and the letter *k* while you say, "This word is /shar/ /k/. What sound is missing?" Wait for a response. Ask, "What letters are missing?" Wait for a response. Repeat this process using the words: *starch, smart, spark,* and *charge.*

Word Discrimination. Write the following on the chalkboard:

hard
hid

Point to the letters *h* and *d* in both *hard* and *hid.* Ask, "What letters are alike in these two words?" Wait for a response. Point to the letters *ar* and *i* in *hard* and *hid.* Ask, "What letters are different?" Wait for a response. Point to the vowel letters in both words again. Ask, "What sounds are different?" Wait for a response. Repeat this process with the word pairs: *card, cod; harm, him; part, pot.*

Dictation. Provide the students with "magic" slate boards, small chalkboards, or scrap paper to write on. Say, "Write the letters that stand for the /ar/ sound that you hear in the word /spar/ /k/. At the count of three hold up what you have written. One . . . two . . . three." Scan the room to assess the accuracy of individual responses. Write the letters *ar* on the chalkboard. Say, "Most of you have written the letters *a* and *r* on your paper. These letters stand for the /ar/ sound we hear in the word *spark.*" Write the letters *sp* before the letters *ar,* and the letter *k* after those letters as you say the word *spark.* Repeat this process with the words *arm, shark,* and *march.*

Final Consonant Sounds

The six steps in a final consonant lesson are designed to help students (a) identify the appropriate vowel sounds in words; (b) blend the beginning consonant sounds in words with the vowel sounds that follow them; (c) identify consonant sounds in the final position of words; and (d) synthesize all of the sounds in the words so the words can be identified.

Association. Write the words *map, hop, nap,* and *lip* on the chalkboard. Underline the letter *p* in each of the words, and say, "Notice that each word I have written on the chalkboard ends with the same letter. Each word also ends with the same sound.

Listen carefully to the words as I read them to see if you can hear how they sound alike at the end." As you say the /p/ sound in each word, point to the letter *p*.

Point to the word *map*. Say, "Listen as I say the word *map* in two parts." Point to the appropriate letters as you say the sounds, and then glide your finger under all the letters as you say, "/ma/ /p/—/map/. Say the word *map* in two parts." Point to the appropriate letters and repeat, "/ma/ /p/—/map/. The letter *p* (point to the letter) in the word *map* stands for the /p/ sound." Keep pointing to the letter *p*. "Say /p/." Repeat this process with the words *hop*, *nap*, and *lip*.

Write the words *cab*, *web*, *bib*, and *cub* on the chalkboard. Repeat the association step using each of the words.

Synthesizing. Write the words *cap*, *hub*, *tip*, *rub*, *pup*, and *rip* on the chalkboard. Say, "We are going to identify these words by their sounds. First, say the vowel sound in each word; second, blend the beginning consonant sound with the vowel sound; third, say the consonant sound after the vowel; and after you have heard all of the sounds in the word, blend them together quickly in your mind to identify the word."

Point to the letter *a* in the word *cap* and say, "Say the sound of this letter." Wait for a response. Point to the letters *ca* in the word *cap*. "Say the sound of the first two letters." Wait for a response. Point to the letter *p* in the word *cap*. "Say the sound of the last letter in the word." Wait for a response. "Say the word." Wait for a response. Repeat the process above with the words *hub*, *tip*, *rub*, *pup*, and *rip*.

Write the words *robe*, *pipe*, *tribe*, *hope*, *soap*, *globe*, and *deep* on the chalkboard and repeat the process above.

Application (Sentences). Write the following sentence on the chalkboard: <u>A</u> *pup* <u>with</u> <u>much</u> *pep* <u>can</u> <u>eat</u> *ripe* grapes. Say, "We will read the underlined words in this sentence and sound out the words that are not underlined." Point to the first word and read it with the students. Point to the letter *u* in the word *pup* and say, "Say the sound of this letter." Wait for a response. Point to the letters *pu* in the word *pup*. "Say the sound of the first two letters." Wait for a response. Point to the letter *p* at the end of the word *pup*. "Say the sound of the last letter in the word." Wait for a response. Ask, "What is the word?" Wait for a response. Continue this process with all of the words in the sentence, and then ask the students to read the entire sentence as quickly as they can.

Write the following sentence on the chalkboard: *Rob* <u>got</u> a *job* <u>driving</u> <u>a</u> *cab*. Have the students read this sentence in the same way.

Word Formation. Write the following on the chalkboard: *ca_* . Run your finger under the *ca* and the _ while you say, "This word is /ka/ /p/. What sound is missing?" Wait for a response. Ask, "What letter is missing?" Wait for a response. Repeat this process using the words *lap*, *dip*, *web*, *mop*, *nap*, *ripe*, *hope*, and *tribe*.

Word Discrimination. Write the following on the chalkboard:

cup
cub

Point to the letters *cu* in both *cup* and *cub* and ask, "What letters are alike in these two words?" Wait for a response. Point to the letters *p* and *b* in *cup* and *cub*. "What letters are different?" Wait for a response. "What sounds are different?" Wait for a response. "What are the words?" Wait for a response. Repeat this process with word pairs: *cab, cap; rope, robe; mop, mob; gap, gab.*

Dictation. Provide the students with "magic" slate boards, small chalkboards, or scrap paper to write on. Say, "Write the letter that stands for the /p/ sound that you hear at the end of the word /ho/ /p/. At the count of three hold up what you have written. One . . . two . . . three." Scan the room to assess the accuracy of individual responses. Write the letter *p* on the chalkboard. "Most of you have written the letter *p* on your paper. The letter *p* stands for the /p/ sound we hear at the end of the word *hop*." Write the letters *ho* before the letter *p* as you say the word *hop*. Repeat this process with the words *leap, globe, rob,* and *hip.*

Beginning Consonant Digraph Sounds

The six steps in a beginning consonant digraph lesson are designed to help students (a) learn to associate specific sounds with specific consonant digraphs; (b) learn to blend consonant digraph sounds in words with the vowel sounds that follow them; (c) identify the consonant sounds in the final position of words; and (d) synthesize all of the sounds in the words so they can be identified.

Association. Write the words *chin, chop, chess, chat,* and *chum* on the chalkboard. Underline the letters *ch* in each of the words and say, "Notice that each word I have written on the chalkboard begins with the same letters. Each word also begins with the same sound. Listen carefully to the words as I read them to see if you can hear the /ch/ sound at the beginning." As you read each word point to the letters *ch* and emphasize the /ch/ sound.

Point to the word *chin*. Say, "Listen as I say the word *chin* in two parts." Point to the appropriate letters as you say the sounds, and then glide your finger under all the letters as you say, "/chi/ /n/—/chin/. Say the word *chin* in two parts." Point to the appropriate letters and repeat, "/chi/ /n/—chin. The letters *c, h, i* (point to the letters) in the word *chin* stand for the /chi/ sound." Keep pointing to the letters *chi*. "Say /chi/." Wait for a response. Point to the appropriate letters as you say, "Say /chi/ /n/—/chin/." Wait for a response. Repeat this process with the words *chop, chess, chat,* and *chum.*

Synthesizing. Write the words *check, chest, chain,* and *cheat* on the chalkboard. Say, "We are going to identify these words by their sounds. First, say the vowel sound in each word; second, blend the /ch/ sound with the vowel sound; and then say the sound or sounds after the vowel. After you have heard all of the sounds in the word, blend them together quickly in your mind, and identify the word."

Point to the letter *e* in the word *check* and say, "Say the sound of this letter." Wait for a response. Point to the letters *che* and say, "Say the sound of the first three letters." Wait for a response. "Say the sound of the last two letters in the word." Wait for a response. Repeat the process above with the words *chest, chain,* and *cheat.*

Application (Sentences). Write the following sentence on the chalkboard: _Do you, by chance, have a chess game in that chest?_ Say, "We will read the underlined words in this sentence and sound out the words that are not underlined." Point to the first three words and read them with the students. Point to the letter _a_ in the word _chance_ and say, "Say the sound of this letter." Wait for a response. Point to the letters _cha_ and say, "Say the sound of the first three letters." Wait for a response. Point to the letters _ce_ and ask, "What is the sound of the last two letters? What is the word?" Wait for a response. Continue this process with all of the words in the sentence, and then ask the students to read the entire sentence as quickly as they can.

Word Formation. Write the following on the chalkboard: _ _ _ p. Run your finger under the _ _ _ and the _p_ while you say, "This word is /cho/ /p/. What sound is missing?" Wait for a response. Ask, "What letters are missing?" Wait for a response. Repeat this process using the words _check, chin, chess, champ,_ and _chum._

Word Discrimination. Write the following on the chalkboard:

> _chart_
>
> _smart_

Point to the letters _art_ in both _chart_ and _smart._ Say, "What letters are alike in these two words?" Wait for a response. Point to the letters _ch_ and _sm_ in _chart_ and _smart_ and ask, "What letters are different?" Wait for a response. "What sounds are different?" Point to the letters _char_ in the word _chart._ Wait for the students to say /char/. Point to the letters _smar_ in the word _smart._ Say, "The sounds of these letters are /smar/." Point to _char,_ then to _smar,_ saying, "Say /char/ and /smar/." Wait for a response. "The ending sound in these words is /t/. What is the first word?" Wait for a response. "What is the second word?" Wait for a response. Repeat this process with word pairs: _chin, spin; chop, drop; cheat, treat; chain, drain._

Dictation. Provide the students with "magic" slate boards, small chalkboards, or scrap paper to write on. Say, "Write the three letters that stand for the /chi/ sound that you hear at the beginning of the word /chi/ /p/. At the count of three hold up what you have written. One . . . two . . . three." Scan the room to assess the accuracy of individual responses. Write the letters _chi_ on the chalkboard and say, "Most of you have written the letters _c, h, i_ on your paper. These letters stand for the /chi/ sound we hear at the beginning of the word _chip._" Write the letter _p_ after the letters _chi_ as you say the word _chip._ Repeat this process with the words _chirp, chop,_ and _choke._

Ending Consonant Digraph Sounds

The six steps in a final consonant digraph lesson are designed to help the students independently decode unfamiliar words that end with consonant digraphs.

Association. Write the words _beach, coach,_ and _teach_ on the chalkboard. Underline the letters _ch_ in each of the words and say, "Notice that each word I have written on the chalkboard ends with the same letters. Each word also ends with the same sound. Listen carefully to the words as I read them to see if you can hear the /ch/

sound at the end of each one." As you say the /ch/ sound in each word, point to the letters *ch*.

Point to the word *beach*. Say, "Listen as I say the word *beach* in two parts." Point to the appropriate letters as you say the sounds, and then glide your finger under all the letters as you say, "/bē/ /ch/—/bēch/. Say the word *beach* in two parts." Point to the appropriate letters and repeat, "/bē/ /ch/—bēch/. The letters *c*, *h* (point to the letters) in the word *beach* stand for the /ch/ sound." Keep pointing to the letters *ch*. "Say /ch/." Repeat this process with the words *coach* and *teach*.

Write the words *catch, witch, fetch,* and *notch* on the chalkboard. Repeat the association step with each of the words.

Synthesizing. Write the words *peach, rich, hatch, ditch,* and *couch* on the chalkboard. Say, "We are going to identify these words by their sounds. First, say the vowel sound in each word; second, blend the beginning consonant sound with the vowel sound; third, say the consonant sound after the vowel; and after you have heard all of the sounds in the word, blend them together quickly in your mind to identify the word."

Point to the letters *ea* in the word *peach*. "Say the sound of these letters." Wait for a response. Point to the letters *pea* and say, "Say the sound of the first three letters." Wait for a response. Point to the letters *ch*. "Say the sound of the last two letters in the word." Wait for a response. "Say the word." Wait for a response. Repeat the process above with the words *rich, hatch, ditch,* and *couch*.

Application (Sentences). Write the following sentence on the chalkboard: <u>Can you</u> catch <u>the</u> witch <u>with</u> the *patch* <u>on her cape</u>? Say, "We will read the underlined words in this sentence and sound out the words that are not underlined." Point to the first two words and read them with the students. Point to the letter *a* in the word *catch* and say, "Say the sound of this letter." Wait for a response. Point to the letters *ca* in the word *catch*. "Say the sound of the first two letters." Wait for a response. Point to the letters *tch* at the end of the word and say, "Say the sound of the last three letters in the word." Wait for a response. Ask, "What is the word?" Wait for a response. Continue this process with all of the words in the sentence, and then ask the students to read the entire sentence as quickly as they can.

Word Formation. Write the following on the chalkboard: *tea _ _* . Run your finger under the *tea* and the _ _ while you say, "This word is /tē/ /ch/. What sound is missing?" Wait for a response. "What letters are missing?" Wait for a response. Repeat this process using the words: *switch, peach, scratch, poach,* and *twitch*.

Note: The sound /ch/ is represented by both the consonant digraphs *tch* and *ch*. The *ch* spelling follows long vowel sounds, such as in the word *peach*, and the *tch* spelling follows short vowel sounds, such as in the word *patch*. (There are only five exceptions to this generalization: *such, much, rich, which,* and *touch*.) Ask your students to listen to the vowel sound to help them know when to write the letters *tch* or *ch* to represent the missing /ch/ sound.

Word Discrimination. Write the following on the chalkboard:

catch

cash

Point to the letters *ca* in both *catch* and *cash*. Ask, "What letters are alike in these two words?" Wait for a response. Point to the letters *tch* and *sh* in *catch* and *cash* and ask, "What letters are different?" Wait for a response. "What sounds are different?" Wait for a response. "What are the words?" Wait for a response. Repeat this process with word pairs: *witch, win; ditch, dig; match, mad.*

Dictation. Provide the students with "magic" slate boards, small chalkboards, or scrap paper to write on. Say, "Write the letters that stand for the /ch/ sound that you hear at the end of the word /kō/ /ch/. At the count of three hold up what you have written. One . . . two . . . three." Scan the room to assess the accuracy of individual responses. Write the letters *ch* on the chalkboard and say, "Most of you have written the letters *c* and *h* on your paper. These letters stand for the /ch/ sound we hear at the end of the word *coach.*" Write the letters *coa* before the letters *ch* as you say the word *coach.* Repeat this process with the words *couch, sketch, ditch,* and *batch.*

Consonant Blends (Approach 1)

Students who have learned their individual consonant sounds well usually have little difficulty in learning to blend two or more of them together when they occur in words like *black, stop, blond, street,* and *last.* This lesson is designed to help students learn to blend consonant sounds together so they can identify words containing consonant clusters that are unfamiliar to them in print.

There are two types of consonant blends. The most common type is when two or more consonant letters are clustered together in words, and each consonant letter represents its individual sound. The words *stand, strip,* and *list* contain examples of this type of blend. The second type of blend is where three consonant letters are clustered together in words, and at least two of those letters represent a consonant digraph sound. For example, the letters *ch* in the consonant cluster *nch* (found in such words as *lunch* and *bench*) are a consonant digraph, so the three letters in the *nch* cluster represent only two sounds rather than three, such as we find in the word *street.*

If students have learned to identify and recall the appropriate sounds of the consonant digraphs presented in previous lessons they should have few problems with consonant clusters, regardless of the type they encounter.

There are two major strategies used to teach students to synthesize consonant blends. The first, presented here, is to blend each consonant one at a time to the vowel in the word. The second strategy (see approach 2, following) is to present words containing one specific blend over and over again. With this approach, students learn to recognize the blend as a unit just as they learned to recognize individual consonant letters and the sounds represented by those letters. Approach 1 is best suited for students who have strong consonant letter/sound knowledge, and strong blending abilities.

Synthesizing. Write the word *slip* on the chalkboard. Draw a line under the letter *i* in the word *slip*. Say, "What is the sound of this letter?" Wait for a response. Draw a line under the letters *li* and ask, "What is the sound of the first two letters?" Wait for a response. Draw a line under the letters *sli* and ask, "What is the sound of the first three letters?" Wait for a response. Draw a line under the letter *p* and ask, "What is the ending sound?" Wait for a response. "What is the word?" Wait for a response.

Write the word *must* on the chalkboard. Draw a line under the letter *u* and ask, "What is the sound of this letter?" Wait for a response. Draw a line under the letters *mu* and ask, "What is the sound of the first two letters?" Wait for a response. Draw a line under the letter *s* and ask, "What is the sound of this letter?" Wait for a response. "What is the sound of the first three letters?" Wait for a response. Draw a line under the letter *t* and ask, "What is the ending sound?" Wait for a response. "What is the word?" Wait for a response.

Continue this synthesizing activity using selected words from the following list, representing all beginning and ending blends.

stiff, sketch, stamp, skimp, step, skin, sled, block, slump, blond, slept, bless, brick, plan, brisk, pledge, bridge, plush, clip, crack, clutch, crash, clash, crutch, glad, grab, gland, grudge, glimpse, gruff, press, trap, print, trick, prank, trust, frog, drop, fresh, dress, frost, drill, flag, smog, flat, smell, flesh, smack, snack, swim, snob, swept, sniff, swift, spend, scab, spill, scat, spin, scuff, stretch, scrub, strip, scrap, strict, scram, spring, thrill, sprint, thrust, sprung, thrift, split, shrub, splash, shrimp, splint, shred, twin, crop, twist, plug, twelve dust, risk, pest, mask, cost, brisk, camp, sense, sent, clamp, spent, limp, mint, pond, honk, band, sink, mend, mink, pinch, felt, bench, tilt, punch, melt, rinse, lift, tract, theft, fact, wept, soft, kept, pact, script, gasp, judge, lisp, dodge, grasp, ledge, hinge, dance, plunge, since, cringe, fence, tense

Word Formation.

Beginning Blends. Write the following on the chalkboard: _ _ _ *p*. Run your finger under the _ _ _ and the *p* while you say, "This word is /ste/ /p/. What sound is missing?" Wait for a response. "What letters are missing?" Wait for a response. Repeat this process using the words *splash, shred, strict, fresh,* and *mask.*

Ending Blends. Write the following on the chalkboard: *pi_ _ _* . Run your finger under the *pi* and the _ _ _ while you say, "This word is /pi/ /n/ /ch/. What sound is missing?" Wait for a response. "What letters are missing?" Wait for a response. Repeat this process using the words *spent, theft, clamp, script,* and *cringe.*

Word Discrimination.

Beginning Blends. Write the following on the chalkboard:

stamp

tramp

Point to the letters *amp* in both *stamp* and *tramp*. Say, "What letters are alike in these two words?" Wait for a response. Point to the letters *st* and *tr* in *stamp* and *tramp* and ask,

"What letters are different?" Wait for a response. "What sounds are different?" Point to the letters *sta* in the word *stamp*. Wait for the students to say /sta/. Point to the letters *tra* in the word *tramp*. Wait for the students to say /tra/. Say, "The ending sound in these words is /mp/. What is the first word?" Wait for a response. "What is the second word?" Wait for a response. Repeat this process with word pairs: *skin, spin; brick, trick; strip, clip.*

Ending Blends. Write the following on the chalkboard:

limp

list

Point to the letters *li* in both *limp* and *list*. Say, "What letters are alike in these two words?" Wait for a response. Point to the letters *mp* and *st* in *limp* and *list* and ask, "What letters are different?" Wait for a response. "What sounds are different?" Point to the letters *mp* in the word *limp*. Wait for the students to say /mp/. Point to the letters *st* in the word *list*. Wait for the students to say /st/. Say, "Say the beginning sound represented by the first two letters in each word. Say the ending sound represented by the last two letters in each word. What is the first word?" Wait for a response. "What is the second word?" Wait for a response. Repeat this process using word pairs: *dust, dump; rinse, risk; wept, west.*

Dictation. Provide the students with "magic" slate boards, small chalkboards, or scrap paper to write on. Say, "Write the four letters that stand for the /spla/ sound you hear at the beginning of the word /spla/ /sh/. At the count of three hold up what you have written. One . . . two . . . three." Scan the room to assess the accuracy of individual responses. Write the letters *spla* on the chalkboard and say, "Most of you have written the letters *s, p, l,* and *a* on your paper. These letters stand for the /spla/ sound we hear at the beginning of the word *splash.*" Write the letters *sh* after the letters *spla* as you say the word *splash.*

Say, "Write the two letters that stand for the /sk/ sound in the word /ma/ /sk/. At the count of three hold up what you have written. One . . . two . . . three." Scan the room to assess the accuracy of individual responses. Write the letters *sk* on the chalkboard and say, "Most of you have written the letters *s* and *k* on your paper. These letters stand for the /sk/ sound we hear at the end of the word *mask.*" Write the letters *ma* before the letters *sk* as you say the word *mask.* Continue the dictation activities using any of the words listed in this lesson.

Consonant Blends in the Initial Position of Words (Approach 2)

These lessons are designed for students who have difficulty blending two or more consonant sounds as presented in Approach 1.

Association. Write the words *stick, stem, stop,* and *step* on the chalkboard. Underline the letters *st* in each of the words, and say, "Notice that each word I have written on the chalkboard begins with the same letters. Each word also begins with the same sound. Listen carefully to the words as I read them to see if you can hear how they sound alike at the beginning." As you read each word point to the letters *st.*

Point to the letter *i* in the word *stick*. Say, "You know the /i/ sound in the word *stick*. When you blend the /s/ and /t/ sounds with the /i/ sound you get /sti/. Listen as I say the word *stick* in two parts." Point to the appropriate letters as you say the sounds, and then glide your finger under all the letters as you say, "/sti/ /k/—/stik/. Say the word *stick* in two parts." Point to the appropriate letters and repeat, "/sti/ /k/—/stik/. The letters *sti* (point to the letters) in the word *stick* stand for the /sti/ sound." Keep pointing to the letters *sti*. "Say /sti/." Wait for a response. Point to the appropriate letters as you continue, "Say /sti/ /k/—/stik/." Wait for a response. Repeat this process with the words *stem, stop,* and *step*.

Synthesizing. Write the words *stamp, stack, stiff,* and *stuff* on the chalkboard. Say, "We are going to identify these words by their sounds." Point to the vowel letters in each word and say, "You know the vowel sounds in each of these words. First, say the vowel sound in each word; second, blend the /s/ and /t/ sounds with the vowel sound; and then I will say the sound or sounds after the vowel. After you hear all of the sounds in the word, blend them together quickly in your mind, and tell me what the word is."

Point to the letter *a* in the word *stamp*. "Say the sound of this letter." Wait for a response. Point to the letters *sta* and say, "Say the sound of the first three letters." Wait for a response. Point to the letters *mp* and say, "The last two letters in the word say /m/ /p/. What is the word?" Wait for a response. Repeat the process with the words *stack, stiff,* and *stuff*.

Application (Sentences). Write the following sentence on the chalkboard: *Stop, don't step on that stamp.* Say, "We will read the underlined words in this sentence and sound out the words that are not underlined." Point to the letter *o* in the word *Stop* and say, "Say the sound of this letter." Wait for a response. Point to the letters *Sto*. "Say the sound of the first three letters." Wait for a response. Point to the letter *p* and ask, "What is the sound of the last letter in this word?" Wait for a response. "What is the word?" Wait for a response. Continue this process with all of the words in the sentence, and then ask the students to read the entire sentence as quickly as they can.

Word Formation. Write the following on the chalkboard: _ _ _*p*. Run your finger under the _ _ _ and the *p* while you say, "This word is /sto/ /p/. What sound is missing?" Wait for a response. "What letters are missing?" Wait for a response. Repeat this process using the words *stem, stitch,* and *storm*.

Word Discrimination. Write the following on the chalkboard:

stop

mop

Point to the letters *op* in both *stop* and *mop*. Ask, "What letters are alike in these two words?" Wait for a response. Point to the letters *st* and *m* in *stop* and *mop* and ask, "What letters are different?" Wait for a response. "What sounds are different?" Encourage the students to say /sto/ and /mo/. Say, "The ending sound in these words is /p/. What is the first word?" Wait for a response. "What is the second word?" Wait for a response. Repeat this process with word pairs: *stock, flock; stitch, hitch; stem, them.*

Dictation. Provide the students with "magic" slate boards, small chalkboards, or scrap paper to write on. Say, "Write the three letters that stand for the /sti/ sound that you hear at the beginning of the word /sti/   /f/. At the count of three hold up what you have written. One . . . two . . . three." Scan the room to assess the accuracy of individual responses. Write the letters *sti* on the chalkboard and say, "Most of you have written the letters *s, t, i* on your paper. These letters stand for the /sti/ sound we hear at the beginning of the word *stiff.*" Write the letters *ff* after the *sti* as you say the word *stiff.* Repeat this process with the words *stuff* and *stamp.*

Advanced Synthesizing. Write the word *start* on the chalkboard. Point to the letters *ar* and say, "What is the sound of these letters?" Glide your finger under the letters *star* and ask, "What is the sound of the first four letters?" Wait for a response. "What is the sound of the last letter?" Wait for a response. "What is the word?" Wait for a response. Continue this process with the words *starch, starve, stay, steal, stern, stew, stir, stone, storm,* and other similar words.

Consonant Blends in the Final Position of Words (Approach 2)

Association. Write the words *cost, nest, fast,* and *dust* on the chalkboard. Underline the letters *st* in each of the words, and say, "Notice that each word I have written on the chalkboard ends with the same letters. Each word also ends with the same sound. Listen carefully to the words as I read them to see if you can hear how they sound alike at the end." As you say the /st/ sound in each word point to the letters *st.*

Point to the word *cost.* Say, "Listen as I say the word *cost* in two parts." Point to the appropriate letters as you say the sounds, and then glide your finger under all the letters as you say, "/ko/   /st/—/kost/. Say the word *cost* in two parts." Point to the appropriate letters and repeat "/ko/   /st/—/kost/. The letters *s* and *t* (point to the letters) in the word *cost* stand for the /st/ sound." Keep pointing to the letters *st.* "Say /st/." Repeat this process with the words *nest, fast,* and *dust.*

Write the words *risk, mask, desk,* and *ask* on the chalkboard. Repeat the association step with each of the words.

Synthesizing. Write the words *test, dusk, lost, task, bust,* and *whisk* on the chalkboard. Say, "We are going to identify these words by their sounds. First, say the vowel sound in each word; second, blend the beginning consonant sound with the vowel sound; third, say the consonant sound after the vowel; and after you have heard all of the sounds in the word, blend them together quickly in your mind to identify the word."

Point to the letter *e* in the word *test.* Say, "Say the sound of this letter." Wait for a response. Point to the letters *te* and say, "Say the sound of the first two letters." Wait for a response. Point to the letters *st* and say, "Say the sound of the last two letters in the word." Wait for a response. "Say the word." Wait for a response. Repeat the process with the words *dusk, lost, task, bust,* and *whisk.*

Application (Sentences). Write the following sentence on the chalkboard: <u>At dusk</u> <u>you</u> *must rest* <u>in</u> <u>my</u> *best* <u>chair.</u> Say, "We will read the underlined words in this sentence and sound out the words that are not underlined." Point to the first word and read it with the students. Point to the letter *u* in the word *dusk* and say, "Say the sound of this letter." Wait for a response. Point to the letters *du*. "Say the sound of the first two letters." Wait for a response. Point to the letters *sk*. "Say the sound of the last two letters in the word." Wait for a response. Ask, "What is the word?" Wait for a response. Continue this process with all of the words in the sentence, and then ask the students to read the entire sentence as quickly as they can.

Word Formation. Write the following on the chalkboard: *fro_ _* . Run your finger under the *fro* and the _ _ while you say, "This word is /fro/ /st/. What sound is missing?" Wait for a response. "What letters are missing?" Wait for a response. Repeat this process using the words *risk, crust, mask, blast, desk,* and *twist.*

Word Discrimination. Write the following on the chalkboard:

> *rust*
>
> *rush*

Point to the letters *ru* in both *rust* and *rush*. Ask, "What letters are alike in these two words?" Wait for a response. Point to the letters *st* and *sh* in *rust* and *rush* and ask, "What letters are different?" Wait for a response. "What sounds are different?" Wait for a response. "What are the words?" Wait for a response. Repeat this process with word pairs: *disk, dish; mast, mask; ask, ash; cast, cash.*

Dictation. Provide the students with "magic" slate boards, small chalkboards, or scrap paper to write on. Say, "Write the letters that stand for the /st/ sound that you hear at the end of the word /lo/ /st/. At the count of three hold up what you have written. One . . . two . . . three." Scan the room to assess the accuracy of individual responses. Write the letters *st* on the chalkboard and say, "Most of you have written the letters *s* and *t* on your paper. These letters stand for the /st/ sound we hear at the end of the word *lost.*" Write the letters *lo* before the letters *st* as you say the word *lost.* Repeat this process with the words *pest, desk, bust,* and *dusk.*

Y as a Vowel

The letter *y* is a consonant when it begins a word or a syllable, as in *yellow* and *canyon.* The letter *y* is a vowel when it occurs in a vowel position in a closed syllable (*myth*); in an open syllable (*my*); or in a vowel-consonant-*e* syllable (*rhyme*).

The letter *y* represents the /i/ sound in a closed syllable (*myth*). It represents the /ī/ sound in an open syllable in single-syllable words or in an accented open syllable in polysyllabic words (*cry, de-ny*). It represents the /ē/ sound in an unaccented syllable in polysyllabic words (*hap-py, ba-by*). Note that in some dialect areas of the country the *y* represents the /i/ sound in unaccented syllables rather than the /ē/ sound.

When teaching *y* as a vowel to students, help them learn that *y* represents the /i/ sound in protected syllables, the /ī/ sound in unprotected single-syllable words, and either /ī/ or /ē/ when it occurs in the last syllable of polysyllabic words.

Association. Write the words *gym*, *hymn*, and *myth* on the chalkboard. Underline the letter *y* in each of the words and say, "Notice that the vowel letter in each word I have written on the chalkboard is *y*. The letter *y* in each of these words represents the /i/ sound. It is the same sound the letter *i* represents in protected syllables. Listen carefully to the words as I read them to see if you can hear the /i/ sound in each one." As you read each word point to the letter *y* and emphasize the /i/ sound.

Write the words *my*, *fly*, and *by* on the chalkboard. Underline the letter *y* in each of the words and say, "Notice that the vowel letter in each word I have written on the chalkboard is *y*. The letter *y* in each of these words represents the /ī/ sound. It is the same sound the letter *i* represents in unprotected syllables. Listen carefully to the words as I read them to see if you can hear the /ī/ sound in each one." As you read each word point to the letter *y* and emphasize the /ī/ sound.

Write the words *deny*, *July*, and *defy* on the chalkboard. Underline the letter *y* in each of the words and say, "Notice that the ending vowel letter in each word I have written on the chalkboard is *y*. The letter *y* in each of these words represents the /ī/ sound. Listen carefully to the words as I read them to see if you can hear the /ī/ sound in each one." As you read each word point to the letter *y* and emphasize the /ī/ sound.

Write the words *jolly*, *happy*, and *baby* on the chalkboard. Underline the letter *y* in each of the words and say, "Notice that the ending vowel letter in each of these words is *y*. This time the *y* represents the /ē/ sound. Listen carefully to the words as I read them to see if you can hear the /ē/ sound in each one." As you read each word point to the letter *y* and emphasize the /ē/ sound.

Say, "When the letter *y* is at the end of words of more than one syllable, *y* can represent either the /ī/ sound or the /ē/ sound."

Synthesizing. Ask the students to say the vowel sounds in the following words; ask them to tell you why they chose the sounds they chose; and ask them to identify the words by sounds. When blending the sounds in polysyllabic words, ask the students to try both sounds until they get a word that makes sense:

fly, by, cy-cle, my, myth, why, gyp-sy, thy, gym, cry, dry, hymn, fry, pry, sly, spy, sty, try, spry, de-ny, hap-py, diz-zy

Application (Sentences). Write the following sentence on the chalkboard: <u>A</u> *dirt-y fly* <u>flew</u> *by* <u>the</u> *hap-py ba-by*. Say, "We will read the underlined words in this sentence and sound out the words that are not underlined." Point to the first word and read it with the students. Point to the letters *ir* in the word *dirt-y* and say, "Say the sound represented by these letters." Wait for a response. Point to the letters *dir*. "Say the sound represented by the first three letters." Wait for a response. Point to the letter *t*. "Say the sound represented by this letter." Wait for a response. Ask, "What is the first syllable in the word?" Wait for a response. Point to the letter *y* in the word and ask, "What is the sound of *y* in this word?" Wait for a response. "What is the word?" Wait for a response. Continue this process with all of the words in the sentence, and then ask the students to read the entire sentence as quickly as they can.

Write the following sentence on the chalkboard: *That cand-y is chunk-y, not cream-y.* Have the students read this sentence the same way they read the first one.

Word Discrimination. Write the following words on the chalkboard:

gem

gym

Point to the letters *g* and *m* in both *gem* and *gym*. Ask, "What letters are alike in these two words?" Wait for a response. Point to the letters *e* and *y* in *gem* and *gym* and ask, "What letters are different?" Wait for a response. Point to the vowel letters in both words again. Ask, "What sounds are different?" Wait for a response. Repeat this process with word pairs: *me, my; sly, slay; free, fry; myth, math; spry, spree; tree, try; be, by; flea, fly.*

Dictation. Provide the students with "magic" slate boards, small chalkboards, or scrap paper to write on. Say, "Write the two letters that stand for the /mi/ sound you hear at the beginning of the word /mi/ /th/. At the count of three hold up what you have written. One . . . two . . . three." Scan the room to assess the accuracy of individual responses. Write the letters *my* on the chalkboard and say, "Most of you have written the letters *m* and *y* on your paper. These letters stand for the /mi/ sound we hear at the beginning of the word *myth*." Write the letters *th* after the letters *my* as you say the word *myth*. Repeat this process using any of the words listed in the synthesizing step.

Application Activities

1. Obtain a copy of any basal first-grade teacher's manual. Find a lesson on beginning consonant sounds. Read the teaching instructions for that lesson. Compare it with the 10-minute phonics lessons described in this chapter. Answer the following questions regarding both approaches: Is phonemic awareness taught? Is segmentation taught? Are children helped to associate sounds with letters? Are children taught how to blend word sounds? How much time will be needed to teach the lesson? Will the children be able to apply what is taught to help them be better readers?

2. Find a child needing help with phonics. Teach an appropriate phonics lesson to this child following the steps outlined in the chapter. Write all of the information you need to teach the lesson on the chalkboard before you begin to teach. Time yourself. Did you teach the lesson in 10 minutes or less?

3. Volunteer to teach a class of first graders one of the 10-minute phonics lessons. After teaching the lesson, ask the children to evaluate their experience. Ask them if they enjoyed the lesson. Ask them if they think it was helpful.

Chapter 11

Assessing Decoding and Reading Comprehension

Assessing Decoding Accuracy and Fluency

Throughout this book, we have emphasized that decoding accuracy and fluency have important positive effects on reading comprehension. Fluent readers recognize words accurately, rapidly, and automatically. Fluent readers comprehend better than children who have poor decoding abilities simply because they have less difficulty translating print into language. You can assess students' decoding abilities by listening to them read. We recommend the following materials be used for testing decoding accuracy and fluency: (1) a specific literature book to be used as the test; (2) individual copies of the book text for you to record reading accuracy data while students read; and (3) a stopwatch.

Readability is a necessary, though not sufficient, criterion to use when choosing testing materials. We recommend that teachers count the number of words in the book(s) selected and calculate the readability level of the book with a readability formula.

Testing Procedures

1. Write the student's name and the test date on one of the text copies prepared for marking.
2. Give the student an unmarked copy of the literature book. Say, "I would like you to read this book for me. Read it with expression if you can. If you come to a word you cannot read, just skip it. (*Do not tell students words they cannot read.*) Do you understand what I want you to do?" Wait for a response. Say, "Begin reading."
3. Push the button on the stopwatch as soon as the child begins to read. In the copy, place a checkmark over each word the child reads correctly. If the child leaves out a word, draw a line through the word. If the child reads a word incorrectly, cross out the word. If the child asks you what a word is, tell him or her to skip the word, and draw a line through the word. If the child reads a word not in the text, write it in where the child placed it.

4. As soon as the child finishes reading the book, push the button on the stopwatch and record the time taken (in seconds) by the child's name.

After the test is completed, count the errors, and calculate the number of words read correctly. Calculate word recognition efficiency scores (Stanovich, Cunningham, & Freeman, 1984b) by dividing the total number of words read correctly by the seconds taken to read them, producing an average number of words read correctly per second. An efficiency score is a combined accuracy and fluency score.

Story Retelling and Questioning

After children have read the literature book, ask them to retell the story as though they were telling it to someone who had never read it before. Tape record their retellings for later analysis. Children's story retellings have proven to be an extremely good indicator of reading comprehension. Since stories have a predictable structure (characters, a setting, a problem, a sequence of events leading to solving the problem, and a solution to the problem), record the number of these elements students include in their retellings as evidence of comprehension.

You may want to develop a story grammar test to get a comprehension score, instead of asking children to retell the story. See Appendix F for a sample test.

Sight Word Assessment

Sight word accuracy and fluency can also be assessed by using the 120 sight word test found in Appendix G. This test was created and validated by the author of this book for a decoding research project undertaken in 1994. All of the words on the test were taken from the Carroll, Davies, and Richman (1971) word frequency book. The words are arranged in four groups of high-frequency, regular graphophonic words; high-frequency, irregular graphophonic words; low-frequency, regular graphophonic words; and low-frequency, irregular graphophonic words. The average number of words read correctly for the subtests and the entire test for children in grades 1, 2, and 3 are as follows:

Test	Part 1	Part 2	Part 3	Part 4	Total
Grade 1	24	21	10	4.6	60
Grade 2	29	27.6	21.5	13.7	92
Grade 3	30	29	25.7	18.8	102.7

After the individual sight word test is completed, word recognition efficiency scores can be calculated as was done for the literature book test.

Phonics Assessment

According to Ehri and Wilce (1983, 1985), the difference between skilled and unskilled readers is that skilled readers possess the phonics knowledge needed to form complete connections between word spellings and word pronunciations in memory, while unskilled readers do not. Skilled readers have stored many written words in lexical memory that they can easily retrieve when seen in print. Unskilled readers, on the other hand, form partial or incomplete word spelling–pronunciation connections because of insufficient phonics knowledge. Their word recognition vocabularies are small and their decoding is slow and inaccurate. Phonics knowledge is necessary for children to form the visual–phonological connections in memory necessary for word storage and retrieval. This knowledge is used by children to learn both regular and irregular words.

Research suggests that students' phonics knowledge can be assessed by giving them pseudowords to read. The speed and accuracy of reading pseudowords is not only a measure of phonics knowledge, but also clearly differentiates students with good reading comprehension from those who do not comprehend well (see Chapter 4).

Appendix H contains an individual phonics test. This test was developed and validated by the author of this book during the 1994 decoding research project. There are three parts to the test. All of the phonics elements and patterns described in Chapter 8 are assessed by this test. After completing the individual phonics test, you may then calculate word recognition efficiency scores.

Appendix I presents a group phonics test. The individual phonics test is more accurate, but not as efficient, as the group test. The test was designed for teachers who want to assess the phonics knowledge of many students at one time. The production tasks required of students on the individual test are more difficult than the recognition tasks on the group test. Therefore, students will get more items correct on the group test than they will on the individual test. However, both tests are significantly related to word recognition and reading comprehension. The correlations of both tests to word recognition and reading comprehension are as follows:

Group phonics test and word recognition $r = .83, p < .01$

Individual phonics and word recognition $r = .88, p < .01$

Group phonics test and comprehension $r = .41, p < .01$

Individual phonics and comprehension $r = .52, p < .01$

Application Activities

1. Assess a selected elementary school child's decoding accuracy and fluency with a literature book, following the steps outlined in the chapter. Assess the child's comprehension of the book using the retelling strategy outlined in the chapter.
2. Assess a child's sight word accuracy and fluency using the sight word test in Appendix G. Share your findings with the child, and if appropriate, with the child's parents and/or teacher.
3. Assess a child's phonics knowledge using the individual phonics test in Appendix H. Share your findings with the child, and if appropriate, with the child's parents and/or teacher.

Appendix A

919 High-frequency Words Obtained from 235 Children's Literature Books

(Listed According to Frequency of Use)

the	then	too	look	that's	along
and	what	asked	cried	head	another
a	me	if	long	am	ate
to	as	came	or	great	bed
said	him	don't	I'm	door	dark
I	have	did	boy	has	three
he	there	over	us	never	let's
you	be	good	well	thought	tree
of	were	house	off	called	than
was	when	away	ran	new	even
it	big	looked	going	yes	sat
in	do	know	saw	eat	give
on	went	by	way	help	heard
she	can	how	think	something	nothing
that	this	bear	two	next	blue
is	down	day	more	only	toad
his	no	Mr.	because	run	wizard
they	will	right	after	can't	its
for	like	it's	again	play	soon
all	your	would	cat	night	been
but	into	who	baby	frog	last
her	man	time	home	first	much
with	now	put	want	dog	witch
we	mother	around	make	still	found
little	from	about	other	water	walked
my	very	come	why	through	red
up	back	oh	take	morning	always
out	could	some	didn't	our	let
at	just	got	made	once	while
had	them	an	I'll	tell	you're
so	old	here	find	king	began
one	see	their	father	must	fast
not	go	where	say	told	bad
are	get	took	Mrs.	rabbit	before

under	I've	side	anything	grandfather	porridge
gave	ice	hat	opened	hole	mean
eyes	lady	four	stood	kitchen	large
room	these	shall	pocket	whole	cry
shouted	fox	suddenly	teeny	straight	bone
dinosaurs	garden	cake	bones	sun	we're
everyone	teeth	goose	own	table	sky
things	really	tail	picked	playing	honey
inside	hill	grasshopper	truck	ball	feel
children	smiled	round	elephant	lost	milk
looking	end	six	himself	bit	stand
stopped	catch	which	grow	book	slowly
small	maybe	work	fine	beautiful	sitting
any	skeleton	name	cow	kind	wish
behind	he's	dinosaur	we'll	police	ready
until	birthday	farmer	course	yellow	mind
girl	street	trees	most	crocodile	kept
fish	met	tried	pretty	such	waited
store	feet	should	voice	quiet	nobody
woman	please	cats	whispered	thank	sorry
couldn't	box	wasn't	brought	far	legs
happy	sleep	enough	jump	girls	arms
young	full	without	try	black	they're
road	across	laughed	faster	story	isn't
together	tiny	need	rain	white	you'll
thing	gingerbread	clothes	read	teacher	sad
left	pumpkin	hard	funny	hungry	wall
better	gone	same	family	balloon	watch
started	top	getting	eggs	doesn't	flying
front	bird	chair	days	world	fat
people	school	mom	skinny	love	town
sure	won't	cream	doing	grass	care
every	umbrella	someone	brown	walrus	car
ever	hear	mouse	almost	horse	asleep
high	may	nose	bunny	friend	five
nice	jumped	window	giant	everybody	lot
each	yelled	open	watched	show	ten
wanted	coming	many	turn	dear	sit
best	those	boys	food	held	past
stop	goat	ground	cave	caught	sea
seen	air	friends	foot	outside	later
knew	walk	wind	today	stay	birds
green	does	lucky	hiccup	happened	says
fell	turned	else	pulled	moon	set
place	lived	hand	flew	bat	felt
keep	poor	tired	parson	climbed	word
sister	fly	everything	running	fun	live
snow	soup	wait	basket	rest	eating

goodnight	mouth	pig	thin	tall	telephone
near	answered	ahead	thinking	dry	smaller
there's	hello	animals	though	bread	meat
cook	city	cheep	quack	zoo	hope
orange	spot	bee	lake	tomorrow	visit
tea	dropped	indeed	goes	listen	nazis
stone	loved	cannot	perhaps	onto	grandmother
shoes	mama	rolled	color	she's	seven
sometimes	gold	chickens	followed	broomstick	real
floor	yet	sound	deep	light	pockets
liked	yard	silly	different	easier	bet
hurry	wouldn't	chocolate	dad	walking	matter
kittens	fire	sick	call	warm	blanket
duck	halloween	pat	crying	quick	swim
talk	I'd	lowly	cloud	pick	moved
brother	quickly	step	wrong	daddy	broke
idea	follow	making	wonderful	row	flat
few	shook	buy	showed	makes	stars
close	pond	what's	robin	marigold	heavy
trumpet	page	breakfast	game	mice	spring
rose	done	being	holding	instead	mallard
chicken	comes	sang	lamb	field	likes
carry	also	change	land	sing	doctor
egg	face	wet	coat	pink	except
button	toward	taking	helped	already	blew
picture	winter	afraid	move	year	song
noise	bag	pie	myself	supper	soldier
grew	vine	stairs	upon	sighed	shopping
star	farm	train	pushed	rabbi	roll
guess	reached	seemed	frightened	mountain	start
ask	ride	money	finally	lunch	line
apple	mad	hot	against	leaves	laughing
might	soft	journey	worry	everywhere	hardly
river	glad	bigger	wearing	strong	okay
sign	son	flowers	loud	shut	finger
miss	boat	closed	berries	biggest	hen
remember	violet	threw	special	gate	here's
alone	surprise	fall	clean	grabbed	above
worm	bring	forget	hide	empty	toys
piece	woods	hold	hurried	become	gets
sorceress	both	pot	hall	nazi	cross
paint	stupid	prince	wood	grandma	club
others	hands	late	climb	lovely	clock
paper	cookies	sheep	surprised	hid	grade
park	corner	men	forgot	waiting	breath
answer	leave	swam	letter	used	bottom
anyone	mother's	trying	life	terrible	steps
party	covered	bottle	short	wants	afternoon

passed	uncle	crowd	owl	free	monkey
bath	filled	became	moth	doll	moving
carried	cars	stepped	mitt	ago	plant
castle	class	higher	leaving	true	private
busy	roof	hung	led	landed	rice
bear's	dinner	louder	rooster	believe	rushed
arm	falling	babies	valley	broom	sandwich
throw	dumb	turkey	knows	hop	send
till	brush	snake	half	closer	sent
smell	bye	bright	onions	coach	ship
pair	bark	case	cents	cut	somebody
palace	wise	fair	fallen	haven't	speak
market	signor	fur	music	hopped	stuck
marsh	second	canoe	trouble	department	talking
jar	part	dug	cupboard	earth	turtle
houses	nest	beside	eater	eight	use
hair	nine	smile	dancing	either	wagon
policeman	kitten	sharp	cold	eye	watching
hey	animal	safe	plants	finished	week
suit	bears	ring	Jewish	glasses	
ladder	cards	stick	join	herself	
butterfly	ears	sugar	dogs	lots	
played	apples	pin	heart	meadow	
easy	lie	pail	dressed	middle	

Appendix B

275 High-frequency Irregular Words Obtained from 235 Children's Literature Books

(Arranged According to Frequency of Use)

the	where	everyone	clothes	mind	done
a	cried	small	chair	sorry	comes
to	I'm	any	someone	they're	also
said	two	behind	many	you'll	toward
you	more	store	friends	wall	son
of	again	woman	tired	watch	violet
was	want	couldn't	anything	care	both
they	other	young	elephant	says	cookies
all	I'll	together	course	word	mother's
one	find	front	most	live	covered
are	father	people	pretty	near	rolled
what	Mrs.	sure	brought	there's	buy
have	great	wanted	doing	shoes	what's
there	door	knew	almost	sometimes	change
were	thought	I've	giant	floor	pie
do	something	full	watched	talk	stairs
your	only	gone	today	brother	money
into	water	school	pulled	idea	journey
mother	through	won't	whole	carry	fall
very	our	hear	straight	picture	hold
could	once	coming	ball	guess	though
old	told	air	beautiful	sign	goes
don't	another	walk	kind	worm	color
know	give	does	police	piece	call
bear	heard	poor	doesn't	others	wrong
Mr.	nothing	soup	world	answer	wonderful
would	wizard	four	love	anyone	holding
who	been	work	walrus	answered	lamb
put	walked	dinosaur	friend	loved	move
come	always	tried	dear	mama	pushed
oh	you're	should	caught	gold	against
some	before	wasn't	climbed	wouldn't	worry
here	eyes	enough	we're	fire	wearing
their	dinosaurs	laughed	honey	I'd	berries

special	field	nazis	pair	babies	believe
hurried	already	grandmother	hair	turkey	haven't
hall	year	moved	policeman	fair	earth
climb	everywhere	soldier	hey	canoe	eight
tall	become	roll	suit	sugar	either
tomorrow	nazi	laughing	falling	knows	eye
listen	grandma	here's	dumb	half	monkey
onto	lovely	above	bye	onions	moving
easier	terrible	carried	signor	trouble	somebody
walking	wants	castle	bears	cupboard	talking
warm	telephone	busy	ears	cold	watching
marigold	smaller	bear's	lie	heart	

Appendix C

Sample Words Containing Low-frequency Letter–Sound Relationships

Graphemes representing the /f/ sound: _phone, laugh, calf_

Graphemes representing the /g/ sound: _ghost, guest_

Graphemes representing the /k/ sound: _ache, mechanic, bisque, walk_

Graphemes representing the /m/ sound: _climb, hymn_

Graphemes representing the /n/ sound: _know, gnat, pneumonia_

Graphemes representing the /r/ sound: _write, rhyme_

Graphemes representing the /s/ sound: _scene, psalm, listen_

Graphemes representing the /sh/ sound: _partial, sugar, precious, machine, session_

Graphemes representing the /ch/ sound: _question, future_

Graphemes representing the /zh/ sound: _measure, azure, division, garage_

Graphemes representing the /a/ sound: _plaid, laugh_

Graphemes representing the /ē/ sound: _seize, money, field, police_

Graphemes representing the /e/ sound: _said, heifer, friend, says, many_

Graphemes representing the /ī/ sound: _aisle, sign, height, pie, aye_

Graphemes representing the /i/ sound: _sieve, build_

Graphemes representing the /ō/ sound: _soul, toe, though_

Graphemes representing the /o/ sound: _cough_

Graphemes representing the /o͞o/ sound: _through, fruit_

Graphemes representing the /u/ sound: _double, come_

Grapheme representing the /oo/ sound: _could_

Grapheme representing the /ou/ sound: _bough_

Appendix D

Readability and Word Analysis Data on 235 Popular Children's Literature Books

Author	Title	Publisher	Readability	Total/Unique Words
Aardama	*Bringing the Rain to Kapiti Plain*	Dial	10.9	747/136
Aardama	*Who's in Rabbit's House*	Dial	1.7	1444/379
Adler	*Cam Jansen and the Mystery of the Stolen Diamonds*	Viking	2.5	4790/841
Ahlberg	*The Baby's Catalogue*	Atlantic	6.5	100/90
Ahlberg	*Each Peach Pear Plum*	Scholastic	20.7	137/63
Ahlberg	*Funny Bones*	Scholastic	2.9	890/227
Ahlberg	*Peek-a-Boo*	Viking	4.7	429/152
Alexander	*I Sure Am Glad to See You, Blackboard Bear*	Dial	1.4	272/135
Alexander	*And My Mean Old Mother Will Be Sorry, Blackboard Bear*	Dial	1.0	403/186
Alexander	*Nobody Asked Me If I Wanted a Baby Sister*	Dial	2.5	222/128
Alexander	*We're in Big Trouble, Blackboard Bear*	Dial	1.3	291/167
Aliki	*Dinosaurs Are Different*	Harper	5.6	1354/519
Aliki	*My Visit to the Dinosaurs*	Crowell	4.9	863/323
Allard	*I Will Not Go to Market Today*	Dial	3.8	441/186
Allard	*The Stupids Step Out*	Houghton/Mifflin	3.9	401/195
Anno	*Anno's Counting Book*	Harper	1.0	18/18
Austin	*Churchkitten Stories and More Kitten Tales*	Dell	2.3	4573/744
Balestrino	*The Skeleton Inside You*	Crowell	3.1	857/292
Bang	*Ten, Nine, Eight*	Viking	1.0	74/66
Barton	*Building a House*	Viking	3.3	88/64
Bauer	*My Mom Travels a Lot*	Viking	2.8	181/73
Benchley	*Red Fox and His Canoe*	Harper	1.0	811/264
Bishop	*Twenty and Ten*	Viking	3.1	12090/1640
Bodecker	*It's Raining Said John Twaining*	Atheneum	2.4	676/288
Bonsall	*The Case of the Cat's Meow*	Harper	1.0	1292/342
Bonsall	*The Case of the Double Cross*	Harper	1.8	1078/291

Author	Title	Publisher	Readability	Total/Unique Words
Bonsall	*The Case of the Hungry Stranger*	Harper	1.0	1366/327
Bonsall	*And I Mean It, Stanley*	Harper	1.0	191/62
Bonsall	*What Spot?*	Harper	1.0	1174/187
Bonsall	*Who's Afraid of the Dark?*	Harper	1.0	216/88
Bornstein	*Little Gorilla*	Clarion	7.4	169/79
Bridwell	*Clifford's Christmas*	Scholastic	3.1	336/170
Briggs	*The Elephant and the Bad Baby*	Putnam	6.2	907/119
Brown	*Arthur's Eyes*	Atlantic	2.6	544/236
Brown	*Arthur Goes to Camp*	Atlantic	2.8	839/361
Brown	*Once a Mouse*	Scholastic	5.0	330/159
Brown	*Goodnight Moon*	Harper	31.0	134/56
Brown	*The Runaway Bunny*	Harper	6.6	408/91
Bulla	*Daniel's Duck*	Harper	1.0	1221/305
Burningham	*Mr. Gumpy's Motor Car*	Viking	1.0	375/171
Burningham	*Mr. Gumpy's Outing*	Viking	1.4	288/110
Burton	*Katy and the Big Snow*	Houghton Mifflin	3.4	695/220
Burton	*The Little House*	Houghton Mifflin	5.9	1394/384
Byars	*Go and Hush the Baby*	Viking	2.7	376/159
Carle	*The Secret Birthday Message*	Harper	1.0	169/75
Carlson	*Harriet and Walt*	Viking	1.0	365/153
Causley	*"Quack," Said the Billy Goat*	Harper	1.0	104/67
Ciardi	*I Met a Man*	Houghton Mifflin	1.0	4559/707
Coerr	*The Big Balloon Race*	Harper	2.2	1412/506
Cohen	*Bee My Valentine*	Dell	3.4	690/276
Cohen	*First Grade Takes a Test*	Dell	3.3	758/301
Cohen	*Lost in the Museum*	Dell	1.8	637/241
Cohen	*When Will I Read?*	Dell	1.7	676/239
Cook	*The Little Fish That Got Away*	Scholastic	2.1	796/124
Coombs	*Dorrie and the Blue Witch*	Dell	2.6	2041/479
Coombs	*Dorrie and the Halloween Plot*	Dell	2.4	3133/725
Crews	*Freight Train*	Viking	3.9	59/43
Crews	*Parade*	Greenwillow	3.8	102/78
Crews	*School Bus*	Viking	1.0	55/38
Crews	*Truck*	Viking	4.0	44/32
Dabcovich	*Sleepy Bear*	Dutton	1.1	53/36
Degen	*Jamberry*	Harper	11.1	114/78
Dennis	*Flip*	Viking	4.0	650/279
DePaola	*Charlie Needs a Cloak*	Prentice-Hall	3.1	194/101
DePaola	*The Legend of Bluebonnet*	Putnam	4.5	962/334
De Regntiers	*It Does Not Say Meow*	Clarion	1.0	376/192
Drescher	*Simon's Book*	Scholastic	5.5	403/202
Dubanevish	*Pigs in Hiding*	Scholastic	2.0	150/83
Duke	*Bedtime*	Dutton	1.0	25/16
Duke	*Clean-up Day*	Dutton	1.0	23/19
Duke	*The Playground*	Dutton	2.0	18/17

Author	Title	Publisher	Readability	Total/Unique Words
Duke	*What Bounces?*	Dutton	2.2	28/25
Elting	*Q Is for Duck*	Clarion	1.0	252/95
Ets	*Gilberto and the Wind*	Viking	1.5	640/228
Ets	*Just Me*	Viking	1.3	789/223
Flack	*Ask Mr. Bear*	Macmillan	1.7	614/124
Flora	*The Great Green Turkey Creek Monster*	Atheneum	3.5	1954/647
Freeman	*A Pocket for Corduroy*	Viking	4.6	870/362
Freeman	*Bearymore*	Viking	5.4	1221/512
Freeman	*Corduroy*	Viking	4.0	671/289
Gackenbach	*A Bag Full of Pups*	Clarion	1.0	279/123
Gaeddert	*Gustav the Gourmet Giant*	Dial	2.9	1431/497
Gag	*Millions of Cats*	Putnam	3.5	973/266
Galdone	*The Gingerbread Boy*	Clarion	3.4	1099/257
Galdone	*Henny Penny*	Clarion	5.3	586/109
Galdone	*Jack and the Beanstalk*	Clarion	3.5	1443/441
Gelman	*Cats and Mice*	Scholastic	1.0	250/96
Gelman	*More Spaghetti, I Say*	Scholastic	1.0	346/110
Gelman	*Wet Cats*	Scholastic	1.0	252/125
Gibbons	*Trucks*	Harper	5.3	192/104
Giff	*Today Was a Terrible Day*	Viking	2.8	677/296
Ginsburg	*Across the Stream*	Viking	1.0	95/51
Goodspeed	*Rhinoceros Wakes Up in the Morning*	Viking	10.4	193/121
Hayes	*This Is the Bear*	Harper	1.0	272/125
Heine	*King Bounce the 1st*	Picture Bk Studio	3.9	418/165
Heyward	*The Country Bunny and the Little Golden Shoes*	Houghton Mifflin	7.1	2519/594
Hoban	*Arthur's Honey Bear*	Harper	2.2	1402/325
Hoban	*A Baby Sister for Frances*	Harper	3.7	1372/361
Hoban	*Count and See*	Macmillan	1.0	43/43
Hughes	*Alfie Gives a Hand*	Greenwillow	3.8	1134/375
Hurd	*Mystery on the Docks*	Harper	1.4	722/321
Hutchins	*Happy Birthday, Sam*	Viking	3.8	224/88
Hutchins	*Don't Forget the Bacon*	Viking	1.3	179/32
Hutchins	*Rosie's Walk*	Macmillan	12.0	36/28
Hutchins	*You'll Soon Grow Into Them, Titch*	Viking	2.6	199/68
Johnson	*A Picture for Harold's Room*	Harper	1.4	557/216
Keats	*The Snowy Day*	Viking	3.2	329/165
Keats	*Peter's Chair*	Harper	1.9	290/152
Keats	*Whistle for Willie*	Viking	3.0	385/170
Kellogg	*Can I Keep Him?*	Dial	1.7	590/266
Kellogg	*Much Bigger than Martin*	Dial	2.7	434/186
Kellogg	*The Mystery of the Flying Orange Pumpkin*	Dial	3.4	439/211

Author	Title	Publisher	Readability	Total/Unique Words
Kellogg	The Mystery of the Missing Red Mitten	Dial	2.6	255/134
Kent	Silly Goose	Prentice Hall	1.5	473/163
Kesselman	Emma	Harper	4.2	590/227
King	Down on the Funny Farm	Random House	1.0	1079/250
Kraus	Leo the Late Bloomer	Simon & Shuster	1.3	170/80
Kraus	Whose Mouse Are You?	Macmillan	1.0	11/58
Kroll	The Biggest Pumpkin Ever	Scholastic	3.7	1017/328
Kuskin	Roar and More	Harper	2.9	359/210
Lawrence	Binky Brothers, Detectives	Harper	1.3	1443/410
Lear	The Owl and the Pussycat	Putnam	5.0	232/114
Leonard	Little Kangaroo's Bad Day	Bantam	2.4	358/163
Leonard	Little Mouse Makes a Mess	Bantam	2.2	303/145
Leonard	Little Owl Leaves the Nest	Bantam	1.5	262/123
Leonard	Little Pig's Birthday	Bantam	2.8	244/128
Levy	Something Queer at the Ball Park	Dell	1.9	1443/461
Levy	Something Queer Is Going On	Dell	2.2	1867/484
Lionni	Swimmy	Knopf	1.7	194/95
Lobel	Frog and Toad Are Friends	Harper	1.1	2296/412
Lobel	Grasshopper on the Road	Harper	2.4	2009/466
Lobel	On Market Street	Scholastic	4.9	129/89
Lobel	The Rose in My Garden	Scholastic	15.5	826/87
Lutton	Little Chicks' Mothers and All the Others	Viking	3.7	238/121
Lynn	Clothes	Atheneum	4.1	15/15
Lynn	Food	Atheneum	1.4	16/16
Lynn	Home	Atheneum	6.5	16/16
Lynn	Toys	Atheneum	2.1	16/16
Manushkin	Baby, Come Out	Harper	1.9	568/205
Mariotti	Hanimals	Green Tiger	Wordless Book	
Maris	My Book	Viking	1.0	19/11
Mark	Fur	Harper	1.0	45/34
Mayer	Ah-Choo	Dial	Wordless Book	
Mayer	Frog on His Own	Dial	Wordless Book	
Mayer	If I Had . . .	Dial	3.8	168/70
Mayer	What Do You Do with a Kangaroo?	Scholastic	4.0	745/283
McCloskey	Blueberries for Sal	Viking	5.2	1044/257
McCloskey	Make Way for Ducklings	Viking	4.2	1161/390
McDermott	Arrow to the Sun	Viking	2.5	406/155
McGovern	Stone Soup	Scholastic	2.1	1047/180
McLeod	The Bear's Bicycle	Viking	2.4	190/100
McPhail	Henry Bear's Park	Viking	4.2	1697/577
Meddaugh	Too Short Fred	Houghton Mifflin	2.0	954/360
Minarik	Little Bear's Visit	Harper	1.6	1446/308

Author	Title	Publisher	Readability	Total/Unique Words
Mooser	The Ghost with the Halloween Hiccups	Avon	2.0	758/256
Mosel	Tikki Tikki Tembo	Scholastic	6.6	1015/270
Murphy	What Next Baby Bear?	Dutton	1.1	319/150
Murphy	Tattie's River Journey	Dial	2.5	1128/362
Noble	The Day Jimmy's Boa Ate the Wash	Dial	2.3	413/179
Noll	Off and Counting	Viking	2.8	137/151
Ormerod	Moonlight	Viking	Wordless Book	
Ormerod	101 Things to Do with a Baby	Viking	27.5	402/199
Ormerod	Sunshine	Viking	Wordless Book	
Parish	Dinosaur Time	Harper	2.5	538/181
Payne	Katy No-Pocket	Houghton Mifflin	3.9	1406/422
Peet	The Caboose Who Got Loose	Houghton Mifflin	5.8	1374/524
Perez	Your Turn Doctor	Dial	1.5	488/216
Perrault	Cinderella or the Little Glass Slipper	Viking	6.8	1715/542
Pinkwater	Roger's Umbrella	Dutton	3.4	945/329
Piatti	The Happy Owls	Atheneum	6.3	467/236
Platt	Big Max	Harper	1.0	1652/358
Potter	The Tale of Benjamin Bunny	Bantam	6.6	1165/406
Potter	The Tale of Peter Rabbit	Bantam	6.8	968/383
Preston	Squawk to the Moon, Little Goose	Viking	1.0	717/170
Provensen	Old Mother Hubbard	Random House	3.9	275/85
Radin	A Winter Place	Atlantic	15.7	215/118
Rey	Curious George	Houghton Mifflin	1.8	938/312
Rice	Goodnight, Goodnight	Viking	6.8	190/88
Riddell	Ben and the Bear	Harper	1.0	175/83
Rockwell	Cars	Dutton	1.7	75/48
Rockwell	My Nursery School	Viking	1.9	239/134
Rockwell	Toolbox	Atheneum	3.0	149/78
Sawyer	Journey Cake, Ho	Viking	2.5	1128/362
Scarry	The Best Mistake Ever	Random House	2.4	1109/314
Schmidt	The Gingerbread Man	Scholastic	2.0	772/119
Schulman	The Big Hello	Dell	1.7	471/201
Schwartz	Busy Buzzing Bumblebees and Other Tongue Twisters	Harper	1.7	329/231
Schwartz	There Is a Carrot in My Ear	Harper	1.4	1070/350
Selsam	A First Look at Dinosaurs	Scholastic	5.6	850/313
Selsam	How Kittens Grow	Scholastic	2.2	774/268
Sendak	Chicken Soup with Rice—A Book of Months	Scholastic	4.6	376/146
Seuling	The Teeny Tiny Woman	Viking	10.9	372/87
Sharmat	A Big Fat Enormous Lie	Dutton	1.5	427/162
Sharmat	Gregory the Terrible Eater	Morrow	3.6	877/305
Shulevitz	One Monday Morning	Atheneum	4.6	285/47

Author	Title	Publisher	Readability	Total/Unique Words
Silverman	*Bear's Big Balloon, A Counting Book*	Putnam	1.0	108/87
Silverman	*Bunny's ABC Boxmouse's Shape Book*	Putnam	3.3	234/137
Silverman	*Ladybug's Color Book*	Putnam	2.5	294/87
Silverman	*Mouse's Shape Book*	Putnam	2.5	253/101
Small	*Imogene's Antlers*	Crown	5.7	295/174
Spier	*Noah's Ark*	Doubleday	2.0	196/36
Tafuri	*All Year Long*	Viking	6.0	41/26
Tafuri	*Early Morning in the Barn*	Viking	1.0	79/32
Testa	*If You Take a Paintbrush*	Dial	2.9	116/58
Testa	*If You Take a Pencil*	Dial	2.9	124/78
Thaler	*A Hippopotamus Ate the Teacher*	Avon	3.4	328/139
Tusa	*Miranda*	Atheneum	4.2	433/204
Wadsworth	*Over in the Meadow*	Scholastic	1.8	397/116
Ward	*The Biggest Bear*	Houghton Mifflin	4.8	982/326
Watanabe	*I Can Build a House*	Philomel	1.0	60/38
Watanabe	*I Can Ride It*	Philomel	1.0	66/33
Watanabe	*I Can Take a Walk*	Philomel	1.0	94/64
Watanabe	*I'm King of the Castle*	Philomel	1.1	72/50
Watanabe	*Where's My Daddy?*	Philomel	1.8	120/54
Watson	*Lollipop*	Viking	13.3	151/62
Weber	*House on East 88th Street*	Houghton Mifflin	4.5	1359/502
Weber	*Lyle, Lyle, Crocodile*	Houghton Mifflin	5.6	1571/559
Weiss	*My Teacher Sleeps in School*	Viking	2.0	947/330
Wells	*Max's Bath*	Dial	2.2	146/73
Wells	*Max's Bedtime*	Dial	2.2	90/50
Wells	*Max's Birthday*	Dial	1.2	77/47
Wells	*Max's Breakfast*	Dial	1.2	89/45
Wells	*Max's First Word*	Dial	1.0	63/27
Wells	*Max's New Suit*	Dial	1.3	142/71
Wells	*Max's Ride*	Dial	2.2	50/34
Wells	*Max's Toys*	Dial	3.1	109/67
Wells	*Goodnight Fred*	Dial	1.0	418/154
West	*Have You Seen the Crocodile?*	Harper	4.4	157/24
West	*Pardon, Said the Giraffe*	Harper	1.0	132/41
Williams	*Something Special for Me*	Greenwillow	4.2	1458/443
Yashima	*Umbrella*	Viking	7.1	538/220
Ylla	*Animal Babies*	Harper	3.7	574/278
Zemach	*It Could Always Be Worse*	Scholastic	3.5	826/228
Ziefert	*So Sick*	Random House	1.2	247/96
Zolotow	*Mr. Rabbit and the Lovely Present*	Harper	2.0	801/141

Appendix E

Word Lists for Chapter 10 Phonics Lessons

Short Vowels:

a

at, an, add, as, am, ash, act, ask, asp, apt, and, ant

hat, pan, fan, lamp, lap, hand, sack, cat, ham, an, bat, wax, back, bad, bag, band, mad, map, rat, sad, sand, sat, rag, ran, had, nap, land, gas, tack, tap, pat, cap, catch

ac-tion, ac-tor, ad-dress, ad-just, ad-mit, af-ter, ap-ple, am-bush, ap-ply

e

Ed, edge, etch, end, else, ebb

web, wet, well, bed, beg, bell, bend, best, set, send, fed, felt, fell, fence, desk, deck, den, men, mend, mess, met, jet, red, hen, neck, nest, next, vest, led, less, let, yes, yell, yet, ten, test, tense, peck, pen, pest, pet, zest, gem

ed-it, ef-fort, en-force, en-try, ex-pel

i

it, in, if, itch, inch, is

wig, win, wish, with, witch, will, wind, bib, big, bid, bit, sit, sick, sin, fix, fin, fish, fist, fit, did, dig, dip, ditch, dish, mix, mill, mint, miss, mist, mitt, jig, rid, rich, risk, rip, hid, hill, hip, hit, lick, lid, lift, lint, lip, list, lit, kick, kill, tin, tip, pill, pin

ig-loo, im-age, ig-nite, im-press, in-crease, it-self, in-deed

o

on, odd, ox, oz, off, oft

box, boss, bond, sob, sock, sod, fox, fog, fond, dog, dock, dodge, dot, mob, mock, mop, job, jot, rob, rock, rod, rot, hog, hop, hot, nod, not, lock, log, loss, lost, lot, got, toss, top, tot, pop, pot, cot, cob, cost

ob-tain, Oc-to-ber, of-fer

u

up, us

bus, bump, bud, budge, bunch, but, sub, suck, sum, fun, fudge, fuss, dust, duck, dug, much, mud, mug, mush, must, just, jump, rub, runt, rush, rut, rust, hum, hug, hush, hut, hunch, hunt, nut, nudge, luck, lug, lump, lunch, luck, gum, gush, tub, puff, pump, punch, pup, punt, cut, cup, cuff, cuss

ug-ly, un-der, un-til, ut-ter, un-bend, up-per, un-mask, up-set

Beginning Consonants:

w

web, wig, went, win, wet, wish, wept, wag, wit, wax, with, witch, wedge, width, wed, will, wilt, weld, well, wind, west, wing, wink, welt, wisp

wade, wage, waist, wait, waive, wake, wave, way, we, weak, wealth, wean, weave, wee, week, weed, weep, wide, wife, wipe, wood, wool, worn, wove, wine

wag-on, wa-ken, wig-gle, win-dow, win-ter, wit-ness, wob-ble, wish-ful

b

back, box, bus, bib, bed, bad, botch, bump, big, beg, badge, boss, bat, buck, bud, bid, bond, budge, bell, bag, bench, ban, bug, bend, band, batch, bath, bum, bun, bunch, bunk, bunt, but, buzz, bit, best, bet, bent

beach, bead, bean, beast, beet, boil, book, boot, born, bound, burst

ban-dit, ban-jo, bash-ful, bas-ket, bo-ny, bot-tle, bu-gle, buc-kle, bun-dle, buz-zer

s

sit, sack, self, sob, sub, sick, sin, sad, sell, sift, sock, such, sag, send, silk, sixth, sod, suck, sand, sense, sill, solve, suds, sang, sent, silt, sum, sank, set, sun, sap, since, sung, sunk, sat, sing, singe, sink

safe, sail, saint, sake, sale, same, sauce, saw, say, sea, seam, seat, serve, so, soak, soap, soil, soon, soothe, sort, sound, south, sown

sa-cred, sad-dle, sat-in, sam-ple, sil-ver, sel-fish, sev-en, sig-nal, sim-ple, si-lent, sis-ter, sud-den

f

fox, fib, fan, fed, fun, fact, felt, fix, fog, fudge, fad, fell, fifth, fond, fence, fig, font, fund, fang, fetch, fill, fuss, fast, fat, film, fin, finch, fish, fist, fit

face, fade, fail, faint, faith, fake, fame, farm, fate, fault, fawn, feast, feat, fee, feed, feel, feet, fete, few, file, fine, firm, first, five, foam, foil, food, fool, foot, for, force, form, fort, forth, foul, found, fowl, fume, fur, fuse

fa-ble, fa-tal, fau-cet, fa-vor, fee-ble, fi-ber, fe-ver, fid-dle, fin-ish, fiz-zle

d

did, dust, dog, desk, dash, dab, debt, dock, dub, dad, deck, dig, dodge, duck, Dutch, daft, dense, dill, damp, dent, dip, doll, dud, Dan, depth, ditch, Don, dug, dance, dish, dot, duff, dash, dull, dam, den, dumb, dump, dunce, dawn, day, daze, dead, deaf, dealt, deal, death, deed, deep, dew, dice, dime, dine, dive, dome

dab-ble, dai-ly, dain-ty, daz-zle, dea-con, de-fy, dim-ple, du-ty, do-nate, diz-zy, di-ver, dip-per, de-ny

m

mad, melt, much, mob, mix, man, men, milk, mock, mud, map, mend, mill, mop, mug, mash, mesh, mink, mum, mass, mess, mint, mumps, met, miss, munch, match, mist, mush, math, mitt, muss, must, mat, midst

maid, mail, maim, make, male, mane, mar, march, mark, maul, may, maze, me, meal, mean, meant, meat, meek, meet, merge, mice, mile, mine, mode, moist, mole, mood, moon, moose, morn, mount, mound, mouse, mouth, mule, my, myth

mag-ic, mag-net, ma-jor, mam-mal, man-age, man-

sion, ma-ple

j

just, job, jig, judge, jam, jack, jet, jug, jag, jilt, jest, jill, jinx, John, jump, jot, junk, jut, jamb, jazz

jail, jar, jaunt, jaw, jeans, jeep, jerk, join, joint, joke, joy

jac-ket, jeal-ous, jel-ly, jew-el, jif-fy, jig-gle, jol-ly, jug-gle, jum-ble, junc-tion, jus-tice

r

rat, red, rob, rug, rid, rack, rich, risk, rub, rag, rent, rock, ram, rest, ridge, rod, rum, ramp, rift, romp, run, ran, rig, rot, rung, ranch, rim, runt, rang, ring, rush, rank, rink, rust, rap, rinse, rut, rash, rip

race, rage, raid, rail, rain, raise, rake, rate, rave, raw, ray, reach, read, realm, ream, reap, reed, reef, reel, rice, ride, right, ripe, rise, road, roam, roast, robe, rode, role, roof, room, roost, root, rope, rose, round, rout, rove, rude, rule, row

rab-bit, rac-coon, ra-cer, ram-ble, rid-dle, ri-der, ri-fle, rob-in, ro-bot

h

hum, had, hid, hog, hedge, hack, hag, heft, help, hill, hilt, hub, huff, hug, hull, husk, hush, hut, ham, hem, him, honk, hump, hand, hen, hinge, hop, hot, hunch, hung, hunk, hunt, hint, hip, his, hiss, hit, hitch, hence, hang, hat, hatch, have, has

hard, harm, harp, harsh, hate, haul, haunt, hawk, hay, haze, head, heal, health, heap, heat, heave, heed, heel, her, herb, herd, hew, hide, hike, hive, hoe, hoist, hole, home, hood, hoof, hook, hoop, hoot, hope, horn, horse, hose, hound, house, how, howl, hue, hurl, hurt

hab-it, ham-mer, ham-ster, han-dle, hap-pen, har-den, hatch-et, ho-tel

n

neck, nod, nag, nick, nudge, nap, nest, nip, not, numb, nab, net, nil, notch, nut, next

nail, name, nay, neat, need, nerve, new, news, nice, night, nine, no, noise, noon, noose, nook, nor, north, nose, note, noun, now, nurse

nap-kin, nas-ty, na-tion, na-vy, nee-dle, neg-lect, nev-er, nib-ble, nim-ble, no-ble, nor-mal, noz-zle, num-ber, ny-lon

v

vest, van, vat, vent, valve, vend, vast, vex

verb, verse, vice, vile, vise, voice, void, vote, vouch, vow

va-cant, va-ca-tion, vac-cin-a-tion, van-ish, va-por, vi-o-lin, vis-it, vow-el, vic-tim, viv-id, vol-ume

l

lap, led, lick, lock, luck, lack, lass, lug, lad, latch, ledge, lid, lodge, lull, lag, lax, left, lift, log, lump, lamp, lamb, leg, limb, loss, lunch, lend, limp, lost, lung, lance, lens, lint, lot, lunge, land, less, lip, luck, lap, lest, lisp, lapse, let, list, lash, lit

lace, laid, lake, lame, lane, large, lark, late, launch, law, lawn, lay, least, leave, leech, life, light, like, line, lo, loaf, loan, loaves, lone, look, loom, loop, loose, loot, loud, lounge, louse, low, lurk

la-bel, la-bor, lad-der, la-dy, lan-tern, laun-dry, law-yer, lead-er, leath-er, lem-on, les-son, lev-el

y

yes, yam, yet, yank, yap, yelp, yank, yell, yak

yard, yarn, yawn, yeast, yoke, yowl, yule

yel-low, yes-ter-day, yo-del, yon-der

k

kick, keg, kiss, kit, kin, kill, kid, kelp, king, kink

kite, keep

ket-tle, ketch-up, ken-nel, ker-nel, kid-nap, kin-dle, kitch-en

g/g/

gum, get, got, gag, gift, gab, gild, gob, gulf, gill, God, gull, gang, golf, gulp, gas, gash, gasp, gap, gush, gust, gut

gage, gain, game, gape, gate, gauze, gave, gaze, geese, goal, goat, good, goose, gorge, gouge, gown

gal-lant, gam-ble, gar-den, gar-gle, gar-lic, gob-ble, gob-lin, go-pher, gos-sip, gut-ter

t

ten, tack, tell, toss, tub, test, tab, Ted, tick, top, till, tuck, tact, tempt, tilt, tot, tug, tag, tin, tan, tend, tinge, tang, tense, tint, tank, tent, tip, tap, tenth, text

toy, type, tail, take, tale, tame, tape, tar, tart, taunt, taut, tea, teach, team, tease, tee, teem, teeth, term, terse, tight, tile, time, toad, toast, toe, toil, tone,

took, tool, toot, tooth, torch, torn, tow, town

ta-ble, tab-let, tac-kle, tai-lor, tar-dy, tar-get, tar-nish, tat-tle, tem-per, tem-ple, ten-der, ten-sion, ti-dy, tick-et, tim-ber

p

pack, peck, pick, pod, puff, pact, peg, pig, pong, pulp, pad, pelt, pill, pop, pulse, pan, pen, pin, pot, pump, pant, pest, pinch, pun, pants, pet, pink, punch, pat, pit, punk, patch, pitch, punt, path, pup, pull

pace, page, paid, pail, pain, paint, pale, pane, park, part, pave, paw, pawn, pay, pea, peace, peak, peek, peel, peep, perch, perk, pew, pile, pine, pipe, poach, point, poise, poke, pole, pool, porch, pork, pouch, pound, pout, purse

pack-et, pad-dle, pam-per, pan-el, pan-ic, pa-per, part-ner, pat-tern, par-ty, pay-ment, pen-cil, pun-ish

c/k/

can, cot, cub, cob, cast, cap, cad, calf, cut, catch, cup, cat, cuff, cog, cash, cuss, cod, camp, cab, cost

carp, carve, cause, coach, coal, coast, coat, coax, code, coil, cook, cool, cork, corn, couch, count, cow, coy, cube, curb, curl, curse, curve, cute

cab-in, ca-ble, cac-tus, cam-el, can-cel, can-dle, can-yon, car-go, cat-tle, com-ic, com-ma, cop-y

c/s/

cent, cinch, cell, cit-y, cen-ter, cig-ar, cin-der, cel-lar, cen-sus, civ-ic, cyn-ic

cite

ce-dar, ce-ment, cir-cle, cir-cus, cy-press, civ-il

z

zap, zest, zip, zonked, zinc, zom-bie, zing

zone, zoo, zoom

ze-bra, ze-ro

qu

quack, quit, quest, quiz, quick, quench, quill, quell, quilt, quip

quail, quaint, quake, queen, quite, quote

ques-tion, qui-et, quit-ter, quiv-er, quo-ta

g/j/—(before *e, i, y*)

gem, gin, gist, gym (gift, get, gild, gill)

gene, germ, gent, (geese)

gen-tle, gin-ger, gen-er-al, gen-er-ous, ge-ni-us, gen-tle-man, gent-ly, gi-ant, gyp-sy, (gig-gle, giz-zard)

Vowel Teams:
ir
firm, dirt, girl, first, bird, third, twirl, swirl, whirl, flirt, shirt, skirt, squirt, fir, sir, gird, chirp, shirk, smirk, stir, thirst, birch, birth

er
fern, verb, germ, stern, herd, her, per, herb, term, serf, perk, pert, clerk

ur
urn, nurse, burn, curb, turn, blur, cur, spur, fur, purr, churn, spurn, purse, curse, hurl, hurt, spurt, curd, curl, curt, turf, surf, lurk, murk, blurt, purge

ar
arm, art, arch, ark, march, bar, car, far, jar, mar, scar, star, tar, mark, starch, card, hard, lar, yar, charge, large, bark, dark, lark, park, shark, spark, charm, farm, harm, barn, darn, yarn, harp, sharp, cart, chart, part, smart, start, tart, barb, snarl

or
or, cord, cork, fork, pork, stork, form, storm, born, corn, horn, morn, scorn, thorn, short, sort, fort, port, sport, torn, for

core, bore, fore, score, shore, swore, tore, wore, snore, store, sore

au
pause, fraud, sauce, caught, clause, launch, vault, cause, taunt, jaunt, fault, taught

aw
lawn, caw, claw, draw, flaw, gnaw, jaw, law, paw, raw, slaw, squaw, straw, thaw, squawk, brawl, crawl, shawl, scrawl, dawn, drawn, yawn, bawl, hawk

ai
drain, frail, gain, hail, jail, maid, mail, main, paid, pail, pain, paint, quail, rail, rain, raise, sail, saint, snail, sprain, stain, straight, strain, tail, train, trait, waist, wait, aim, bait, braid, brain, chain, claim, drain, fail, faint, faith, nail, wail, grain, lain, plain, aid, laid, maim, taint, praise

ay
stay, day, gay, hay, jay, lay, may, nay, pay, ray, say, way, bray, clay, flay, gray, play, tray, spray, slay, pray, bay, stray

ee
freeze, bee, free, knee, see, three, tree, bleed, deed, feed, need, seed, speed, tweed, weed, cheek, creek, meek, peek, seek, week, eel, feel, heel, kneel, peel, reel, steel, wheel, seem, green, keen, queen, screen, seen, creep, deep, keep, peep, sheep, sleep, sweep, weep, steep, beet, feet, meet, sheet, sleet, breeze, sneeze, squeeze, wheeze, fee, flee, glee, greed, greet, jeep, screech, sleek, sleeve, speech, street, sweet, tweet, beef

oa
coach, poach, roach, load, road, toad, loaf, oaf, cloak, oak, soak, coal, foal, shoal, loan, moan, roan, soap, boast, coast, roast, toast, boat, coat, float, gloat, goat, oats, throat, coax, croak, foam, groan, oath, goal, hoax

oi
coin, choice, voice, boil, broil, coil, foil, oil, soil, spoil, toil, join, noise, poise, joint, point, void, foist, groin, hoist, loin, moist

oy
toy, boy, coy, joy, en-joy, des-troy, an-noy, em-ploy, de-coy, loy-al, voy-age

ea
heat, flea, plea, sea, tea, beach, bleach, each, peach, preach, reach, teach, bead, lead, plead, deal, heal, meal, seal, squeal, steal, veal, beam, dream, gleam, scream, steam, stream, team, clean, lean, mean, wean, cheap, heap, leap, reap, please, tease, east, feast, least, yeast, beat, cheat, eat, meat, neat, peat, seat, treat, wheat, feat, freak, grease, heave, leaf, leak, lean, league, lease, leave, peace, peach, peal, please, plead, pleat, ream, seam, sneak, speak, squeak, streak, tease, weak, weave, teak, beast, bleach, cease, cream, dean, ease

bread, breadth, meant, breath, cleanse, dead, deaf, dealt, death, dread, head, health, spread, sweat, thread, threat, tread, wealth, realm, stead, read

ou
trout, couch, crouch, ouch, pouch, slouch, cloud, loud, proud, shroud, bound, found, ground, hound, mound, pound, round, sound, count, mount, flour, our, scour, sour, clouse, house, louse, mouse, out, pout, scout, snout, spout, stout, noun, south, foul

ow

brown, cow, bow, how, plow, row, vow, fowl, growl, howl, owl, prowl, scowl, brown, clown, crown, down, drown, frown, gown, town

snow, bow, mow, row, sow, blow, crow, flow, glow, grow, know, low, show, slow, stow, throw, bowl, blown, flown, grown, known, own, strown, sown

oo

fool, roof, proof, cool, drool, pool, school, spool, loose, tool, bloom, boom, broom, gloom, loom, room, goose, coon, croon, moon, noon, spoon, soon, coop, moose, droop, hoop, loop, scoop, stoop, swoop, troop, noose, boot, hoot, loot, shoot, toot

good, hood, stood, wood, hoof, book, brook, crook, hook, look, shook, took

ew

chew, flew, grew, knew, stew, brew, new, crew, drew, slew, threw, shrew, blew, screw, dew, news, shrewd, strewn

few, hew, mew, pew

ue

glue, clue, true, blue, sue, due, rue

cue, hue

igh

light, blight, bright, right, sight, tight, fight, might, night, flight, fright, knight, plight, slight, high, sigh, nigh

are

fare, flare, glare, hare, mare, pare, rare, scare, share, snare, spare, square, care

air

chair, fair, flair, hair, lair, pair, air

eer

cheer, deer, jeer, peer, sheer, sneer, steer

ear

clear, dear, ear, fear, gear, hear, rear, shear, smear, spear, year

Final Consonants:

p

cap, pep, tip, top, cup, tap, hep, zip, sop, sup, zap, sip, pop, pup, sap, rip, mop, rap, quip, hop, nap, pip, map, dip, lap, lip, gap, hip, up, nip, lop

ape, cape, drape, grape, scrape, shape, pipe, dope, hope, rope, slope, gape, nape, tape, wipe, cope, lope, mope, snipe, tripe, grope, scope, slope, stripe, swipe

seep, soap, weep, peep, reap, leap, loop, coop, deep, heap, hoop, jeep, keep

b

hub, gob, dub, jab, rub, job, sub, mob, dab, rob, tub, nab, fib, sob, tab, rib, cob, cub, cab, web, bib, bob, bub

globe, robe, gibe, lobe, tribe, probe, scribe

x

tax, six, fox, tux, wax, Rex, box, sax, hex, fix, pox, Max, vex, ox, lax, ax, mix, sex

f

puff, off, puff, if, muff, doff, huff, buff

safe, life, fife, wife, knife, strife, beef, roof, reef

n

ban, ten, bin, Don, ran, bun, can, yen, tin, sun, tan, pen, sin, run, van, den, pin, pun, pan, man, fin, nun, man, dun, fan, gun, Dan, fun, gin, in, win

lane, plane, shine, dine, line, bone, cone, lone, cane, mane, pane, sane, vane, wane, gene, mine, nine, pine, vine, wine, tone, zone, crane, scene, whine, brine, spine, swine, thine, twine, drone, prone, shone, shrine, throne, stone, phone

bean, been, seen, wean, noon, noun, pain, pawn, rain, roan, lain, lawn, lean, loan, loin, loon, main, mean, moan, moon, boon, coin, dawn, dean, down, fain, fawn, gain, gown, jean, join, keen

ck

buck, back, peck, wick, sock, suck, tack, neck, sick, rock, puck, sack, deck, quick, dock, duck, rack, heck, pick, mock, muck, quack, Dick, lock, luck, pack, lick, hock, tuck, hack, nick, jack, tick, lack

k

shake, wake, bake, brake, cake, fake, flake, make, rake, snake, dike, hike, like, choke, poke, lake, sake, take, bike, coke, joke, woke, drake, slake, spake, spike, broke, choke, smoke, spoke, strike, stroke

beak, seek, soak, week, weak, took, nook, peak, peek, reek, leak, look, meek, book, cook, hawk, hook

t

bat, bet, bit, tot, but, cat, yet, sit, rot, cut, vat, pet, wet, quit, pot, rut, sat, set, pit, not, putt, rat, mitt, dot, nut, pat, net, hit, lot, mutt, nat, met, fit, got, gut, mat, let, wit, hot, hut, hat, fat, get, jot

kite, ate, date, fate, slate, gate, hate, late, mate, plate, rate, vote, note, cute, fete, mete, bite, mite, site, dote, mote, rote, mute, crate, grate, skate, slate, state, white, smite, spite, trite, smote, sprite, quote, write, wrote

bait, beat, beet, boat, root, seat, soot, toot, wait, loot, lout, mail, maim, maul, meal, meat, meet, moat, neat, boot, bout, coat, feat, feet, foot, goat, heat, hoot

bot-tle, bat-tle, cat-tle, ket-tle, lit-tle, rat-tle, set-tle, at-om, met-al, bet-ter, bot-tom, bat-ter, but-ter, but-ton, bit-ter, gut-ter, pat-tern, mot-to, wit-ness, kit-ten, let-ter, mit-ten, mat-ter

m

sum, yam, gem, him, mum, ram, hem, mom, hum, ham, vim, bum, gum, jam, rim, yum, Sam, dim, rum

shame, blame, came, fame, flame, frame, game, lame, name, same, slime, crime, dime, grime, home, dame, tame, lime, time, dome, Rome, fume, theme, chime, prime, slime, scheme

beam, room, seam, seem, team, zoom, ream, roam, maim, boom, deem, doom, down, foam

dim-ple, fum-ble, gam-ble, hum-ble, jum-ble, mum-ble, nim-ble, sam-ple, sim-ple, cam-er-a, com-ic, dam-age, im-age, lem-on, lim-it, mem-o, mim-ic, com-ma, com-pound, dum-my, em-ploy, ham-per, mum-my, mem-ber, num-ber, tim-ber

l

mill, bell, dull, doll, cell, till, moll, lull, tell, will, gull, yell, sill, well, pill, sell, dill, quell, gill, dell, jell, hill, fill, fell, bill, loll, kill, cull

smile, tile, male, file, mile, pile, stole, hole, mole, pole, mule, bale, gale, hale, pale, sale, tale, vale, bile, vile, wile, dole, role, sole, yule, scale, shale, stale, whale, while, stile, whole

bail, seal, soil, tail, toil, tool, veal, wool, pail, pool, rail, mail, maul, meal, nail, boil, bowl, coal, coil, cool, fail, feel, foal, foul, foil, fool, foul, fowl, hail, haul, heal, heel

col-umn, frol-ic, jol-ly, mel-on, sol-id, bel-low, bal-lot,

bol-ster, cel-lar, cul-prit, fil-ter, hel-lo, hol-low, hel-met, hol-ly, yel-low, mil-dew, pil-low, sil-ver, sil-ly, sel-dom, vel-vet, wel-come

d

bad, pad, bed, bid, cod, bud, cad, wed, rid, sod, mud, sad, red, did, rod, dad, led, hid, pod, mad, fed, nod, lad, had, fad, kid, lid, cud, God

blade, fade, grade, made, side, slide, bride, hide, ride, jade, wade, cede, bide, tide, wide, ode, bode, code, lode, mode, rode, glade, shade, spade, trade, Swede, chide, glide, stride, strode, guide

bead, seed, toad, void, weed, wood, paid, raid, read, reed, road, laid, laud, lead, load, loud, tweed, maid, mood, need, dead, deed, feed, feud, food, good, heed, hood

cud-dle, fid-dle, grid-dle, hud-dle, mud-dle, med-dle, mid-dle, pad-dle, rid-dle, sad-dle, bod-y, cred-it, mod-ern, mod-el, med-al, mod-est, prod-uct, stud-y, ad-mit, ad-vice, ad-vance, dad-dy, sud-den, glad-den, hid-den, kid-nap, kid-ney, lad-der, mud-dy, mid-night

g

fog, bag, big, bog, bug, tag, peg, zig, dog, rug, zag, meg, wig, log, dug, wag, leg, rig, hog, mug, sag, pig, jog, lug, rag, dig, hug, nag, fig, lag, gag, jig, hag, jag

wag-on, big-ger, beg-ger, dag-ger, sig-nal, drag-gle, gig-gle, hag-gle, jug-gle, jig-gle, snug-gle, drag-on, fig-ure, bug-gy, drug-gist, drag-net, dag-ger, fog-gy, mag-net

ge

stage, cage, gage, page, rage, huge, age, sage, wage, verge, forge, gorge, large, merge, purge, surge

s

mess, mass, yes, miss, boss, bus, hiss, toss, cuss, lass, less, kiss, moss, pus, sass, Bess, loss, muss, fuss, pass, Russ, us

base, case, chase, dose, vase, curse, verse, terse, horse, purse, loose, house, louse, moose, mouse, noose, geese, goose, lease, blouse, crease, grease, grouse, spouse, sparse

(*s* after voiceless consonants) pups, ducks, hats, locks, maps, cuffs, socks, sacks

bas-ket, blos-som, blis-ter, clas-sic, clus-ter, cus-tom, dis-cuss, dis-tant, des-troy, dras-tic, dis-turb, dis-tort, dis-like, dis-count, sis-ter, ves-sel, whis-per, wit-ness, plas-tic, roos-ter, res-cue, es-cape, es-say, es-cort, es-tate, es-teem, flus-ter, fos-sil, fos-ter, frus-trate, gos-sip, gos-pel, hos-tage, les-son, las-so, lus-ter, les-sen, mis-hap, mus-ket, mus-tang, mas-ter, mes-sage, mis-take, nas-ty, nos-tril, con-sists, car-cass, sys-tem, e-rase, de-crease, en-dorse

s/z/
has, as, is, his

fuse, hose, chose, rise, close, rose, ruse, muse, wise, nose, pose, use, phase, prose, these, those, whose, phrase

choose, clause, noise, pause, poise, raise, tease, please, praise

(*s* after voiced consonants) jobs, pigs, hams, bells, dogs, beds, guns, hills

pris-on, vis-it, hus-band, com-pose, sup-pose, sur-prise, be-cause, dis-please, ex-er-cise, en-close, ad-ver-tise, like-wise

z
quiz, razz, fuzz, jazz, fizz, daze, gaze, glaze, graze, haze, doze, maze, raze, size, craze, prize, froze, blaze

haz-ard, liz-ard, wiz-ard, daz-zle, driz-zle, fiz-zle, muz-zle, puz-zle, bliz-zard, buz-zard, buz-zer, diz-zy, giz-zard

ce
ace, ice, lace, lice, dice, face, race, rice, mice, nice, pace, vice, brace, grace, place, price, slice, spacc, spice, trace, truce, twice, splice, spruce, thrice

farce, force, peace, sauce, voice, choice, fleece, Greece

ap-ple-sauce, clock-face, en-force, re-trace, dis-place, re-place, de-face, dis-grace

ve
eve, five, gave, hive, cave, cove, dive, dove, pave, rave, save, wave, wove, brave, crave, drive, drove, grave, grove, clove, knave, strove, shave, slave, stove, strive, thrive

carve, curve, delve, valve, heave, leave, waive, weave, cleave, groove, sleeve, eaves, elves, sheaves

cav-ern, bev-el, clev-er, civ-ic, crev-ice, driv-en, grav-el, gav-el, hav-oc, liv-er, lev-el, riv-er, sev-en, trav-el, nov-ice, bee-hive, de-prive

Consonant Digraphs:
ch—beginning
chop, chat, chap, chaff, check, chess, chick, chill, chin, chip, chub, chuck, chug, chum, champ, chance, chant, chest—chain, charge, charm, chart, chase, cheap, cheat, cheep, cheese, chime, chirp, choice, choke, choose, chow, church, churn

chan-nel, chap-ter, char-coal, chat-ter, chick-en, chim-ney, chi-na, cho-sen, chow-der, chuc-kle, chal-lenge, chap-el, charm-ing, char-ter, chas-tise, cheap-en, check-ers, chil-ly, chim-pan-zee, chis-el, chub-by, en-chant-ing, en-chant-ment, mer-chant, mer-chan-dise, pur-chase, un-chain, wood-chuck

ch & tch—ending
beach, leech, peach, beech, poach, pouch, coach, couch, reach, teach, vouch, bleach, breach, broach, crouch, grouch, preach, slouch, speech

rich, which, such, much

ditch, catch, batch, witch, blotch, clutch, etch, pitch, patch, notch, snatch, fetch, stitch, hatch, hitch, batch, thatch, sketch, snitch, latch, itch, crotch, crutch, stretch, match, switch, splotch, Dutch, wretch, scratch, twitch, Scotch, hutch

arch-er, at-tach, bleach-ers, sand-wich, coach-man, cock-roach, grouch-y, rich-es, hatch-et, treach-er-ous, treach-er-y, dis-patch, im-peach

sh—beginning
shut, shop, sham, shack, shag, shall, shed, shell, ship, shod, shock, shot, shun, shuck, shaft, shalt, shank, shelf, shift—shade, shake, shale, shame, shape, shark, sharp, shave, shawl, she, sheaf, sheen, sheep, sheet, shine, shirk, shirt, shone, shoo, shook, shoot, short, shout, show, shown

shab-by, shad-ow, sha-dy, shag-gy, sha-ky, shal-low, sham-bles, sharp-en, shiv-er, show-er, shac-kle, sha-ding, sha-ken, sham-poo, shat-ter, shel-ter, sher-bet, shi-ny, ship-ment, shiv-er, short-en, shop-ping, shoot-ing, short-cake, ship-yard, shop-keep-er, shift-less

sh—ending
rush, cash, rash, blush, wish, flesh, gosh, brush, dish, fresh, bosh, sash, fish, thresh, clash, slush, swish, mesh, slash, crush, crash, flush, splash, gush, dash, hush, flash, mush, smash, plush, thrash, gash, trash, hash, lash, bash, mash, ash

leash, harsh

sel-fish, cash-ew, fin-ish, Dan-ish, ab-o-lish, ad-mon-ish, ban-ish, bash-ful, blem-ish, boy-ish, dem-ol-ish, fool-ish, dim-in-ish, fash-ion, fash-ion-a-ble, fresh-ness, fur-nish, gar-nish, harsh-ness, pol-ish, pun-ish, rad-ish, round-ish, snob-bish, tar-nish, tick-lish, rel-ish, pun-ish-ment

wh—beginning

whiz, whip, whack, when, whiff, whet, whim, whit, which, whisk—whale, wheat, wheel, while, whine, whirl, white, why

wheez-y, wheth-er, which-ev-er, whim-per, whim-sic-al, whirl-pool, whirl-wind, whis-ker, whis-per, whit-tle

ng

long, sing, bang, bring, flung, rang, bong, rung, string, clang, song, cling, hung, slang, slung, fang, strong, ding, dong, lung, tang, sling, sprung, swing, gang, gong, fling, stung, sang, spring, strung, thing, hang, prong, king, sung, sprang, pong, swung, wing, pang, throng, ring, clung, sting, bung, ting, zing, wring, wrong

king-dom, cong-ress, gang-ster, ang-ry, hung-ry, ang-le, ang-er, fing-er, fung-us, hung-er, jing-le, jung-le, ling-er, mang-le, ming-le, sing-le, tang-le

NOTE: When the first syllable of a two-syllable word ends in ng and the second syllable begins with a vowel sound, the /g/ sound begins the second syllable.

th—beginning

voiceless: thin, thick, thong, thud, thence, thug, thank, thing, think, thump, thumb, thaw, theme, third, thirst, thorn

thir-ty, thir-teen, thun-der, thank-ful, ther-mom-et-er, ther-mos-tat, thick-en, thick-et, thick-ness, thim-ble, think-er, thirst-y, thorn-y, thous-and, thun-der-cloud, thun-der-storm, Thurs-day, thy-roid, e-ther, leng-then, leng-thy, streng-then, syn-thet-ic

voiced: that, than, them, then, this, thus, these, thine, those

fur-ther, far-ther, them-selves, hea-then

th—ending

voiceless: bath, broth, with, Beth, path, cloth, lath, moth, pith, hath, smith, math, froth, myth, wroth, wrath, mouth, booth, death, faith, south, teeth,

tooth, growth, sleuth, wreath, wealth, twelfth

meth-ods, ath-lete, ath-let-ic, auth-or, auth-en-tic, auth-or-ize, death-ly, sab-bath, eth-ic-al, eth-ics, math-em-at-ics, meth-od-ic-al, mouth-ful, orth-od-ox, sev-enth, sym-path-et-ic, sym-path-ize

voiced: loath, smooth, soothe

gath-er, wheth-er, hith-er

Consonant Blends:
st—beginning

stop, stick, stab, stack, staff, stag, stem, step, stiff, still, stock, stub, stuck, stuff, stun, stamp, stance, stand, stench, stilt, sting, stint, stomp, stink, stitch, stump, stung, stunk, stunt

star, starch, start, starve, state, stay, steal, steam, steel, steep, stern, stew, stir, stone, stood, stool, storm, stove

sta-ble, stam-mer, stam-pede, sta-ple, sta-tion, stee-ple

sk—beginning

skin, sketch, skip, skunk, skill, skull, skim, skid, skiff, skit, skimp

skirt, sky, state

skel-et-on, skin-ny, skill-ful, skip-per, sky-line

sl—beginning

slap, slim, sled, slid, slot, slum, slam, slob, slack, slip, slug, slag, slick, slit, slop, slog, slang, slant, slash, sledge, slept, sling, slink, sludge, slump, slush, slat

slate, slave, slay, sleek, sleep, sleet, sleeve, slew, slice, slide, slight, slime, slope, slouch, slow, sly, slur

slan-der, slen-der, slug-gish, slum-ber

bl—beginning

bless, blush, black, bled, blip, bliss, blob, block, blot, bluff, bland, blank, blast, blend, blimp, blink, blond, blotch, blunt

bleak, bleed, blight, bloat, blood, bloom, blouse, blow, blown, blue, blur, blurt

bleach-ers, blem-ish, bless-ing, blis-ter, bliz-zard, blos-som, blow-er, blub-ber, blun-der

br—beginning

bronze, brat, brag, bran, brass, bred, brick, brig, brim, brand, branch, bridge, bring, brink, brisk, broth, brunt, brush

brace, braid, brake, brave, brawl, brawn, breach,

bread, breath, breeze, brew, bribe, bride, bright, broil, broke, bronze, brood, brook, broom, brow, brown, browse, brute

brace-let, breez-y, bri-dle, bright-en, brit-tle, bro-ken, bron-co, bru-net, bru-tal

pl—beginning

plot, pled, plod, pluck, plug, plum, plus, plank, plant, pledge, plump, plunge, plush, plan

place, plain, plane, plate, play, plea, plead, please, pleat, plight, plow, plume, ply

plan-et, plas-tic, plas-ter, plen-ty, plat-ter, Plu-to

cl—beginning

clip, clack, clam, clan, clap, class, clef, click, cliff, clock, clod, clog, clot, cluck, club, clamp, clang, clasp, clash, clench, cleft, clinch, cling, clink, clump, clutch, clung

claim, clause, claw, clay, clean, cloud, clown, clue, cleanse

clas-sic, clat-ter, clev-er, cli-mate, clip-per, clos-et, clo-ver, clum-sy, clus-ter

cr—beginning

crop, crack, crag, crab, cram, crib, crock, cross, craft, cramp, crank, crash, crept, crest, cringe, crisp, crotch, crumb, crunch, crush, crutch

crate, crave, crawl, craze, cream, crease, creek, creel, creep, crew, crime, cry, croak, crook, croon, crouch, crow, crowd, crown, crude

cra-dle, crank-y, cra-ter, cra-yon, cra-zy, cred-it, crick-et, crip-ple, crum-ble, cru-sade, crys-tal

gl—beginning

glum, glad, glen, glib, gloss, glass, glance, gland, glimpse, glint

glaze, gleam, glee, glide, glean, gloat, globe, gloom, glow, glue

gli-der, glim-mer, glit-ter, glut-ton

gr—beginning

grip, grab, gram, grass, grill, grid, grim, grin, grit, grub, gruff, graft, grand, grant, graph, grasp, grudge, grunt, grump

grace, grade, grain, grape, grave, graze, grease, greed, green, greet, grew, grime, groan, groom, groove, grope, grouch, ground, grove, grow, growl,

grown, growth

gram-mar, grav-el, gra-vy, grid-dle, griz-zly, gro-cer

pr—beginning

prop, press, prim, prick, prod, prom, prance, prank, prince, print, prong, prompt

praise, pray, preach, price, pride, prime, prize, pro, probe, prone, proof, proud, prowl, prine, pry

prin-cess, prob-lem, prof-it, pro-gram, pro-noun, pro-nounce, prop-er

tr—beginning

trot, tram, trap, trek, trick, trill, trim, trip, truss, truck, track, tract, tramp, trance, trash, trench, trend, trump, trund, trust

trace, trade, trail, train, trait, tray, tread, treat, tree, tribe, trite, troop, trounce, trout, truce, true, try

trac-tor, tra-der, traf-fic, tram-ple, trans-fer, trans-late, trap-eze, trav-el, trem-ble, tric-kle

fr—beginning

frog, fret, frill, frizz, frock, from, frank, French, fresh, fringe, frisk, frost

frail, frame, fraud, freak, free, freeze, fright, fro, frown, froze, fry

frac-tion, fra-grance, fran-tic, frec-kle, free-dom, fren-zy, fric-tion

dr—beginning

drip, drop, drab, dram, drag, dreg, dress, drill, dross, drug, drub, drum, draft, drank, dredge, drench, drift, drink, drunk, drudge

drain, drape, draw, drawl, drawn, dread, dream, drew, drive, drone, droop, drove, dry

drag-on, dras-tic, draw-er, dream-er, driv-en, dri-ver, driz-zle, drow-sy, drummer

fl—beginning

flat, flag, flap, flax, fled, fleck, flex, flick, flit, flip, flock, flog, floss, flop, fluff, flank, flash, flask, flesh, flinch, fling, flint, flung, flunk, flush

flake, flame, flaunt, flaw, flea, flee, fleece, fleet, flew, fly, flight, flirt, float, flood, flout, flow, flown, flu, flute

flan-nel, flat-ter, fla-vor, flim-sy, flow-er, flut-ter

sm—beginning

smog, smug, smut, smock, smack, smell, smash, smudge, smelt

smart, smile, smirk, smite, smoke, smooth, smote

smel-ter, smo-ky, smug-gle

sn—beginning

snack, sniff, snob, snub, snatch, snap, snip, snug, snag, snuff

snail, snake, snarl, sneak, sneeze, snipe, snoop, snooze, snort, snout, snow

snap-py, snap-shot, snif-fle, snob-bish, snor-kel, snug-gle, snoop-ing

sw—beginning

swift, swim, swam, swell, switch, swum, swish, swank, swept, swung, swing, swift, Swiss

sway, sweat, sweep, sweet, swerve, swirl, swoon, sworn

swiv-el

sp—beginning

spend, spot, span, spat, speck, sped, spell, spill, spin, spit, spun, spank, spent, spilt, spunk

space, Spain, spake, spark, sparse, spawn, speak, speech, speed, spice, spike, spine, spite, spoil, spoke, spook, spool, spoon, sport, spout, spy

spa-cious, spar-kle, spi-cy, spi-der, spin-dle, spin-ster, spin-et, spon-sor

sc—beginning

scat, scuff, scab, scoff, scan, scum, Scott, Scotch, scamp, scud

scale, scar, scarf, scoop, scoot, scope, scorch, scorn, scout, scowl

scaf-fold, scam-per, scan-dal, scant-y, scar-let, scat-ter, scoot-er, scoun-drel

str—beginning

stretch, strap, stress, strip, struck, strut, strand, strict, string, strong, strung

strain, strait, straw, stray, streak, stream, street, strewn, stride, strife, strike, stripe, stroke

strad-dle, stretch-er, stri-king, strug-gle

scr—beginning

scrub, scrap, scrag, scram, scrim, scruff, scratch, scrimp, script, scrunch, scrod

scrape, scrawl, scream, screech, screen, scribe, screw

scrab-ble, scram-ble, scrib-ble, scru-ples

spr—beginning

spring, sprig, sprag, sprung, sprint, sprang

sprain, sprawl, spray, spread, spree, sprite, sprout, spruce, spry

thr—beginning

thrill, throb, thrash, thresh, thrift, thrust, throng, thrush

thread, threat, three, threw, thrice, thrive, throat, throne, throw

threat-en, thrift-y, throt-tle

spl—beginning

splash, split, splotch, spling, splat

spleen, splice

splat-ter, splen-did, splin-ter

shr—beginning

shrub, shrill, shred, shrug, shrank, shrunk, shrink, shrimp

shrew, shrine, shrewd

shriv-el

tw—beginning

twin, twig, twill, twang, twelve, twinge, twist, twitch

tweed, twice, twine, twirl

st—ending

zest, dust, just, nest, past, cost, rest, blast, frost, fist, bust, best, fast, lost, twist, crust, vast, list, rust, chest, last, mist, thrust, west, cast, gist, gust, crest, mast, trust, jest, must, vest, pest, test

sk—ending

risk, mask, ask, brisk, desk, dusk, flask, disk, husk, frisk, musk, task, bask, whisk, cask

mp

damp, camp, bump, skimp, stomp, pump, stamp, dump, imp, hemp, rump, clamp, hump, limp, slump, romp, cramp, jump, shrimp, stump, clomp, lamp, lump, crimp, thump, chomp, ramp, plump, pomp, trump

nt

sent, bent, ant, tent, blunt, tint, font, chant, went, bunt, hint, vent, grant, dent, grunt, lint, pent, plant, rent, hunt, mint, slant, punt, print, pant, spent, runt, splint, stint, can't, lent, flint, glint, cent, stunt, sprint, rant, scent, squint

nd

tend, sand, and, bend, blond, fund, band, blend, bond, strand, bland, end, fond, brand, lend, pond, gland, mend, grand, send, hand, spend, land, stand, trend

nk

honk, bank, blink, bunk, blank, rink, flank, brink, chunk, crank, zonk, sunk, drink, drunk, drank, sink, trunk, ink, hunk, frank, stink, flunk, kink, plank, junk, think, stunk, link, punk, rank, wink, tank, pink, shrunk, sank, clink, thank, shrink, spunk, spank, mink, clank

lt

felt, belt, jilt, quilt, knelt, stilt, melt, tilt, pelt, wilt, smelt, hilt, welt, lilt, milt, silt

ft

lift, craft, drift, left, soft, tuft, draft, gift, theft, loft, raft, deft, oft, sift, shaft, shift, heft, daft, graft, swift, thrift, rift

ct

tract, fact, act, pact, tact, duct, strict

pt

slept, kept, script, wept, crept, swept

sp

lisp, wisp, clasp, gasp, grasp, hasp, rasp, crisp

nge

hinge, lunge, binge, plunge, singe, tinge, fringe, twinge, cringe

nce

dance, fence, mince, glance, dunce, lance, hence, since, whence, wince, stance, prince, trance, pence, chance, thence, prance

nse

rinse, sense, dense, tense

nch

pinch, bench, clench, branch, munch, scrunch, trench, ranch, punch, clinch, winch, French, wench, crunch, finch, cinch, quench, hunch, flinch, drench, bunch, lunch, inch, brunch, wrench, lynch

dge

judge, fudge, bridge, badge, budge, dodge, edge, ridge, madge, grudge, lodge, hedge, fridge, ledge, nudge, pledge, smudge, wedge, sludge, sledge, drudge, fledge

Y as a Vowel:

fly, by, my, why, thy, cry, dry, fry, pry, sly, spy, sty, try, spry

myth, hymn, gym

de-ny, de-fy, re-ly, Ju-ly, im-ply, cyn-ic, cy-cle, gyp-sy, wood-y, room-y, starch-y, speed-y, chunk-y, mud-dy, fun-ny, snap-py, slop-py, hap-py, pen-ny, sun-ny, jol-ly, sil-ly, ba-by, po-ny, la-dy, ti-ny, gra-vy, na-vy, ho-ly, mush-y, fish-y, storm-y, rain-y, bod-y, bo-ny, cand-y, cook-y, dirt-y, diz-zy, dress-y, dum-my, dust-y, du-ty, emp-ty, weed-y, frost-y, leaf-y, brain-y, spook-y, cloud-y, gloom-y, bump-y, crisp-y, cream-y, rat-if-y, oc-cu-py, mag-nif-y, i-den-tif-y, syl-la-ble, sys-tem, sym-bol, cyl-in-der, cym-bal, syc-a-more, syn-thet-ic, sym-path-et-ic, sym-path-ize, typ-ic-al, sym-path-y, sym-pho-ny, symp-tom, syn-dic-ate, hyp-no-sis, hyp-no-tize, hyp-oc-ris-y, phys-ics, phys-ic-al, pyg-my, mys-ter-y, mys-tic, mys-tic-al, myth-ic-al

Appendix F

Sample Story Grammar Test

for Peter's Chair, *by Ezra Jack Keats*
(Harper & Row, 1967)

1. Where did this story take place?
   a. Mostly inside Peter's house—one point
   b. Some of the story took place outside Peter's house—another point
2. Who was this story mostly about?
   a. Peter—one point
   b. Peter's dog—another point
   c. Peter's family—mom and dad and Susie, his sister—give another point for identifying his family, or one or more family member(s)
3. What was bothering Peter in this story?
   a. His father was painting Peter's things pink so they could be given to his new baby sister, Susie—one point
   b. If the student mentions that the father was painting Peter's *cradle, high chair,* or *crib* pink—give another point
   c. If the student mentions that Peter did not want his father to paint his *old blue chair* pink—give another point
4. What did Peter decide to do because he was unhappy?
   a. He decided to run away—one point
   b. If the student says he decided to run away with his *dog,* or his *blue chair,* or with some of his things—give another point
5. How did Peter solve his problem?
   a. When he tried to sit in his old blue chair he couldn't because he was too big—one point
   b. He decided to ask his dad to paint his old blue chair pink for his sister—another point
   c. He played a trick on his mother by putting his shoes under the curtain to make her think he was hiding behind the curtain—another point

TOTAL POINTS_____(13 Possible)

Appendix G

Individual Sight Word Test, Parts 1, 2, 3, and 4

Teacher Directions
Materials Needed:

1. Two copies of the test (one for the teacher to use for marking, and one for the student to read)
2. Stopwatch

Administration of the Test:

1. Write the student's name on one test. Keep this copy.
2. Give the student the other copy of the test.
3. Say, "Look at the words on Part 1 of this test." Allow the student a few seconds to look at the words. "Touch each word as you read it, and read the words on this test as quickly as you can. If you feel you can't read a word on the test, just say 'SKIP' and go to the next word."
4. Say, "Put your finger on the first word and begin reading."
5. Push the button on the stopwatch as soon as the student begins to read. On your test copy: write a *C* next to each word read correctly; write an *I* next to each word read incorrectly; and write an *S* next to each word skipped.
6. As soon as the student finishes with word number 30 on Part 1 of the test, push the button on the stopwatch and record the time taken (in seconds) by the student's name.
7. Repeat steps 1 through 6 with Parts 2, 3, and 4 of the test. Note that each part has 30 items.

Sight Word Test, Part 1

1. that	16. than
2. with	17. first
3. this	18. made
4. when	19. down
5. can	20. way
6. will	21. just
7. each	22. get
8. how	23. back
9. out	24. man
10. them	25. day
11. like	26. same
12. him	27. right
13. see	28. came
14. time	29. part
15. make	30. place

Sight Word Test, Part 2

1. to	16. other
2. you	17. two
3. they	18. could
4. from	19. who
5. have	20. people
6. one	21. only
7. what	22. find
8. were	23. use
9. there	24. water
10. your	25. very
11. their	26. words
12. said	27. where
13. many	28. most
14. some	29. through
15. would	30. our

Sight Word Test, Part 3

1. gunshot
2. outlast
3. cookout
4. pocketful
5. handcart
6. trucking
7. spade
8. waistline
9. refill
10. salesgirl
11. mousetrap
12. freezer
13. toothbrush
14. minnow
15. mixer
16. bathrobe
17. noose
18. hiked
19. cobweb
20. spaceman
21. rainstorm
22. trapeze
23. insults
24. hinted
25. snowflake
26. houseboat
27. hanger
28. unpaid
29. unselfish
30. bleach

Sight Word Test, Part 4

1. inconvenient
2. custodian
3. seagull
4. stoneworker
5. persecute
6. invention
7. innocent
8. fluent
9. elevate
10. inquire
11. unforgettable
12. withhold
13. conflicting
14. creamy
15. alerted
16. tinted
17. licorice
18. inflation
19. deodorant
20. duet
21. stingy
22. defy
23. shoeshine
24. bachelor
25. badger
26. resented
27. workroom
28. beverage
29. salads
30. watercolor

Appendix H

Individual Phonics Test, Parts 1, 2, and 3

Teacher Directions

Materials Needed:

1. Two copies of the test (one for the teacher to use for marking, and one for the student to read)
2. Stopwatch

Administration of the Test:

1. Write the student's name on one test. Keep this copy.
2. Give the student the other copy of the test.
3. Say, "Look at the words on this test." Allow the student a few seconds to look at the words. "They are not real words, but they were made just like real words are made. Try to read the words on this test just like you would read real words. Touch each word as you read it, and read the words as quickly as you can. If you feel you can't read a word on the test, just say 'SKIP' and go to the next word."
4. Say, "Put your finger on the first word and begin reading."
5. Push the button on the stopwatch as soon as the student begins to read. On your test copy: write a *C* next to each word read correctly; write an *I* next to each word read incorrectly; and write an *S* next to each word skipped.
6. As soon as the student finishes with word number 22 on part 1 of the test, push the button on the stopwatch and record the time taken (in seconds) by the student's name.
7. Repeat steps 1 through 6 with parts 2 and 3 of the test. Note that there are 33 items on part 2 of the test, and 28 items on part 3.

Individual Phonics Test, Part 1

1. bab	12. pux
2. cem	13. nell
3. cuzz	14. dag
4. tive	15. mot
5. ved	16. lin
6. yat	17. gam
7. zin	18. heb
8. wep	19. juck
9. soss	20. kix
10. ruff	21. fot
11. quix	22. geb

Individual Phonics Test, Part 2

1. glact
2. scash
3. squist
4. crith
5. smilt
6. splesk
7. scradge
8. strisp
9. frept
10. slift
11. twing
12. drent
13. brunk
14. stend
15. snamp
16. spitch
17. prench
18. blence
19. plense
20. springe
21. swush
22. clomp
23. skint
24. gratch
25. tredge
26. flost
27. shunk
28. choft
29. whinse
30. thesk
31. thung
32. thrug
33. shreb

Individual Phonics Test, Part 3

1. lope
2. ye
3. knod
4. phope
5. wrem
6. gnad
7. cly
8. shay
9. paim
10. feep
11. heach
12. toak
13. curge
14. reath
15. birt
16. herk
17. har
18. saud
19. sawn
20. coise
21. boun
22. plowl
23. groot
24. dewn
25. strow
26. tood
27. voy
28. hight

Appendix I

Group Phonics Test, Parts 1, 2, and 3

Teacher Directions, Part 1

Distribute place markers and a test to each student. Tell students, "Look at the words on your test. Most of the words are nonsense words. However, they can be read as if they were real words. I am going to read one of the words on each row. Please circle each word that I read."

Print the words *tep, mep, tup,* and *teb* on the chalkboard. Say, "Place your markers under the Sample row on your test. It looks like this row." Point to the chalkboard row of words. Check to be sure that each student has the marker under the sample row. Say, "Circle the word *tep*." Wait for the students to respond. Circle the word *tep* in the chalkboard sample. Ask, "Did you circle this word?" Point to the word *tep.* Say, "If you did, you circled the correct word. Now, place your markers under Row 1 and circle the word *bab.*" Repeat the word: *"bab."* Continue dictating words for the students to circle:

2.	cem	(pronounced /sem/)
3.	cuzz	(rhymes with *fuzz*)
4.	tive	(rhymes with *give*)
5.	ved	(rhymes with *bed*)
6.	yat	(rhymes with *fat*)
7.	zin	(rhymes with *tin*)
8.	wep	(rhymes with *pep*)
9.	soss	(rhymes with *boss*)
10.	ruff	(rhymes with *cuff*)
11.	quix	(pronounced /kwiks/)
12.	pux	(rhymes with *tux*)
13.	nell	(rhymes with *tell*)
14.	dag	(rhymes with *bag*)
15.	mot	(rhymes with *hot*)
16.	lin	(rhymes with *sin*)
17.	gam	(rhymes with *ham*)
18.	heb	(rhymes with *web*)
19.	juck	(rhymes with *duck*)
20.	kix	(rhymes with *fix*)
21.	fot	(rhymes with *hot*)
22.	geb	(pronounced /jeb/)

Group Phonics Test, Part 1

Sample:	tep	mep	tup	teb
1.	bab	dab	beb	bap
2.	kem	cen	cem	cam
3.	cizz	cuzz	cux	guzz
4.	tive	bive	tave	tiff
5.	veb	vid	med	ved
6.	yut	zat	yat	yad
7.	yin	zin	zan	ziff
8.	wep	vep	wip	weg
9.	noss	sess	sozz	soss
10.	roff	rux	ruff	luff
11.	quax	quiss	quix	pix
12.	pum	pux	gux	pex
13.	nell	zell	noll	nep
14.	dap	pag	deg	dag
15.	mit	mox	mot	fot
16.	vin	len	lig	lin
17.	cam	gom	gam	gat
18.	heb	beb	hib	hed
19.	jeck	jut	juck	yuck
20.	kizz	kix	pix	kex
21.	fet	yot	foss	fot
22.	geb	gib	gep	keb

Teacher Directions, Part 2

Distribute place markers and a test to each student. Tell students, "Look at the words on your test. Most of the words are nonsense words. However, they can be read as if they were real words. I am going to read one of the words on each row. Please circle each word that I read."

Print the words *plint, phint, plent,* and *plift* on the chalkboard. Say, "Place your markers under the Sample row on your test. It looks like this row." Point to the chalkboard row of words. Check to be sure that each student has the marker under the sample row. Say, "Circle the word *plint*." Wait for the students to respond. Circle the word *plint* in the chalkboard sample. Ask, "Did you circle this word?" Point to the word *plint*. Say, "If you did, you circled the correct word. Now, place your markers under Row 1 and circle the word *glact.*" Repeat the word: *"glact."* Continue dictating words for the students to circle:

2.	scash	(rhymes with *cash*)
3.	squist	(rhymes with *fist*)
4.	crith	(rhymes with *with*)
5.	smilt	(rhymes with *built*)
6.	splesk	(rhymes with *desk*)
7.	scradge	(rhymes with *badge*)
8.	strisp	(rhymes with *crisp*)
9.	frept	(rhymes with *kept*)
10.	slift	(rhymes with *lift*)
11.	twing	(rhymes with *sing*)
12.	drent	(rhymes with *bent*)
13.	brunk	(rhymes with *sunk*)
14.	stend	(rhymes with *bend*)
15.	snamp	(rhymes with *damp*)
16.	spitch	(rhymes with *pitch*)
17.	prench	(rhymes with *bench*)
18.	blence	(rhymes with *fence*)
19.	plense	(rhymes with *sense*)
20.	springe	(rhymes with *singe*)
21.	swush	(rhymes with *mush*)
22.	clomp	(rhymes with *stomp*)
23.	skint	(rhymes with *flint*)

24.	gratch	(rhymes with *patch*)
25.	tredge	(rhymes with *wedge*)
26.	flost	(rhymes with *frost*)
27.	shunk	(rhymes with *trunk*)
28.	choft	(rhymes with *soft*)
29.	whinse	(rhymes with *rinse*)
30.	thesk	(pronounced /thesk/)
31.	thung	(pronounced /thung/)
32.	thrug	(rhymes with *rug*)
33.	shreb	(rhymes with *web*)

Group Phonics Test, Part 2

Sample: plint   phint   plent   plift

1.	glact	gract	gluct	glaft
2.	swash	scosh	scask	scash
3.	squest	squift	swist	squist
4.	crint	crith	clith	crath
5.	shilt	smilt	smalt	smint
6.	splisk	splesh	spresk	splesk
7.	scradge	stradge	scridge	scrand
8.	strist	strasp	stisp	strisp
9.	fropt	flept	frept	frest
10.	skift	slift	slaft	slith
11.	tring	twing	twang	twint
12.	drent	trent	drunt	drend
13.	brund	brank	brunk	blunk
14.	stund	stend	stemp	strend
15.	snand	slamp	snamp	snump
16.	pritch	spetch	spitch	spith
17.	spench	princh	prench	pretch
18.	blance	flence	blent	blence
19.	plinse	plench	plense	prense
20.	squinge	springe	sprenge	sprinse
21.	swesh	swust	swush	spush
22.	glomp	climp	clomp	clonk
23.	skift	skint	slint	skent
24.	gritch	glatch	gratch	grath
25.	twedge	tredge	tresk	tridge
26.	flost	flopt	flist	slost
27.	slunk	shink	shunk	shund
28.	cheft	choth	choft	cloft
29.	shinse	whinse	whint	whense
30.	thesk	twesk	thisk	thept
31.	thang	thunk	thung	tung
32.	trug	thrug	thrag	thrup
33.	sheb	shreb	shrab	shrep

Teacher Directions, Part 3

Distribute place markers and a test to each student. Tell students, "Look at the words on your test. Most of the words are nonsense words. However, they can be read as if they were real words. I am going to read one of the words on each row. Please circle each word that I read."

Print the words *scrade, scade, scride,* and *scrafe* on the chalkboard. Say, "Place your markers under the Sample row on your test. It looks like this row." Point to the chalkboard row of words. Check to be sure that each student has the marker under the sample row. Say, "Circle the word *scrade*." Wait for the students to respond. Circle the word *scrade* in the chalkboard sample. Ask, "Did you circle this word?" Point to the word *scrade.* Say, "If you did, you circled the correct word. Now, place your markers under Row 1 and circle the word *lope.*" Repeat the word: "*lope.*" Continue dictating words for the students to circle:

2.	ye	(rhymes with *we*)
3.	knod	(pronounced /nod/)
4.	phope	(pronounced /fop/)
5.	wrem	(pronounced /rem/)
6.	gnad	(pronounced /nad/)
7.	cly	(rhymes with *my*)

8.	shay	(rhymes with *may*)
9.	paim	(rhymes with *game*)
10.	feep	(rhymes with *keep*)
11.	heach	(rhymes with *teach*)
12.	toak	(rhymes with *cloak*)
13.	curge	(rhymes with *merge*)
14.	reath	(rhymes with *death*)
15.	birt	(rhymes with *dirt*)
16.	herk	(rhymes with *jerk*)
17.	har	(rhymes with *tar*)
18.	saud	(rhymes with *fraud*)
19.	sawn	(rhymes with *lawn*)
20.	coise	(rhymes with *noise*)
21.	boun	(rhymes with *town*)
22.	plowl	(rhymes with *howl*)
23.	groot	(rhymes with *boot*)
24.	dewn	(rhymes with *noon*)
25.	strow	(rhymes with *grow*)
26.	tood	(rhymes with *good*)
27.	voy	(rhymes with *boy*)
28.	hight	(rhymes with *night*)

Group Phonics Test, Part 3

Sample:	scrade	scade	scride	scrafe
1.	lop	lope	loip	lupe
2.	ye	yue	yo	yew
3.	noad	nood	knod	knode
4.	phope	fop	foop	foip
5.	ruem	wrem	reem	reme
6.	gnad	nade	gnod	naid
7.	clee	clo	cly	clu
8.	shaw	shi	shar	shay
9.	gaim	pam	peam	paim
10.	flep	feep	fep	fuep
11.	huech	heach	heak	hoach
12.	toak	tok	tock	toap
13.	corge	curge	curn	carge
14.	rith	reath	roath	reat
15.	bort	girt	bart	birt
16.	herk	herm	hork	hark
17.	hir	har	hor	hur
18.	sud	saud	soad	saun

19.	soan	sain	sawn	rawn
20.	coase	coise	coese	cose
21.	boun	boin	boan	buen
22.	plaul	plown	plool	plowl
23.	groot	groat	gloot	grot
24.	deen	dewn	dewd	doan
25.	strue	strow	strew	stroy
26.	tode	tod	tood	tord
27.	voy	vay	vo	vow
28.	hoat	hight	huet	haught

References

Adams, M. J. (1990). *Beginning to read, thinking and learning about print.* Cambridge, MA: MIT Press.

Adams, M. J. (1991). A talk with Marilyn Adams. *Language Arts, 68,* 206–212.

Allington, R. L. (1977). If they don't read much, how they ever gonna get good? *Journal of Reading, 21,* 57–61.

Allington, R. L. (1980). Poor readers don't get to read much in reading groups. *Language Arts, 57,* 872–876.

Allington, R. L. (1984). Content coverage and contextual reading in reading groups. *Journal of Reading Behavior, 16,* 85–96.

Almasi, J. F., Palmer, B. M., Gambrell, L. B., & Pressley, M. (1991, December). *Toward disciplined inquiry: A methodological analysis of whole language research.* Paper presented at the meeting of the National Reading Conference, Palm Springs, CA.

Alwerger, B., Edelsky, C., & Flores, B. (1987). Whole language: What's new? *The Reading Teacher, 41,* 144–155.

Amlund, J. T., Kardash, C. A. M., & Kulhavy, R. W. (1986). Repetitive reading and recall of expository text. *Reading Research Quarterly, 21,* 49–58.

Anderson, R. C., Hiebert, E. H., Scott, J. A., & Wilkinson, I. A. G. (1985). *Becoming a nation of readers.* Washington, DC: National Institute of Education.

Arnold, R. D. (1972). *A comparison of the neurological impress method, the language experience approach, and classroom teaching for children with reading disabilities* (Final Report). Purdue Research Foundation, Lafayette, IN.

Backman, J., Bruck, M., Herbert, M., & Seidenberg, M. S. (1984). Acquisition and use of spelling–sound correspondences in reading. *Journal of Experimental Child Psychology, 38,* 114–133.

Baghban, M. (1984). *Our daughter learns to read and write.* Newark, DE: International Reading Association.

Ball, E. W., & Blachman, B. A. (1991). Does phoneme segmentation training in kindergarten make a difference in early word recognition and developmental spelling? *Reading Research Quarterly, 26,* 49–66.

Balota, D., Pollatsek, A., & Rayner K. (1985). The interaction of contextual constraints and parafoveal visual information in reading. *Cognitive Psychology, 17,* 364–390.

Barr, R. C. (1972). The influence of instructional conditions on word recognition errors. *Reading Research Quarterly, 7,* 509–529.

Barron, R. W. (1981). Reading skill and spelling strategies. In A. Lesgold & C. A. Perfetti (Eds.), *Interactive processes in reading* (pp. 299–327). Hillsdale, NJ: Erlbaum.

Barron, R. W. (1986). Word recognition in early reading: A review of the direct and indirect access hypotheses. *Cognition, 24,* 93–119.

Beers, J., & Henderson, E. (1977). A study of developing orthographic concepts among first graders. *Research in Teaching English, 11,* 133–148.

Bergeron, B. (1990). What does the term whole language mean? Constructing a definition from the literature. *Journal of Reading Behavior, 22,* 301–329.

Biemiller, A. (1970). The development of the use of graphic and contextual information as children learn to read. *Reading Research Quarterly, 6,* 75–96.

Biemiller, A. (1979). Changes in the use of graphic and contextual information as functions of passage difficulty and reading achievement level. *Journal of Reading Behavior, 11,* 307–319.

Bissex, G. (1980). *Gyns at wrk: A child learns to write and read.* Cambridge, MA: Harvard University Press.

Blachman, B. (1983). Are we assessing the linguistic factors critical in early reading? *Annals of Dyslexia, 33,* 91–109.

Blachman, B. (1984). Language analysis skills and early reading acquisition. In G. Wallach & K. Butler (Eds.), *Language learning disabilities in school-age children* (pp. 271–287). Baltimore, MD: Williams & Wilkins.

Blachman, B. (1989). Phonological awareness and word recognition: Assessment and intervention. In A. G. Kamhi & H. W. Catts (Eds.), *Reading disabilities: A developmental language perspective* (pp. 133–158). Boston: College-Hill.

Blachman, B. (1991). Phonological awareness: Implications for prereading and early reading instruction. In S. A. Brady & D. P. Shankweiler (Eds.), *Phonological processes in literacy: A tribute to Isabelle Y. Liberman* (pp. 29–36). Hillsdale, NJ: Erlbaum.

Blachman, B., & James, S. (1985). Metalinguistic abilities and reading achievement in first-grade children. In J. Niles & R. Lalik (Eds.), *Issues in literacy: A research perspective. Thirty-fourth yearbook of the National Reading Conference* (pp. 280–286). Washington, DC: National Reading Conference.

Bond, G. L., & Dykstra, R. (1967). The cooperative research program in first-grade reading instruction. *Reading Research Quarterly, 6,* 75–96.

Bradley, L., & Bryant, P. E. (1983). Categorizing sounds and learning to read: A causal connection. *Nature, 30,* 419–421.

Bradley, L., & Bryant, P. E. (1985). *Rhyme and reason in reading and spelling.* Ann Arbor: University of Michigan Press.

Bridge, C., & Burton, B. (1982). Teaching sight vocabulary through patterned language materials. In J. A. Niles & L. A. Harris (Eds.), *New inquiries in reading research and instruction: Thirty-first yearbook of the National Reading Conference* (pp. 119–123). Washington, DC: National Reading Conference.

Bridge, C., Winograd, P., & Haley, D. (1983). Using predictable materials vs. preprimers to teach beginning sight words. *The Reading Teacher, 36,* 884–891.

Bruner, J. S. (1978). The role of dialogue in language acquisition. In A. Sinclair, R. J. Jarvella, & W. M. Levelt (Eds.), *The child's conception of language* (pp. 241–256). New York: Springer-Verlag.

Bryant, P., & Bradley, L. (1980). Why children sometimes write words which they do not read. In U. Frith (Ed.), *Cognitive processes in spelling* (pp. 355–370). New York: Academic Press.

Burns, J., & Richgels, D. (1989). An investigation of task requirements associated with invented spellings of 4-year-olds with above average intelligence. *Journal of Reading Behavior, 21,* 1–14.

Byrne, B. & Fielding-Barnsley, R. (1989). Phonemic awareness and letter knowledge in the child's acquisition of the alphabetic principle. *Journal of Educational Psychology, 81,* 313–321.

Calfee, R. C., & Drum, P. (1986). Research on teaching reading. In M. C. Wittrock (Ed.), *Handbook of Research on Teaching* (pp. 804–849). New York: Macmillan.

Calfee, R. C., & Lindamood, P., & Lindamood, C. (1973). Acoustic-phonetic skill and reading–kindergarten through twelfth grade. *Journal of Educational Psychology, 64,* 293–298.

Calkins, L. M. (1982). Writing taps a new energy source: The child. In R. D. Walsh (Ed.), *Donald Graves in Australia.* Portsmouth, NH: Heinemann Educational Books.

Carbo, M. (1978). Teaching reading with talking books. *The Reading Teacher, 32,* 267–273.

Carnine, L., Carnine, D., & Gersten, R. (1984). Analysis of oral reading errors made by economically disadvantaged students taught with a synthetic-phonics approach. *Reading Research Quarterly, 19,* 343–356.

Carroll, J. B., Davies, P., & Richman, B. (1971). *The American heritage word frequency book.* Boston, MA: Houghton Mifflin.

Cattell, J. M. (1886). The time it takes to see and name objects. *Mind, 11,* 63–65.

Chall, J. (1967). *Learning to read: The great debate.* New York: McGraw-Hill.

Chomsky, C. (1971). Write first, read later. *Childhood Education, 47,* 296–299.

Chomsky, C. (1976). After decoding: What? *Language Arts, 53,* 288–296.

Chomsky, C. (1978). When you still can't read in third grade: After decoding, what? In S. J. Samuels (Ed.), *What research has to say about reading instruction* (pp.

13–30). Newark, Delaware: International Reading Association.

Clarke, L. K. (1988). Invented versus traditional spelling in first graders' writings: Effects on learning to spell and read. *Research in the Teaching of English, 22,* 281–309.

Clay, M. (1983). Getting a theory of writing. In B. M. Kroll & G. Wells (Eds.), *Explorations in the development of writing, theory, research, and practice* (pp. 23–32). New York: Wiley.

Cohen, A. S. (1974–1975). Oral reading errors of first-grade children taught by a code-emphasis approach. *Reading Research Quarterly, 10,* 616–650.

Cohen, D. (1968). The effect of literature on vocabulary and reading achievement. *Elementary English, 45,* 209–213, 217.

Content, A., Kolinsky, R., Morais, J., & Bertelson, P. (1986). Phonetic segmentation in prereaders: Effect of corrective information. *Journal of Experimental Child Psychology, 42,* 49–72.

Cook, J. E., Nolan, G., & Zanotti, R. J. (1965). *The effect of neurological impress on reading disabled children with auditory perception impairments.* Arlington, VA. (ERIC Document Reproduction Service No. ED 128 781)

Cook, J. E., Nolan, G., & Zanotti, R. J. (1980). Treating auditory perception problems: The NIM helps. *Academic Therapy, 15,* 473–481.

Cullinan, B., Jaggar, A., & Strickland, D. (1974). Language expansion for black children in the primary grades: A research report. *Young Children, 29,* 98–112.

Cunningham, P. M., & Cunningham, J. W. (1978). Investigating the "print to meaning" hypothesis. In P. D. Pearson & J. Hansen (Eds.), *Reading: Disciplined inquiry in process and practice. Twenty-seventh Yearbook of the National Reading Conference* (pp. 116–120). Clemson, SC: National Reading Conference.

Dahl, P. (1974). *An experimental program for teaching high speed word recognition and comprehension skills* (Final Report Project #3-1154). Washington, DC: National Institute of Education. (ERIC Document Reproduction Service No. ED 099 812)

Dahl, P., & Samuels, J. (1974). *A mastery based experimental program for teaching poor readers high speed word recognition skills.* Unpublished manuscript.

Dale, E., & Chall, J. S. (1948). A formula for predicting readability. *Educational Research Bulletin, 27,* 11–20; *28*:37–54.

Dale, E., & O'Rourke, J. (1976). *The living word vocabulary.* Elgin, IL: Dorne.

Dank, M. E. (1976). *A study of the relationship of miscues to the mode of formal reading instruction received by selected second graders.* Unpublished doctoral dissertation, University of Massachusetts. (ERIC Document Reproduction Service No. ED 126 431)

DeLawter, J. A. (1975). Three miscue patterns: The relationship of beginning reading instruction and miscue patterns. In W. D. Page (Ed.), *Help for the reading teacher: New directions in research.* Urbana, IL: National Conference on Research in English, ERIC Clearinghouse on Reading and Communication Skills, National Institute of Education.

Devries, T. (1970). Reading, writing frequency and expository writing. *Reading Improvement, 7,* 14–15.

Dionisio, M. (1983). Write? Isn't this reading class? *The Reading Teacher, 36,* 746–750.

Doake, D. L. (1987). Learning to read: It starts in the home. In D. R. Tovey & J. E. Kerber (Eds.), *Roles in literacy learning* (pp. 2–9). Newark, DE: International Reading Association.

Doctorow, M., Wittrock, M. C., & Marks, C. (1978). Generative processes in reading comprehension. *Journal of Educational Psychology, 70,* 109–118.

Doehring, D. G., Trites, R. L., Patel, P. G., & Fiedorowicz, C. A. M. (1981). *Reading disabilities: The interaction of reading, language, and neuropsychological deficits.* New York: Academic Press.

Dolch, E. W. (1936). A basic sight vocabulary. *Elementary School Journal, 36,* 456–460.

Dolch, E. W. (1948). *Problems in reading.* Champaign, IL: Garrard.

Dowhower, S. L. (1987). Effects of repeated reading on second-grade transitional readers' fluency and comprehension. *Reading Research Quarterly, 22,* 389–406.

Edelsky, C. (1990). Whose agenda is this anyway? A response to McKenna, Robinson, and Miller. *Educational Researcher, 19,* 7–11.

Ehri, L. C. (1992). Reconceptualizing the development of sight word reading and its relationship to recoding. In P. B. Gough, L. C. Ehri, & R. Treiman (Eds.), *Reading acquisition* (pp. 107–143). Hillsdale, NJ: Erlbaum.

Ehri, L.C., & Robbins C. (1992). Beginners need some decoding skill to read words by analogy. *Reading Research Quarterly, 27,* 13–26.

Ehri, L. C., & Wilce, L. (1983). Development of word identification speed in skilled and less skilled beginning readers. *Journal of Educational Psychology, 75,* 3–18.

Ehri, L. C., & Wilce, L. (1985). Movement into reading: Is the first stage of printed word learning visual or phonetic? *Reading Research Quarterly, 20,* 163–179.

Ehri, L. C., & Wilce, L. (1987). Does learning to spell help beginners learn to read words? *Reading Research Quarterly, 12,* 47–65.

Eldredge, J. L. (1988–1989). A fifty-two-year-old dyslexic learns to read. *Journal of Reading, Writing & Learning Disabilities International, 4,* 101–106.

Eldredge, J. L. (1990a). Increasing the performance of poor readers in the third grade with a group-assisted strategy. *Journal of Educational Research, 84,* 69–77.

Eldredge, J. L. (1990b). "You'll never get me in the corner again!": Effective practices in literature-based instruction. *The California Reader, 23,* 2–21.

Eldredge, J. L. (1991). An experiment with a modified whole language approach in first grade classrooms. *Reading Research and Instruction, 30,* 21–38.

Eldredge, J. L., & Butterfield, D. D. (1984). *Sacred cows make good hamburger: A report on a reading research project titled "Testing the sacred cows in reading."* ED 255 861. Arlington, VA: ERIC Document Reproduction Service.

Eldredge, J. L., & Butterfield, D. D. (1986). Alternatives to traditional reading instruction. *The Reading Teacher, 40,* 32–37.

Eldredge, J. L., & Quinn, D. W. (1988). Increasing reading performance of low-achieving second graders by using dyad reading groups. *Journal of Educational Research, 82,* 40–46.

Eldredge, J. L., Quinn, D. W., & Butterfield, D. D. (1990). Causal relationships between phonics, reading comprehension, and vocabulary achievement in the second grade. *Journal of Educational Research, 83,* 201–214.

Elkonin, D. B. (1963). The psychology of mastering the elements of reading. In B. Simon & J. Simon (Eds.), *Educational psychology in the U.S.S.R.* (pp. 165–179). London: Routledge & Kegan Paul.

Elkonin, D. B. (1973). U.S.S.R. In J. Downing (Ed.), *Comparative reading* (pp. 551–580). New York: Macmillan.

Embrey, A. (1968). *A study of the effectiveness of neurological impress as a remedial reading technique.* Unpublished master's thesis, Central Washington State College, Ellenburg, WA.

Evanechko, P., Ollila, L., & Armstrong, R. (1974). An investigation of the relationships between children's performance in written language and their reading ability. *Research in the Teaching of English, 8,* 315–326.

Evans, M. A., & Carr, T. H. (1985). Cognitive abilities, conditions of learning, and the early development of reading skill. *Reading Research Quarterly, 20,* 327–347.

Farris, P. J., & Kaczmarski, D. (1988). Whole language: A closer look. *Contemporary Education, 59,* 77–81.

Ferguson, C. A. (1986). Discovering sound units and constructing sound systems: It's child's play. In J. S. Perkell & D. H. Klatt (Eds.), *Invariance and variability in speech processes* (pp. 36–51). Hillsdale, NJ: Erlbaum.

Ferreiro, M., & Teberosky, A. (1982). *Literacy before schooling.* Exeter, NH: Heinemann Educational Books.

Ferroli, L., & Shanahan, T. (1987). Kindergarten spelling, Explaining its relationship to first-grade reading. In J. E. Readence & R. S. Baldwin (Eds.), *Research in literacy: Merging perspectives. Thirty-sixth yearbook of the National Reading Conference* (pp. 93–99). Rochester, NY: National Reading Conference.

Fielding, L. G., Wilson, P. T., & Anderson, R. C. (1986). A new focus on free reading: The role of trade books in reading instruction. In T. E. Raphael (Ed.), *The contexts of school-based literacy* (pp. 149–160). New York: Random House.

Fitzgerald, J. (1984). The relationship between reading ability and expectations for story structure. *Discourse Processes, 7,* 211–241.

Fitzgerald, J., & Spiegel, D. L. (1983). Enhancing children's reading comprehension through instruction in narrative structure. *Journal of Reading Behavior, 15,* 1–17.

Fitzgerald, J., & Teasley, A. B. (1986). Effects of instruction in narrative structure on children's writing. *Journal of Education Psychology, 78,* 424–432.

Fountas, I. C., & Hannigan, I. L. (1989). Making sense of whole language: The pursuit of informed teaching. *Childhood Education, 65,* 133–137.

Fowler, A. E. (1991). How early phonological development might set the stage for phoneme awareness. In S. A. Brady & D. P. Shankweiler (Eds.), *Phonological processes in literacy: A tribute to Isabelle Y. Liberman* (pp. 97–117). Hillsdale, NJ: Erlbaum.

Fox, B., & Routh, D. K. (1975). Analyzing spoken language into words, syllables and phonemes: A developmental study. *Journal of Psycholinguistic Research, 4,* 331–342.

Fox, B., & Routh, D. K. (1976). Phonemic analysis and synthesis as word attack skills. *Journal of Educational Psychology, 68,* 70–74.

Fox, B., & Routh, D. K. (1980). Phonemic analysis and severe reading disability in children. *Journal of Psycholinguistic Research, 9,* 115–119.

Fox, B., & Routh, D. K. (1984). Phonemic analysis and synthesis as word attack skills: Revisited. *Journal of Educational Psychology, 76,* 1059–1061.

Freedman, S. W., & Calfee, R. C. (1984). Understanding and comprehending. *Written Communication, 1,* 459–490.

Frith, U. (1980). Unexpected spelling problems. In U. Frith (Ed.), *Cognitive processes in spelling* (pp. 495–516). New York: Academic Press.

Frith, U. (1985). Beneath the surface of developmental dyslexia. In K. Patterson, J. Marshall, & M. Coltheart (Eds.), *Surface dyslexia* (pp. 301–330). London: Erlbaum.

Fry, E. (1980). The new instant word list. *The Reading Teacher, 34,* 284–289.

Gardner, C. E. (1963). *Sonoma county schools office research project.* Unpublished.

Gardner, C. E. (1965). *The experimental use of the impress method of reading habilitation* (U.S. Office of Education Co-op Reading Project No. S167). Arlington, VA. (ERIC Document Reproduction Service No. ED 003 838)

Gibbs, V., & Proctor, S. (1977). Reading together: An experiment with the neurological-impress method. *Contemporary Education, 48,* 156–157.

Giddings, L. R. (1992). Literature-based reading instruction: An analysis. *Reading Research and Instruction, 31,* 18–30.

Goldenberg, C. (1991). Learning to read in New Zealand: The balance of skills and meaning. *Language Arts, 68,* 555–562.

Golinkoff, R. M. (1978). Phonemic awareness skills and reading achievement. In F. B. Murray & J. H. Pikulski (Eds.), *The acquisition of reading: Cognitive, linguistic, and perceptual prerequisites* (pp. 23–41). Baltimore: University Park.

Gonzales, P. G., & Elijah, D. V. (1975). Rereading: Effect on error patterns and performance levels on the IRI. *The Reading Teacher, 28,* 647–652.

Goodman, K. S. (1967). Reading: A psycholinguistic guessing game. *Journal of Reading Specialist, 6,* 126–135.

Goodman, K. S. (1986). *What's whole in whole language.* Portsmouth, NH: Heinemann Educational Books.

Goodman, K. S. (1989). Whole language is whole: A response to Heymsfeld. *Educational Leadership,* (March), 69–70.

Goodman, K. S. (1992a). I didn't found whole language. *The Reading Teacher, 46,* 188–199.

Goodman, K. S. (1992b). Why whole language is today's agenda in education. *Language Arts, 69,* 354–363.

Goodman, K. S., & Goodman, Y. M. (1979). Learning to read is natural. In L. B. Resnick & P. A. Weaver (Eds.), *Theory and practice of early reading* (Vol. 1, pp. 137–154). Hillsdale, NJ: Erlbaum.

Gordon, C. J. (1985). Modeling inference awareness across the curriculum. *Journal of Reading, 28,* 444–447.

Goswami, U. (1986). Children's use of analogy in learning to read: A developmental study. *Journal of Experimental Child Psychology, 42,* 73–83.

Goswami, U. (1988). Orthographic analogies and reading development. *Quarterly Journal of Experimental Psychology, 40,* 239–268.

Gough, P. B., Ehri, L. C., & Treiman, R. (Eds.) (1992). *Reading acquisition.* Hillsdale, NJ: Erlbaum.

Gough, P. B., & Hillinger, M. L. (1980). Learning to read: An unnatural act. *Bulletin of the Orton Society, 30,* 179–196.

Gough, P. B., Juel, C., & Griffith, P. L. (1992). Reading, spelling, and the orthographic cipher. In P. B. Gough, L. C. Ehri, & R. Treiman (Eds.), *Reading acquisition* (pp. 35–48). Hillsdale, NJ: Erlbaum.

Gough, P. B., & Tunmer, W. E. (1986). Decoding, reading, and reading disability. *Remedial and Special Education, 7,* 6–10.

Gough, P. B., & Walsh, M. A. (1991). Chinese, Phoenicians, and the orthographic cipher of English. In S. A. Brady & D. P. Shankweiler (Eds.), *Phonological processes in literacy: A tribute to Isabelle Y. Liberman* (pp. 199–209). Hillsdale, NJ: Erlbaum.

Graves, D. H. (1983). *Writing: teacher and children at work.* Portsmouth, NH: Heinemann Educational Books.

Griffith, P. L. (1991). Phonemic awareness helps first graders invent spellings and third graders remember correct spellings. *Journal of Reading Behavior, 23,* 215–233.

Griffith, P. L., & Olson, M. W. (1992). Phonemic awareness helps beginning readers to break the code. *The Reading Teacher, 45,* 517–522.

Gunning, T. G. (1992). *Creating reading instruction for all children.* Boston: Allyn & Bacon.

Hall, M. (1981). *Teaching reading as a language experience.* Columbus, OH: Merrill.

Halliday, M. A. K. (1973). *Explorations in the functions of language.* London: Edward Arnold.

Harris, A. J., & Sipay, E. R. (1980). *How to increase reading ability.* White Plains, NY: Longman.

Harste, J. C., Woodward, V. A., & Burke, C. L. (1984). *Language stories and literacy lessons.* Portsmouth, NH: Heinemann Educational Books.

Heckelman, R. G. (1962). *A neurological impress method of reading instruction.* Merced, CA: Merced County Schools Office.

Heckelman, R. G. (1966). The phonics bound child. *Academic Therapy Quarterly, 1,* 12–13.

Heckelman, R. G. (1968). Is reading an instantaneous memory process? *Academic Therapy Quarterly, 3,* 231–232.

Heckelman, R. G. (1969). A neurological-impress method of remedial-reading instruction. *Academic Therapy, 4,* 277–282.

Helfgott, J. (1976). Phoneme segmentation and blending skills of kindergarten children: Implications for beginning reading acquisition. *Contemporary Educational Psychology, 1,* 157–169.

Herman, P. A. (1985). The effect of repeated readings on reading rate, speech pauses, and word recognition accuracy. *Reading Research Quarterly, 20,* 553-565.

Hohn, W., & Ehri, L. (1983). Do alphabet letters help prereaders acquire phonemic segmentation skills? *Journal of Educational Psychology, 75,* 752–762.

Holbrook, H. T. (1987). Writing to learn in the social studies. *The Reading Teacher, 41,* 216–219.

Holdaway, D. (1979). *The foundations of literacy.* Sydney, Australia: Ashton Scholastic.

Hollingsworth, P. M. (1970). An experiment with the impress method of teaching reading, *The Reading Teacher, 24,* 112–114, 187.

Hollingsworth, P. M. (1978). An experimental approach to the impress method of teaching reading. *The Reading Teacher, 31,* 624–626.

Hoover, W., & Gough, P. B. (1990). The simple view of reading. *Reading and Writing: An Interdisciplinary Journal, 2,* 127–160.

Hopkins, C. J. (1979). The spontaneous oral vocabulary of children in grade 1. *The Elementary School Journal, 79,* 240–249.

Horn, E. (1926). *A basic writing vocabulary—10,000 words most commonly used in writing.* Iowa City, Iowa: State University of Iowa.

Hoskisson, K. (1974). Should parents teach their children to read? *Elementary English, 51,* 295–299.

Hoskisson, K. (1975a). The many facets of assisted reading. *Elementary English, 52,* 312–315.

Hoskisson, K. (1975b). Successive approximation and beginning reading. *The Elementary School Journal, 75,* 443–445.

Hoskisson, K., & Krohm, B. (1974). Reading by immersion: Assisted reading. *Elementary English, 51,* 832–836.

Hoskisson, K., Sherman, T. M., & Smith, L. L. (1974). Assisted reading and parent involvement. *The Reading Teacher, 27,* 710–714.

Huey, E. B. (1908). *The psychology and pedagogy of reading.* New York: Macmillan.

Huxford L., Terrell, C., & Bradley, L. (1991). The relationship between the phonological strategies employed in reading and spelling. *Journal of Research in Reading, 14,* 99–105.

Irwin, J. W. (1991). *Teaching reading comprehension processes.* Englewood Cliffs, NJ: Prentice Hall.

Jeffrey, W. E., & Samuels, S. J. (1967). The effect of method of reading training on initial learning and transfer. *Journal of Verbal Learning and Verbal Behavior, 6,* 354–358.

Jenkins, J. R., Bausell, R. B., & Jenkins, L. M. (1972). Comparison of letter name and letter sound training as transfer variables. *American Educational Research Journal, 9,* 75–86.

Johnson, D. D., & Baumann, J. F. (1984). Word identification. In P. D. Pearson (Ed.), *Handbook of reading research.* White Plains, NY: Longman.

Jordan, W. C. (1965). Prime-O-Tec: A new approach to reading. *Instructor, 7,* 108–111.

Jordan, W. C. (1966). Six-year olds reading faster, better with electronic aids. *Audio-Visual Instructor, 11,* 542–543.

Jordan, W. C. (1967). Prime-O-Tec: The new reading method. *Academic Therapy Quarterly, 2,* 248–250.

Jorm, A. F., & Share, D. L. (1983). Phonological recoding and reading acquisition. *Applied Psycholinguistics, 4,* 103–147.

Jorm, A. F., Share, D. L., Maclean, R., & Matthews, R. (1984). Phonological recoding skills and learning to read: A longitudinal study. *Applied Psycholinguistics, 5,* 201–207.

Juel, C. (1988). Learning to read and write: A longitudinal study of 54 children from first through fourth grades. *Journal of Educational Psychology, 80,* 437–447.

Juel, C., Griffith, P., & Gough, P. B. (1986). Acquisition of literacy: A longitudinal study of children in first and second grade. *Journal of Educational Psychology, 78,* 243–255.

Jusczyk, P. (1986). Toward a model of the development of speech perception. In J. Perkell & D. Klatt (Eds.), *Invariance and variability in speech perception* (pp. 1–33). Hillsdale, NJ: Erlbaum.

Just, M. A., & Carpenter, P. A. (1980). A theory of reading: From eye fixations to comprehension. *Psychological Review, 4,* 329–354.

Just, M. A., & Carpenter, P. A. (1987). *The psychology of reading and language comprehension.* Boston, MA: Allyn & Bacon.

Kahneman, D. (1973). *Attention and effort.* Englewood Cliffs, NJ: Prentice Hall.

Kowal, S., O'Connell, D., O'Brian, E., & Bryant, E. (1975). Temporal aspects of reading aloud and speaking: Three experiments. *American Journal of Psychology, 88,* 549–569.

Kucera, H., & Francis, W. N. (1967). *Computational analysis of present-day American English.* Providence, RI: Brown University Press.

LaBerge, D., & Samuels, S. J. (1974). Toward a theory of automatic information processing in reading. *Cognitive Psychology, 6,* 293–323.

Langford, K., Slade, K., & Barnett, A. (1974). An examination of impress techniques in remedial reading. *Academic Therapy, 9,* 309–319.

Leong, C. K., & Haines, C. F. (1978). Beginning readers' awareness of words and sentences, *Journal of Reading Behavior, 10,* 393–407.

Lesgold, A. M., & Curtis, M. E. (1981). Learning to read words efficiently. In A. M. Lesgold & C. A. Perfetti (Eds.), *Interactive processes in reading.* Hillsdale, NJ: Erlbaum.

Lesgold, A. M., Resnick, L. B., & Hammond, K. (1985). Learning to read: A longitudinal study of word skill development in two curricula. In G. E. Mackinnon & T. G. Waller (Eds.), *Reading research: Advances in theory and practice* (Vol. 4, pp. 107–138). San Diego, CA: Academic Press.

Liberman, A. M. (1989). Reading is hard just because listening is easy. In C. von Euler (Ed.), *Wenner-Gren International Symposium series: Brain and reading.* Basingstoke, England: Macmillan.

Liberman, A. M., Cooper, F. S., Shankweiler, D., & Studdert-Kennedy, M. (1967). Perception of the speech code. *Psychological Review, 74,* 731–761.

Liberman, I. Y. (1971). Basic research in speech and lateralization of language: Some implications for reading disability. *Bulletin of the Orton Society, 21,* 72–87.

Liberman, I. Y. (1973). Segmentation of the spoken word and reading acquisition. *Bulletin of the Orton Society, 23,* 65–67.

Liberman, I. Y. (1983). A language-oriented view of reading and its disabilities. In H. R. Mykebust (Ed.), *Progress in learning disabilities* (Vol. 5, pp. 81–101). New York: Grune & Stratton.

Liberman, I. Y., & Liberman, A. M. (1990). Whole language vs. code emphasis: Underlying assumptions and their implications for reading instruction. *Annals of Dyslexia, 40,* 51–76.

Liberman, I. Y., & Liberman, A. M. (1992). Whole language versus code emphasis: Underlying assumptions and their implications for reading instruction. In P. B. Gough, L. C. Ehri, & R. Treiman (Eds.), *Reading acquisition* (pp. 343–366). Hillsdale, NJ: Erlbaum.

Liberman, I. Y., Shankweiler, S., Fischer, F. W., & Carter, B. (1974). Explicit syllable and phoneme segmentation in the young child. *Journal of Experimental Child Psychology, 18,* 201–212.

Liberman, I. Y., Shankweiler, D., & Liberman, A. M. (1989). The alphabetic principle and learning to read. In D. Shankweiler & I. Y. Liberman (Eds.), *Phonology and reading disability: Solving the reading puzzle* (pp. 1–33). Ann Arbor, MI: University of Michigan Press.

Lindfors, J. (1987). *Children's language and learning* (2nd ed.). Englewood Cliffs, NJ: Prentice Hall.

Lomax, R. G., & McGee, L. M. (1987). Young children's concepts about print and reading: Toward a model of word reading acquisition. *Reading Research Quarterly, 22,* 237–256.

Lorenz, L., & Vockell, E. (1979). Using the neurological impress method with learning disabled readers. *Journal of Learning Disabilities, 12,* 420–422.

Lovett, M. W. (1987). A developmental approach to reading disability: Accuracy and speed criteria of normal and deficient reading skill. *Child Development, 58,* 234–260.

Lundberg, I., Frost, J., & Petersen, O. (1988). Effects of an extensive program for stimulating phonological awareness of preschool children. *Reading Research Quarterly, 23,* 263–284.

Lundberg, I., Olofsson, A., & Wall, S. (1980). Reading and spelling skill in the first school years predicted from phonemic awareness skills in kindergarten. *Scandinavian Journal of Psychology, 21,* 159–173.

Maclean, M., Bryant, P., & Bradley, L. (1987). Rhymes, nursery rhymes, and reading in early childhood. *Merrill-Palmer Quarterly, 33,* 266–281.

Mandler, J. M., & Johnson, N. S. (1977). Remembrance of things parsed: Story structure and recall. *Cognitive Science, 9,* 111–151.

Manis, F. R., & Morrison, F. J. (1985). Reading disability: A deficit in rule learning? In L. S. Siegel & F. J. Morrison (Eds.), *Cognitive development in atypical children* (pp. 1–26). New York: Springer-Verlag.

Manis, F. R., Szeszulski, P. A., Howell, M. J., & Horn, C. C. (1986). A comparison of analogy- and rule-based decoding strategies in normal and dyslexic children. *Journal of Reading Behavior, 18,* 203–218.

Mann, V. A. (1984). Longitudinal prediction and prevention of early reading difficulty. *Annals of Dyslexia, 34,* 117–136.

Mann, V. A., & Liberman, I. Y. (1984). Phonological awareness and verbal short-term memory: Can they presage early reading problems? *Journal of Learning Disabilities, 17,* 592–599.

Mann, V. A., Tobin, P., & Wilson, R. (1987). Measuring phonological awareness through the invented spellings of kindergarten children. *Merrill-Palmer Quarterly, 33,* 365–391.

Marsh, G., Friedman, M., Desberg, P., & Saterdahl, K. (1981). Comparison of reading and spelling strategies in normal and reading disabled children. In M. P. Friedman, J. P. Das, & N. O'Connor (Eds.), *Intelligence and learning* (pp. 363–367). New York: Plenum.

Marsh, G., Friedman, M. Welch, V., & Desberg, P. (1981). A cognitive developmental theory of reading acquisition. In G. E. Mackinnon & T. G. Waller (Eds.), *Reading research: Advances in theory and practice* (Vol. 3, pp. 199–221). New York: Academic Press.

May, F. B. (1994). *Reading as communication.* New York: Macmillan.

McCutcheon, D., Bell, L. C., France, I. M., & Perfetti, C. A. (1991). Phoneme-specific interference in reading: The tongue-twister effect revisited. *Reading Research Quarterly, 26,* 87–103.

McGee, L. M., & Lomax, R. G. (1990). On combining apples and oranges: A response to Stahl and Miller. *Review of Educational Research, 60,* 133–140.

McGee, L. M., Lomax, R. G., & Head, M. (1988). Young children's written language knowledge: What environmental and functional print reading reveals. *Journal of Reading Behavior, 20,* 99–118.

McKenna, M. C., Robinson, R. D., & Miller, J. W. (1990). Whole language: A research agenda for the nineties. *Educational Researcher, 19,* 3–6.

McKenna, M. C., Robinson, R. D., & Miller, J. W. (1992, December). *Whole language: The case for caution.* Paper presented at the annual meeting of the National Reading Conference, San Antonio, TX.

McNeill, D. (1968). Production and perception: The view from language. *Ontario Journal of Educational Research, 10,* 181–185.

Menyuk, P., & Menn, L. (1979). Early strategies for the perception and production of words and sounds. In P. Fletcher & M. Garman (Eds.), *Language acquisition* (pp. 49–70). Cambridge, England: Cambridge University Press.

Meyer, V. (1982). Prime-O-Tec: A successful strategy for adult disabled readers. *Journal of Reading, 25,* 512–515.

Miller, M. Z. (1969). Remediation by neurological impress, *Academic Therapy Quarterly, 4,* 313–314.

Mills, E. (1974). Children's literature and teaching written composition. *Elementary English, 51,* 971–973.

Moe, A. J., Hopkins, C. J., & Rush, R. T. (1982). *The vocabulary of first-grade children.* Springfield, IL: Charles C. Thomas.

Moorman, G. B., Blanton, W. E., & McLaughlin, T. M. (1992). The rhetoric of whole language: Part one. *Reading Psychology, 13,* 3–15.

Morais, J. (1991). Constraints on the development of phonemic awareness. In S. A. Brady & D. P. Shankweiler (Eds.), *Phonological processes in literacy* (pp. 5–27). Hillsdale, NJ: Erlbaum.

Morais, J., Cary, L., Alegria, J., & Bertelson, P. (1979). Does awareness of speech as a sequence of phones arise spontaneously? *Cognition, 7,* 323–331.

Morris, D. (1983). Concept of word and phoneme awareness in the beginning reader. *Research in the Teaching of Reading, 17,* 359–373.

Muller, D. (1973). Phonic blending and transfer of letter training to word reading in children. *Journal of Reading Behavior, 5,* 13–15.

Nathan, R. G., & Stanovich, K. E. (1991). The causes of consequences of differences in reading fluency. *Theory Into Practice, 30,* 176–184.

Newman, J. (1985). *Whole language: Theory in use.* Portsmouth, NH: Heinemann Educational Books.

Newman, J. M., & Church, S. M. (1990). Myths of whole language. *The Reading Teacher, 44,* 20–26.

Nicholson, T., Lillas, C., & Rzoska, M. (1988). Have we been misled by miscues? *The Reading Teacher, 42,* 6–10.

Norton, D. E. (1976). A comparison of the oral reading errors of high and low ability first and third graders taught by two approaches—synthetic phonic and analytic-eclectic. (Doctoral dissertation, University of Wisconsin–Madison). *Dissertation Abstracts International, 37,* 3399A.

Norton, D. E., & Hubert, P. (1977). *A comparison of the oral reading strategies and comprehension patterns developed by high, average, and low first grade students taught by two approaches—phonic emphasis and eclectic basal.* College State: Texas A & M University. (ERIC Document Reproduction Service No. ED 145 393)

Olofsson, A., & Lundberg, I. (1985). Evaluation of long term effects of phonemic awareness training in kindergarten: Illustrations of some methodological problems in evaluation research. *Scandinavian Journal of Psychology, 26,* 21–34.

O'Shea, L. J., Sindelar, P. T., & O'Shea, D. J. (1985). The effects of repeated readings and attentional cues on reading fluency and comprehension. *Journal of Reading Behavior, 17,* 129–142.

Paul, R. (1976). Invented spelling in kindergarten. *Young Children, 21,* 195–200.

Pearson, P. D., & Fielding, L. (1991). Comprehension instruction. In R. Barr, M. Kamil, P. Mosenthal, & P. Pearson (Eds.), *Handbook of reading research* (Vol. 2, pp. 815–860). White Plains, NY: Longman.

Perfetti, C. A. (1985). *Reading ability.* New York: Oxford University Press.

Perfetti, C. A. (1986). Cognitive and linguistic components of reading ability. In B. R. Foorman & A. W. Siegel (Eds.), *Acquisition of reading skills: Cultural constraints and cognitive universals* (pp. 1–40). Hillsdale, NJ: Erlbaum.

Perfetti, C. A. (1992). The representation problem in reading acquisition. In P. B. Gough, L. C. Ehri, & R. Treiman (Eds.), *Reading acquisition* (pp. 145–174). Hillsdale, NJ: Erlbaum.

Perfetti, C. A., Goldman, S., & Hogaboam, T. (1979). Reading skill and the identification of words in discourse context. *Memory and Cognition, 7,* 273–282.

Perfetti, C. A., & Hogaboam, T. W. (1975). The relationship between single word decoding and reading comprehension skill. *Journal of Educational Psychology, 67,* 461–469.

Peterson, M. E., & Haines, L. P. (1992). Orthographic analogy training with kindergarten children: Effects on analogy use, phonemic segmentation, and letter-sound knowledge. *Journal of Reading Behavior, 24,* 109–124.

Pflaum, S. W., Walberg, H. J., Karegianes, M. L., & Rasher, S. P. (1980). Reading instruction: A quantitative analysis. *Educational Researcher, 9,* 12–18.

Pollatsek, A., Rayner, K., & Balota, D.A. (1986). Inferences about eye movement control from the perceptual span in reading. *Perception and Psychophysics, 40,* 123–130.

Quandt, I., & Selznick, R. (1984). *Self-concept and reading.* Newark, DE: International Reading Association.

Railsback, L. (1969). Use of automated aural-oral techniques to teach functional illiterates who are upper age level adolescents. *The psychology of reading behavior: Eighteenth yearbook of the National Reading Conference,* 207–211.

Rayner, K., & Bertera, J.H. (1979). Reading without a fovea. *Science, 206,* 468–469.

Rayner, K., & Pollatsek, A. (1989). *The psychology of reading.* Englewood Cliffs, NJ: Prentice Hall.

Read, C. (1971). Pre-school children's knowledge of English phonology. *Harvard Educational Review, 41,* 1–34.

Read, C. (1986). *Children's creative spellings.* London: Routledge & Kegan Paul.

Read, C., Zhang, Y., Nie, H., & Ding, B. (1986). The ability to manipulate speech sounds depends on knowing alphabetic writing. *Cognition, 24,* 31–44.

Reitsma, P. (1983). Printed word learning in beginning readers. *Journal of Experimental Child Psychology, 36*, 321–339.

Reitsma, P. (1988). Reading practice for beginners: Effects of guided reading, reading-while-listening, and independent reading with computer-based speech feedback. *Reading Research Quarterly, 23*, 219–235.

Reutzel, D. R., & Cooter, R. B. (1992). *Teaching children to read: From basals to books.* New York: Merrill/Macmillan.

Rich, S. J. (1985). Restoring power to teachers: The impact of "whole language." *Language Arts, 62*, 717–724.

Rinsland, H. D. (1945). *A basic vocabulary of elementary school children.* New York: Macmillan.

Robin, K. (1977). *A study of the effectiveness of two impress methods of instruction with elementary school children.* Unpublished manuscript. Highland Park, IL.

Robinson, S. S. (1991, April). *Reading achievement: Contributions of invented spelling and alphabetic knowledge.* Paper presented at the annual meeting of the American Educational Research Association, Chicago, IL.

Rohl, M., & Tunmer, W. E. (1988). Phonemic segmentation skill and spelling acquisition. *Applied Psycholinguistics, 9*, 335–350.

Rosenshine, B., & Meister, C. (1992). The use of scaffolds for teaching higher-level cognitive strategies. *Educational Leadership, 49*, 26–33.

Rosner, J., & Simon, D. (1971). The auditory analysis test: An initial report. *Journal of Learning Disabilities, 4*, 384–392.

Rozin, P., & Gleitman, L. (1977). The structure and acquisition of reading II: The reading process and the acquisition of the alphabetic principle. In A. Reber & D. Scarborough (Eds.), *Toward a psychology of reading* (pp. 55–141). Hillsdale, NJ: Erlbaum.

Samuels, S. J. (1976). Automatic decoding and reading comprehension. *Language Arts, 53*, 323–325.

Samuels, S. J. (1979). The method of repeated readings. *The Reading Teacher, 32*, 403–408.

Scardamalia, M. (1981). How children cope with the cognitive demands of writing. In C. H. Frederickson & J. F. Dominic (Eds.), *Writing: The nature, development and teaching of written communication.* Vol. 2: *Writing: Process, development and communication* (pp. 81–104). Hillsdale, NJ: Erlbaum.

Schickendanz, J. A. (1990). The jury is still out on the effects of whole language and language experience approaches for beginning reading: A critique of Stahl and Miller's study. *Review of Educational Research, 60*, 127–131.

Schneeberg, H. (1977). Listening while reading: A four year study. *The Reading Teacher, 30*, 629–635.

Seidenberg, M. S. (1985). The time course of phonological code activation in two writing systems. *Cognition, 19*, 1–30.

Shanahan, T. (1988). The reading–writing relationship: Seven instructional principles. *The Reading Teacher, 41*, 636–647.

Shankweiler, D. (1991). The contribution of Isabelle Y. Liberman. In S. A. Brady & D. P. Shankweiler (Eds.), *Phonological processes in literacy: A tribute to Isabelle Y. Liberman* (pp. 29–36). Hillsdale, NJ: Erlbaum.

Share, D. J., Jorm, A. F., Maclean, R., & Mathews, R. (1984). Sources of individual differences in reading achievement. *Journal of Educational Psychology, 76*, 466–477.

Simpson, G. B., & Foster, M. R. (1986). Lexical ambiguity and children's word recognition. *Developmental Psychology, 22*, 147–154.

Slaughter, H. (1988). Indirect and direct teaching in a whole language program. *The Reading Teacher, 42*, 30–34.

Smith, D. E. P., & Carrigan, P. (1959). *The nature of reading disability.* New York: Harcourt, Brace & Co.

Smith, F. (1971). *Understanding reading.* New York: Holt, Rinehart & Winston.

Smith, F. (1973). *Psycholinguistics and reading.* New York: Holt, Rinehart & Winston.

Smith, F. (1975). *Comprehension and learning.* New York: Holt, Rinehart & Winston.

Smith, F. (1976). Learning to read by reading. *Language Arts, 53*, 297–299, 322.

Snowling, M. (1980). The development of grapheme–phoneme correspondences in normal and dyslexic readers. *Journal of Experimental Child Psychology, 29*, 294–305.

Snowling, M. (1981). Phonemic deficits in developmental dyslexia. *Psychological Research, 43*, 219–234.

Snowling, M. (1985). The assessment of reading and spelling skills. In M. Snowling (Ed.), *Children's written language difficulties* (pp. 80–95). Windsor, England: NFER-Nelson.

Spiegel, D. L. (1992). Blending whole language and systematic direct instruction. *The Reading Teacher, 46*, 38–44.

Stahl, S. A. (1990). Riding the pendulum: A rejoinder to Schickendanz and McGee and Lomax. *Review of Educational Research, 60,* 141–151.

Stahl, S. A., & Miller, P. D. (1989). Whole language and language experience approaches for beginning reading: A quantitative research synthesis. *Review of Educational Research, 59,* 87–116.

Stanovich, K. E. (1980). Toward an interactive-compensatory model of individual differences in the development of reading fluency. *Reading Research Quarterly, 16,* 32–71.

Stanovich, K. E. (1984). The interactive-compensatory model of reading: A confluence of developmental, experimental and educational psychology. *Remedial and Special Education, 5,* 11–19.

Stanovich, K. E. (1985). Explaining the variance in reading ability in terms of psychological processes: What have we learned? *Annals of Dyslexia, 35,* 67–96.

Stanovich, K. E. (1986). Matthew effects in reading: Some consequences of individual differences in the acquisition of literacy. *Reading Research Quarterly, 21,* 360–406.

Stanovich, K. E. (1991). Word recognition: Changing perspectives. In R. Barr, M. L. Kamil, P. B. Mosenthal, & P. D. Pearson (Eds.), *Handbook of reading research* (Vol. 2, pp. 418–452). White Plains, NY: Longman.

Stanovich, K. E. (1992). Speculations on the causes and consequences of individual differences in early reading acquisition. In P. B. Gough, L. C. Ehri, & R. Treiman (Eds.), *Reading acquisition* (pp. 307–342). Hillsdale, NJ: Erlbaum.

Stanovich, K. E., Cunningham, A. E., & Cramer, B. B. (1984). Assessing phonological awareness in kindergarten children: Issues of task comparability. *Journal of Experimental Child Psychology, 38,* 175–190.

Stanovich, K. E., Cunningham, A. E., & Freeman, D. J. (1984a). Intelligence, cognitive skills and early reading progress. *Reading Research Quarterly, 19,* 278–303.

Stanovich, K. E., Cunningham, A. E., & Freeman, D. J. (1984b). Relation between early reading acquisiting and word decoding with and without context: A longitudinal study of first-grade children. *Journal of Educational Psychology, 76,* 668–677.

Stanovich, K. E., & West, R. F. (1989). Exposure to print and orthographic processing. *Reading Research Quarterly, 24,* 402–433.

Stanovich, K. E., West, R. F., & Freeman, D. J. (1981). A longitudinal study of sentence context effects in second-grade children: Tests of an interactive-compensatory model. *Journal of Experimental Child Psychology, 32,* 185–199.

Stinner, M. C. (1979). *The use of neurological impress method in accelerating reading levels in selected disabled children.* Unpublished master's project. University of Florida.

Stotsky, S. (1983). Research on reading/writing relationships: A synthesis and suggested directions. *Language Arts, 60,* 627–642.

Studdert-Kennedy, M. (1986). Sources of variability in early speech development. In J. S. Perkell & D. H. Klatt (Eds.), *Invariance and variability of speech processes.* Hillsdale, NJ: Erlbaum.

Studdert-Kennedy, M. (1987). The phoneme as a perceptumotor structure. In A. Allport, D. Mackay, W. Prinz, & E. Scheerer (Eds.), *Language perception and production* (pp. 67–84). London: Academic Press.

Sulzby, E., & Teale, W. (1991). Emergent literacy. In R. Barr, M. L. Kamil, P. B. Mosenthal, & P. D. Pearson (Eds.), *Handbook of reading research, vol. II.* White Plains, NY: Longman.

Tangel, D. M., & Blachman, B. A. (1992). Effect of phoneme awareness instruction on kindergarten children's invented spelling. *Journal of Reading Behavior, 24,* 233–261.

Tannenhaus, M. K., Flanigan, H., & Seidenberg, M. S. (1980). Orthographic and phonological code activation in auditory and visual word recognition. *Memory and Cognition, 8,* 513–520.

Taylor, B., & Berkowitz, S. (1980). Facilitating children's comprehension of content material. In M. Kamil & A. Moe (Eds.), *Perspectives on reading research and instruction: Twenty-ninth yearbook of the National Reading Conference* (pp. 64–68). Washington, DC: National Reading Conference.

Taylor, I., & Taylor, M. M. (1983). *The psychology of reading.* New York: Academic Press.

Taylor, N. E., Wade, M. R., & Yekovich, F. R. (1985). The effects of text manipulation and multiple reading strategies on the reading performance of good and poor readers. *Reading Research Quarterly, 20,* 566–574.

Teale, W. (1991). Dear readers. *Language Arts, 68,* 184–187.

Temple, C., Nathan, R., Temple, F., & Burris, N. A. (1993). *The beginnings of writing.* Boston, MA: Allyn & Bacon.

Thompson, G. B. (1986). When nonsense is better than sense: Non-lexical errors to word reading tests. *British Journal of Educational Psychology, 56,* 216–219.

Thompson, R. A. (1992). A critical perspective on whole language. *Reading Psychology: An International Quarterly, 13,* 131–155.

Thorndike, E. L., & Lorge, I. (1944). *The teacher's word book of 30,000 words.* New York: Teacher's College Press, Columbia University.

Tierney, R. J., & Cunningham, J. W. (1984). Research on teaching reading comprehension. In P. D. Pearson, R. Barr, M. L. Kamil, & P. Mosenthal (Eds.), *Handbook of reading research* (pp. 609–655). White Plains, NY: Longman.

Tierney, R. J., & Shanahan, T. (1991). Research on the reading–writing relationship: Interactions, transactions, and outcomes. In R. Barr, M. L. Kamil, P. B. Mosenthal, & P. D. Pearson (Eds.), *Handbook of reading research* (Vol. 2, pp. 246–280). White Plains, NY: Longman.

Torneus, M. (1984). Phonological awareness and reading: A chicken and egg problem? *Journal of Educational Psychology, 76,* 1346–1358.

Treiman, R., & Baron, J. (1983). Individual differences in spelling: The Phoenician-Chinese distinction. *Topics in Learning and Learning Disabilities, 3,* 33–40.

Treiman, R., & Breaux, A. (1982). Common phoneme and overall stimulating relations among spoken syllables. Their use by children and adults. *Journal of Psycholinguistic Research, 11,* 569–597.

Tulving, E., & Gold, C. (1963). Stimulus information and contextual information as determinants of tachistoscopic recognition of words. *Journal of Experimental Psychology, 66,* 319–327.

Tunmer, W. E. (1989). The role of language-related factors in reading disability. In D. Shankweiler & I. Y. Liberman (Eds.), *Phonology and reading disability: Solving the reading puzzle* (pp. 91–131). Ann Arbor: University of Michigan Press.

Tunmer, W.E., Herriman, M.L., & Nesdale, A.R. (1988). Metalinguistic abilities and beginning reading. *Reading Research Quarterly, 23,* 134–158.

Tunmer, W. E., & Nesdale, A. R. (1985). Phonemic segmentation skill and beginning reading. *Journal of Educational Psychology, 77,* 417–427.

Vellutino, F. R., & Scanlon, D. M. (1984). Converging perspectives in the study of the reading process:

Reactions to the papers presented by Morrison, Siegel and Ryan, and Stanovich. *Remedial and Special Education, 5,* 39–44.

Vellutino, F. R., & Scanlon, D. M. (1987). Phonological coding, phonological awareness, and reading ability: Evidence from a longitudinal and experimental study. *Merrill-Palmer Quarterly, 33,* 321–363.

Venezky, R. L. (1976). *Theoretical and experimental base for teaching reading.* The Hague: Mouton.

Vygotsky, L. S. (1978). *Mind in society.* Cambridge, MA: Harvard University Press.

Vygotsky, L. S. (1986) *Thought and language.* Cambridge, MA: MIT Press.

Wagner, R. (1986). Phonological processing abilities and reading: Implications for disabled readers. *Journal of Learning Disabilities, 19,* 623–630.

Wagner, R., & Torgesen, J. (1987). The nature of phonological processing and its causal role in the acquisition of reading skills. *Psychological Bulletin, 101,* 192–212.

Walker, C. M. (1979). High frequency word list for grades 3 through 9. *The Reading Teacher, 32,* 803–812.

Watson, D. J. (1989). Defining and describing whole language. *Elementary School Journal, 90,* 129–142.

Weber, R. M. (1970). A linguistic analysis of first-grade errors. *Reading Research Quarterly, 5,* 427–451.

Wepman, J. M., & Hass, W. (1969). *A spoken word count (children—ages 5, 6 and 7).* Chicago, IL: Language Research Associates.

West, R. F., & Stanovich, K. E. (1978). Automatic contextual facilitation in readers of three ages. *Child Development, 49,* 717–727.

Williams, J. P. (1986). The role of phonemic analysis in reading. In J. Torgesen & B. Wong (Eds.), *Psychological and educational perspectives on learning disabilities* (pp. 399–416). Orlando: Academic Press.

Yopp, H. K. (1992). Developing phonemic awareness in young children. *The Reading Teacher, 45,* 696–703.

Zhurova, L. E. (1963). The development of analysis of words into their sounds by preschool children. *Soviet Psychology and Psychiatry, 72,* 17–27.

Zifcak, M. (1981). Phonological awareness and reading acquisition. *Contemporary Educational Psychology, 6,* 117–126.

Zinna, D. R., Liberman, I. Y., & Shankweiler, D. (1986). Children's sensitivity to factors influencing vowel reading. *Reading Research Quarterly, 21,* 465–480.

Index